Refining
Design
for Business

**USING ANALYTICS, MARKETING, AND TECHNOLOGY
TO INFORM CUSTOMER-CENTRIC DESIGN**

MICHAEL KRYPEL

Adobe

Refining Design for Business:
Using analytics, marketing, and technology to inform customer-centric design

Michael Krypel

This Adobe Press book is published by Peachpit.
For information on Adobe Press books and other products, contact:

Peachpit
www.peachpit.com

For the latest on Adobe Press books, go to www.adobepress.com
To report errors, please send a note to errata@peachpit.com
Peachpit is a division of Pearson Education.

Project Editor: Valerie Witte
Production Editor: Becky Winter
Developmental and Copyeditor: Anne Marie Walker
Proofreader: Liz Welch
Composition: Danielle Foster
Indexer: James Minkin
Cover and Interior Design: Mimi Heft
Cover and Interior Illustrations: Paul Mavrides

ISBN-13: 978-0-321-94088-9
ISBN-10:   0-321-94088-1

9 8 7 6 5 4 3 2 1
Printed and bound in the United States of America

To Darren Johnson, Jennifer Sun, Kripa Nerlikar,

Ramona Meyer-Piagentini, and Stephen Ratpojanakul:

Thank you for your guidance and enthusiasm over the last eight years,

and for your tremendous contributions to building the optimization field.

Acknowledgments

I will be forever grateful to all the wonderful people from Adobe, Omniture, and Offermatica for allowing me to be part of their exceptional teams, including Aaron Graham, Adam Fayne, Adam Justis, Adam Wood, Alan Gurock, Amy Lam, Andre Prevot, Ann Chen, Aseem Chandra, Barbara Dawson, Bianca Slade, Bill Ozinga, Bill Peabody, Brad Kay, Brent Dykes, Brian Hawkins, Brian Ivanovick, Brittany Chandler, Cameron Barnes, Christi Terjesen, Christine Yarrow, Christy Armstrong, Colin Lewis, Colleen Nagle, Daniel Hopkins, Daniel Wright, Darren Johnson, Darrin Poole, David Baker, David Hoye, David Humphrey, Debra Adams, Derek Bryce, Don Abshire, Doni Lillis, Doug Mumford, Drew Burns, Drew Phillips, Eddie Ramirez, Ehren Hozumi, Garrett Ilg, Gene Holcombe, Georgia Frailey, Heather Razukas, Hiro Awanohara, Jacob Favre, James Roche, Jameson O'Guinn, Jamie Stone, Jason Haddock, Jason Hickey, Jason Holmes, Jeff Fuhriman, Jennifer Sun, Jim Sink, John Kucera, John Mosbaugh, Jonathan Mendez, Jonathan Weissbard, Justin Patrick, Ka Swan Teo, Kaela Cusack, Katie Cozby, Kellie Snyder, Kendra Jenkins, Kevin Lindsay, Kevin Scally, Kevin Smith, Kripa Nerlikar, Kyle Ellis, Kyle Johnson, Lacey Bell, Lambert Walsh, Lance Jones, Lily Chiu, Liz Quinn, Mandeep Sidhu, Mark Boothe, Matthew Lowden, Matthew Roche, Matthew Smedley, Matthew Thurber, Michael Curry, Michael Evensen, Mikel Chertudi, Neha Gupta, Norman Dabney, Paige Burton, Peter Callahan, Rachel Elkington, Rameen Taheri, Ramona Piagentini, Rand Blair, Reuben Poon, Richard Oto, Rob Cantave, Ron Breger, Rotem Ben-Israel, Russell Lewis, Sachie Reichbach, Sarah Ferrick, Serge St. Felix, Shoaib Alam, Stephen Frieder, Stephen Ratpojanakul, Steve O'Neil, Thejas Varier, Tiffany Olejnik, Tom Ratcliff, Tony DiLoreto, Tracy Harvey, Vincent Cortese, Vladimir Sanchez Olivares, Wallace Rutherford, Whitney Littlewood, and Zoltan Liu.

I am extremely thankful to everyone who agreed to be interviewed or who helped connect me with people to interview, including Justin Ramers from Active Network; Andrew Switzer from Ally Bank; Tom Lau from American Express®; Kevin Gallagher and Thomas Gage from AutoTrader; Adam Crutchfield from Axcess Financial; Brandon Proctor and Justin Bergson from Build.com; Chris Kahle from Caesars; Joanne Pugh and Stephanie Paulson from Central Restaurant Products; Kyle Power from CHG Healthcare;

Christine Cox, John Williamson, Jonathan Stein, and Ruth Zinder from Comcast; Ed Wu, Emily Campbell, Étienne Cox, Isabelle Mouli-Castillo, Joel Wright, Lester Saucier, Nazli Yuzak, and Will Close from Dell; Sandy Martin from Dollar Thrifty; Zimran Ahmed from Electronic Arts; Nate Bolt and Slater Tow from Facebook; Thomas Jankowski from FlightNetwork; Karina van Schaardenburg and Simon Favreau-Lessard from Foursquare; Jerome Doran, Jon Wiley, and Krisztina Radosavljevic-Szilagyi from Google; Linda Tai from Hightail; Phil Corbett from IBM; Ajit Sivadasan, Ashish Braganza, Lewis Broadnax, and Siping Roussin from Lenovo; Amy Parnell and Lea Ann Hutter from LinkedIn; Pete Maher from the Luma Institute; Kenyon Rogers from Marriott; Peter Davio and Steven Webster from Microsoft; Kyle Rush from Obama for America; Blake Brossman, Natalie Bonacasa, and Ujjwal Dhoot from PetCareRx; Amit Gupta from Photojojo; John Pace from RealNetworks; Chris Krohn, Phil Volini, and Sarah Nelson from Restaurant.com; Matt Curtis and Roger Scholl from Saks Fifth Avenue; Ryan Pizzuto from T-Mobile; Eileen Krill and Mary Bannon from The Washington Post; and Matthew Pereira and Rob Blakeley from WebMD.

Thank you to Kelly Patterson for her fabulous editing, to Rosemary Knes for her careful proofing, and to Jeff Patterson for introducing me to them. Thank you also to everyone at the Adobe Press and Pearson Education for their hard work, including Anne Marie Walker, Becky Winter, Damon Hampson, Danielle Foster, Jim LeValley, Liz Welch, Mimi Heft, Ted Waitt, Valerie Witte, Victor Gavenda, and Vidya Subramanian Ravi.

Thank you to my mom, Merrill Janover, whose curiosity, creativity, and love of learning are an inspiration, and to my brothers, David Krypel and Brian Krypel, for their encouragement and comfort. Thank you to Alan Schorn, Bob Klein, Chayym Zeldis, David Roth, Elizabeth Metz, Jarek Koniusz, Jeffrey Gilden, Jerry Denzer, John Cave, John Zannos, Joseph Rutkowski, Nina Zeldis, Philip Sorgen, Robert Abrams, and all my other wonderful teachers for their guidance, confidence, and inspiration. Thank you also to Daniel Schweitzer, Bonnie Walters, Greg Lowder, and Scott Epstein for their feedback on drafts of the book and for their amazing support.

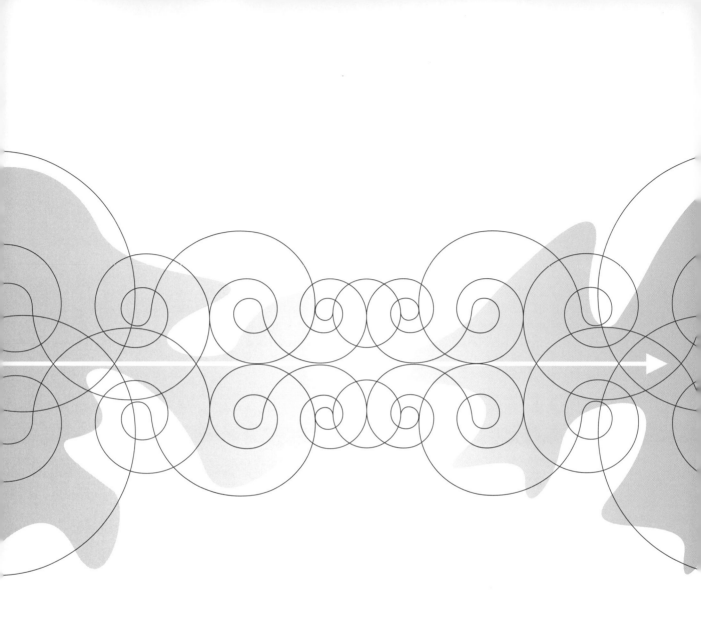

Contents at a Glance

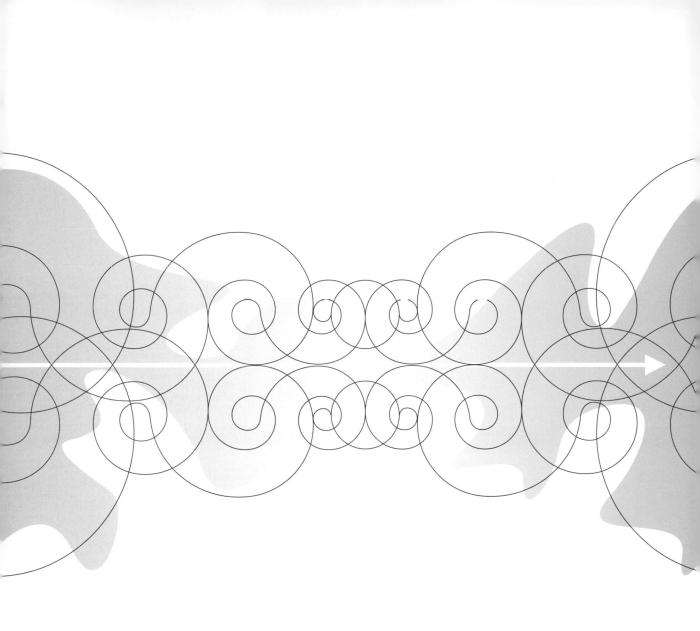

Contents

PART 1   Creating Engaging Customer Experiences   1

Introduction

The Age of Optimization

This book aims to help businesspeople apply a comprehensive and powerful new way of building business and customer value online, using a proven methodology that works for any size of business, in any industry. Highly interdisciplinary in nature, the Iterative Optimization Methodology will be especially useful to:

- ▶ **Business executives.** Aiming to meet online customer needs through a rigorous research and evaluation process that also fosters creativity, the optimization method is appealing to business leaders of all ranks, including C-Level executives.

- ▶ **Marketers, designers, and information architects.** Great marketers and designers were among the first professional groups to embrace the customer-centric design techniques described in this book.

- ▶ **Data analysts.** Data analysts are essential to the success of almost every step of the Iterative Optimization Methodology. They provide users throughout the business with access to crucial data and help them to act on analytics-based insights.

- ▶ **Engineers and solutions architects.** Engineers and solutions architects are often the unsung heroes of online business. They spend much of their time setting up systems to deploy designs without knowing whether what they're working on is helping the company and its customers. The optimization method allows them to find out whether or not their efforts have been fruitful.

- ▶ **Students, including MBA candidates.** Students can learn more about an exciting new field—one in which there is high demand for people who excel at creating great wireframes, running optimization programs, and other skills described in this book.

How This Book Is Structured

This book is divided into three parts:

Part 1: Creating Engaging Customer Experiences. This part discusses the level of importance design now plays in the business world, challenges the standard design process implemented by most companies, and introduces the Iterative Optimization Methodology by showing how design testing can lead to more creative and impactful designs.

Part 2: The Iterative Optimization Methodology. Using real-life examples, this part describes how to drive business and customer value in step-by-step detail. It shows how companies can integrate qualitative and quantitative customer research, prioritize website sections and design ideas for testing, experiment with new designs under real market conditions, and scale optimization techniques across their organization.

Part 3: Visual Business Cases. In this part, business leaders from 20 companies, including Google, Facebook, Comcast, Marriott, and American Express®, share examples of their favorite design tests and discuss practical approaches for using data to inform customer-centric design.

PART 1

Creating Engaging Customer Experiences

This book is about how to build a successful online business by creating engaging and measurable customer experiences. It focuses on the principles and real-world application of technology, data analysis, marketing, and design, and shows how these disciplines are emerging as critical factors in any company's drive toward becoming a business leader.

This section discusses the new level of importance design now plays in the business world, and how changing the standard design process most companies follow can enhance accountability for generating business and customer value, while creating new opportunities for collaboration and innovation.

CHAPTER 1

The Art and Science of Business

As a company's online presence plays an increasingly vital role in everything from marketing and customer outreach to sales and delivery, website design has emerged as a powerful and important aspect of any business. Now more than ever, businesses need an effective framework for web design that will help them keep a finger on the pulse of their customers, experiment with evolving business models, and innovate, drawing on the core set of interdisciplinary skills within their companies.

In doing so, they must marry the art of creating designs that meet customers' needs effectively, with the science of business, objectively evaluating those designs using data and experimental techniques. It can be a difficult mix, and there are to date few frameworks to help guide organizations through this new challenge. This chapter outlines an effective and easy-to-use framework companies can use to navigate the digital space. The framework is also highly adaptable, in recognition of today's rapidly changing business landscape: while it is unclear what businesses will look like five to ten years from now, significant change is highly probable, and customers will almost certainly interact with companies in entirely new ways. Companies ranging from start-ups to today's market leaders are applying these methods not only to meet their present needs, but also to reimagine the future of online business—and then to try to build it.

The Importance of Design to Business

Innovation and technology have forever changed what it means to be a business. Some businesses now exist only online; increasingly, companies are being built with new technologies that require new skills; and customers are engaging with them in novel ways, accessing businesses through interactive visual and audio experiences such as webpages or apps, using computers, mobile devices, and televisions.

These experiences are based on design, which has never been so important to the business world. Customers interact with designs by looking, clicking, typing, listening, speaking to, and touching them. These interactions largely occur where and when the customer chooses: alone on the couch at home, at work, at sporting and social events, while traveling on an airplane, and so on. When people say they "read an article," "checked reviews," "bought a friend a gift," "paid a bill," "watched a video," "booked a hotel," or "replied to an invite," they're talking about engaging with businesses by interacting with their designs.

The translation of a business idea into a design is the core part of creating an online presence for that company. Customers decide within the first few seconds of visiting a website whether they will stay or leave. No matter how great a business idea is, or what technology it relies on behind the scenes, a company needs to express itself visually in a way customers will understand and be able to interact with easily—all without ever having seen it before—in order to become successful online (**Figure 1.1**).

However, there is as yet no standard model on which to build appealing designs and to measure their efficacy accurately. While some literature exists on this topic, most companies simply develop their own approaches to web design by trial and error, with mixed results.

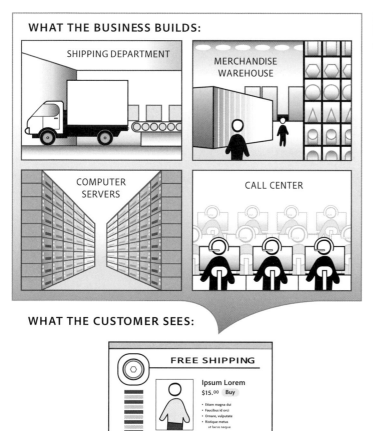

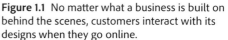

Figure 1.1 No matter what a business is built on behind the scenes, customers interact with its designs when they go online.

This book aims to help fill this gap, offering a methodological framework for creating designs and evaluating their effectiveness. The framework is based on a set of best practices developed over many years by a cross-functional team at Adobe and has since been adopted by hundreds of other businesses; it also draws on other highly effective design practices used by a range of companies online, distilling these disparate discoveries into a single central framework on which any company—big or small—can build its own unique approach to web design.

Customer-Centric Design

It is crucial for online businesses to determine which designs customers will use and find engaging, and which ones will drive them away. The single most important principle companies must observe here is to develop designs that will satisfy both the goals of the business *and* those of their customers. This can be difficult: customers' goals—such as finding a product or service they need, gathering information, supporting a cause, or simply seeking entertainment—are often different from a business's main goal, which is, typically, to make money, through direct sales, reservations, account creations, the collection of information, etc.

It is all too easy for a business to focus on its main goal and lose sight of its customers' goals. So the central question here is: there is an infinite number of ways to translate an idea into a design that could drive business value, but which designs will also drive customer value?

The most accurate way to determine this is to test multiple versions of a design against one another in a controlled experiment. In this book, these design *tests* are also referred to as *campaigns*, *experiments*, and *optimizations*. Any element of a design can be tested, including layout, products, services, features, functionality, messaging, story headlines, copy, prices, flows between pages, colors, and many others.

For example, let's say a businessperson thinks designing a new version of their company's homepage will increase sales. They will first gather and analyze qualitative and quantitative data to understand what their customers are trying to accomplish, and where they may be struggling. They may interview individual customers, or watch them interact with the site; they may look at data showing how most customers arrived at the homepage, what they then clicked on, where they may have abandoned the site, and what they did or didn't buy.

Using these insights, they'll hypothesize ways to improve the business while giving customers a better experience, and their hypotheses will be turned into a new design for the homepage. They will then split the customer traffic arriving on the homepage so that some visitors will be sent to the new design and the rest will be sent to the old design (**Figure 1.2**). Using data from real customers, they can then measure which version of the homepage offers better customer and business value.

In a more complex variation of this approach, the business may segment customer traffic to test the value of providing more personalized experiences. For example, a company could test a design that offers visitors different experiences based on whether they've been to the site or app before, what products or articles they've viewed, or even what the weather is where they're located.

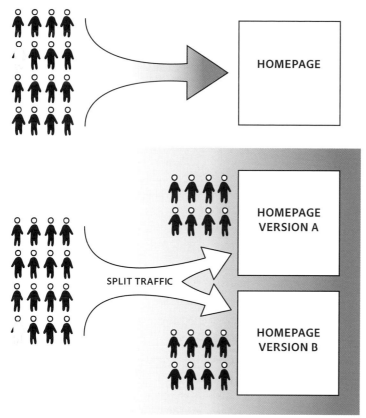

Figure 1.2 Instead of all customers seeing the same homepage, different customers can simultaneously experience different versions of the site.

Designed to Evolve:
The Iterative Optimization Methodology

The framework proposed in this book incorporates the customer-centric design principles just described into a repeatable process, called the *Iterative Optimization Methodology*. Adopted by businesses ranging from startups to some of the world's largest corporations, this methodology has brought in hundreds of millions of dollars in added value for those companies, by making the testing and refining of new designs an integral part of the process.

Businesses using this framework would ideally have at least one test running in every major area of the company (the amount of traffic a site receives may limit the number of tests it can run at once; this will be addressed later in the book). For example, a company could run one campaign testing different layouts for the homepage, another exploring ways to personalize recommended products, and global campaigns testing prices for top-selling items—all at the same time.

Within each section of a website, waves of successive tests drive improvements for that area: while one campaign is up and running, results from the previous test are analyzed and recommendations proposed; these recommendations are in turn added to the queue for evaluation. Overall, a business will compound the net positive impact from rounds of testing and gain a better understanding of how its designs influence its customers' behavior, both within each area individually and across the company.

This Iterative Optimization Methodology, described in detail later in the book, uses a framework that is lightweight, flexible, and scalable. It's lightweight in order to allow adequate, but not endless, time for analysis and planning, while staying focused on taking action. It's flexible, to allow plenty of room for creativity and innovation. Finally, it's scalable so that the same methodology can be applied to companies of any size, and at any stage of their growth, from infancy through to maturity, including large multinational corporations with business units spanning several countries.

The core principles of the methodology are:

▸ Starting from a helpful and customer-centric point of view

▸ Making use of both qualitative and quantitative customer research

▸ Regularly realigning the business's goals with those of the customers

▸ Experimenting with products and services by testing designs

Businesses, and designs, exist to help customers

The importance of starting from *a foundation of helpfulness* cannot be overstated. Before a successful business can exist, a customer for that company must exist. Customers are goal-oriented: they want to be able to do something they currently can't do, or accomplish something more easily than they currently can.

Businesses help customers accomplish their goals, or fulfill their unmet needs, by building *products* or *services* that customers use. It is important to recognize that, although interactive designs are sometimes—incorrectly—regarded as holding purely aesthetic value, they are in fact *products* or *services* that customers *use* when they are looking for help from businesses online.

Qualitatively and quantitatively understanding customer goals

Carefully studying customers can reveal a wealth of information about their unmet needs. Quantitative customer research is a highly effective means of finding out *what* customers do on a website, where they go, and where they may be struggling to achieve their goals. Online analytics systems can track information across every customer session, including entry points, clicks, page views, paths, searches, time spent on site, and purchases. They also allow analysts to examine the data in aggregate or at the individual customer level.

However, analytics systems have their limitations. If a business isn't providing a product or service that helps its customers, there's no quantitative financial or analytics report that will explain what the business should be building instead.

By contrast, qualitative inquiry, such as observational customer research, can reveal *why* customers come to a business for help with a specific problem in the first place, and *why* they may be struggling with certain sections of a site. Qualitative research can be nuanced, as customers don't always *articulate* their needs in a way a business can immediately address. Often they cannot put their finger on exactly why they became frustrated or disinterested and left a site; an external party can more easily make those observations. However, customers are very good at *demonstrating* where they have a need for more help.

Experts at qualitative observational research look for what customers are trying to accomplish, and pinpoint any obstacles they encounter, whether or not customers notice them. Skilled researchers listen carefully, look for nonverbal cues from body language, and read between the lines to identify the differences between what customers say and how they behave.

There is no substitute for watching actual customers when a business is trying to find out about their unmet needs; nor is there any substitute for aggregating site data when trying to analyze customer usage patterns. When paired together, both qualitative and quantitative research are extremely powerful tools for understanding customers' goals.

Continually realigning business and customer goals

As noted, a key part of the challenge of building a business online is first gaining an understanding of an obstacle that customers face, and then figuring out how to build a product or service to help them overcome that obstacle, while also satisfying the business's goal of making money.

This is difficult, as business and customer goal alignment is always in flux and misalignment is common. The most basic error businesses make is building something customers don't want, or more often, continuing to build a product, or to provide a service, customers used to want but no longer do.

Businesses that fail to make it easy and convenient for customers to achieve their goals open up a competitive weakness that can be exploited by another company. In a world where businesses are racing to provide customers with ever more convenient experiences, at lower costs, only the most customer-centric businesses survive.

Experimenting with new products and services

The only reliable way to determine whether a product or service is helpful is to see how customers respond to it under real market conditions. Businesses can build all the financial projections and conduct all the customer research they want, but there is no substitute for testing ideas in the open marketplace.

Companies with an online presence have an advantage over traditional brick-and-mortar businesses in that their customers interact with them virtually, and they can therefore change aspects of their business models (for example, what products they offer, what prices they charge, how they communicate with customers, and so on) more quickly.

Rather than waiting for competitors to offer more customer-centric products or services, *market-leading* companies distinguish themselves by continually redefining how effective they can be. They regularly ask: could we be even more helpful to our customers? And if the answer is yes, as it most always is, they test potential solutions to their customers' problems.

Visual Business Cases

This book draws on "visual business cases," in which images play a central role in laying out the different stages of decision making. The cases illustrate the approaches different companies have taken to solving problems by reviewing the before-and-afters of *what the businesses themselves actually looked like*, rather than ideas expressed solely in words, tables, and charts—a fitting approach for the highly visual, interactive world of online business.

The visual business cases outlined in this book will typically show how a company applied the following steps:

1. Identify the business goals.
2. Identify the customer goals, as informed by qualitative and quantitative customer research.
3. Generate hypotheses about how to better satisfy the business and customer goals through new designs, and define how success will be measured.
4. Create designs that isolate potentially impactful elements of the page to test each hypothesis, and display them visually for comparison.
5. Analyze the test results and provide business recommendations.

Given the rapidly evolving nature of the online business landscape, these examples will necessarily be dated by the time of publication. Even if they were not, however, they should serve as examples of what's possible rather than as specific designs that can be applied directly to other companies. Every business—and every customer—is unique.

For those who love taking action over endless analysis and wrapping their heads around puzzles related to expressing ideas interactively, visual business cases can act as a source of inspiration. To help explain the ideas discussed in this chapter, the next section provides two such cases as examples.

The Washington Post: Social Networking Links

As a global media company specializing in newspaper print and online publishing, *The Washington Post* is having to adapt to the virtual world: many customers now prefer to read articles for free on their phones and computers, rather than pay for print newspapers; new online publishers, competitors for classified listings, and digital advertising models are disrupting former revenue mainstays. With their traditional revenue models upset by the emergence of technology, organizations such as *The Washington Post* need to figure out how to evolve into successful online businesses.

In 2013, Jeff Bezos, the founder and CEO of Amazon.com, bought *The Washington Post*, and in his first interview about the purchase, said the following about testing to align the business with the customer: "In my experience, the way invention, innovation, and change happen, is a team effort... You develop theories and hypotheses, but you don't know if readers will respond. You do as many experiments as rapidly as possible."

This business case is an example of early experimentation by *The Washington Post* and centers on its article pages, as viewed from a desktop web browser, as opposed to a mobile one. The test took place in 2009, the year Facebook surpassed MySpace as the largest social network, based on monthly unique visitors.

In an interview for this book, Eileen Krill, Senior Marketing Research Manager for *The Washington Post*, noted, "We analyzed our online data, and noticed that social networking sites were becoming an important source of incoming traffic. The *Post* had already added links to each article, to try to make it easy for our readers to share stories on social networks, but our analytics showed that very few customers were clicking on these links. The goal of this design test was to increase clicks to share articles, in the hopes of generating even more traffic from social networks." Since viewing articles was the primary customer goal, more traffic from social networks would hopefully lead to more articles viewed, which would in turn lead to more advertising revenue for the business.

An example of the default article page appears in **Figure 1.3**. The links to share an article on social networks were offered in a page element called the "toolbox," and appeared above the fold on most screens ("the fold" refers to the bottommost part of the page viewable before the customer has to scroll to see more). A link to share on the social network Yahoo! Buzz appeared within the toolbox, but a reader had to click on "Save/Share+" to expose the additional sharing links. In 2009, this "Save/Share+" element was a popular design pattern used to contain social sharing links.

The *Post*'s overarching hypothesis was that alternate page layouts that better exposed the links would lead to increased clicks to share articles. This hypothesis was translated into several different designs; each was tested against the default experience across all articles for a period of several weeks. Each design is displayed below with a sample article; the default design is referred to as Recipe A, and the alternate options are called Recipes B, C, D, E, and F.

Figure 1.3 The default article template for *The Washington Post*. The test was run across all article pages simultaneously; the above screenshot, with a tongue-in-cheek headline about Susan Boyle, is just one example.

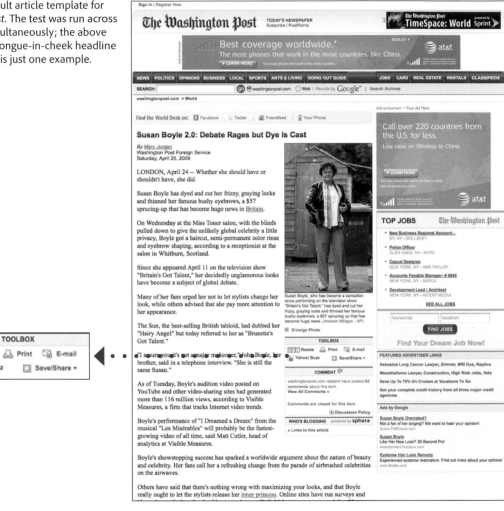

Alternate design: Recipe B

The alternate design for Recipe B, pictured in **Figure 1.4**, was built based on the following analysis:

Hypothesis:

▶ Customers are familiar with the toolbox as a way of accessing important links like those for printing or emailing articles, so this is still the most appropriate place on the page for social sharing links. Placing each link directly within the toolbox, as opposed to behind a "Save/Share+" link, will better expose the links, leading to more sharing. This will also ensure the links appear above the fold on most screen sizes.

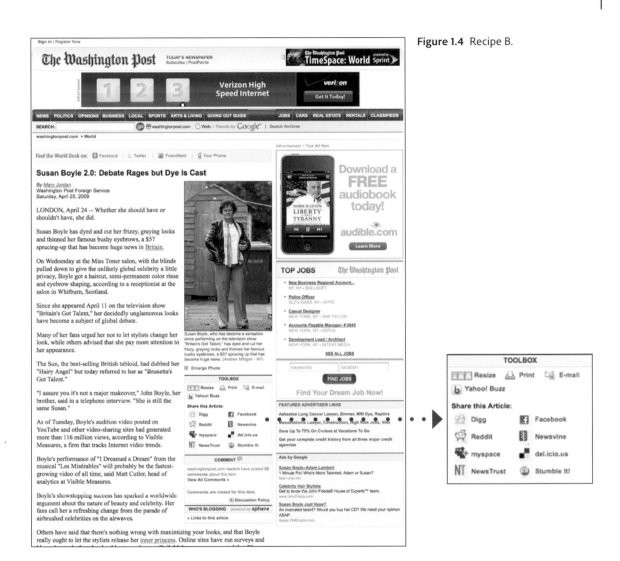

Figure 1.4 Recipe B.

Design:

▶ The "Save/Share+" element has been removed. Except for the Yahoo! Buzz link, which remains in the same place in each recipe, all of the sharing links have been placed under text reading, "Share this Article." Each link also appears next to an icon representing the different social networks.

Risks:

▶ Customers are primarily focused on the article and may ignore the toolbox unless they want to print or email an article.

▶ As it appears next to the right-hand column of the page, which is filled with advertisements, customers may mistake the toolbox for an advertisement and ignore it.

Alternate design: Recipe C

The alternate design for Recipe C, pictured in **Figure 1.5**, was built based on the following analysis:

Figure 1.5 Recipe C.

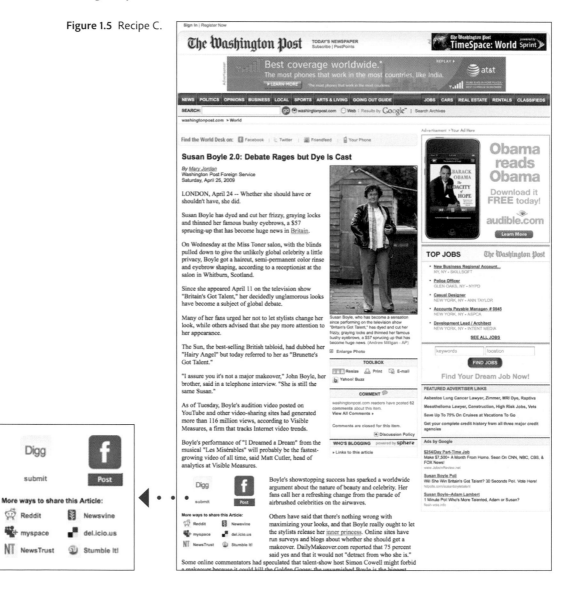

Hypotheses:

This version incorporates two hypotheses into one design:

▶ Since customers are engaged with the article, inserting the links into the article, rather than having them only in the toolbox, will place them in the line of sight of the reader, and increase the likelihood that customers will click on them.

▶ The two most popular links account for many of the shares; therefore, making those links more prominent than the others will increase overall clicks to share.

Design:

▶ The social sharing links have been inserted into the body of every article.

▶ Digg and Facebook, the two most popular sharing links based on site analytics at the time, are prominent icons, with buttons to "submit" or "post," appearing under each, respectively.

Risks:

▶ Customers may find this design unnecessarily disruptive to reading the article, leading to irritation, fewer clicks, and fewer page views.

Alternate design: Recipe D

The alternate design for Recipe D, pictured in **Figure 1.6**, was built based on the following analysis:

Hypothesis:

▶ The same as for Recipe C, except that this hypothesis posits that showing all the links at once may overwhelm customers to the point where a decision becomes hard to make. Instead, prominently showing only the two most popular links will make customers more likely to share.

Design:

▶ The sharing links, except for Digg and Facebook, have been hidden. When customers click the link reading, "More ways to share this Article..." the other links will appear.

▶ Since this design does not take up as much space as Recipe C, the Digg and Facebook links have been oriented vertically, in order to be slightly less disruptive to the reader.

Risks:

▶ Even though the links take up less space, customers may still find this design unnecessarily intrusive.

Figure 1.6 Recipe D.

Alternate design: Recipe E

The alternate design for Recipe E, pictured in **Figure 1.7**, was built based on the following analysis:

Hypothesis:

▶ Customers will be more likely to share an article once they have completed reading it; therefore, placing the sharing links at the bottom of the article will lead to increased clicks to share.

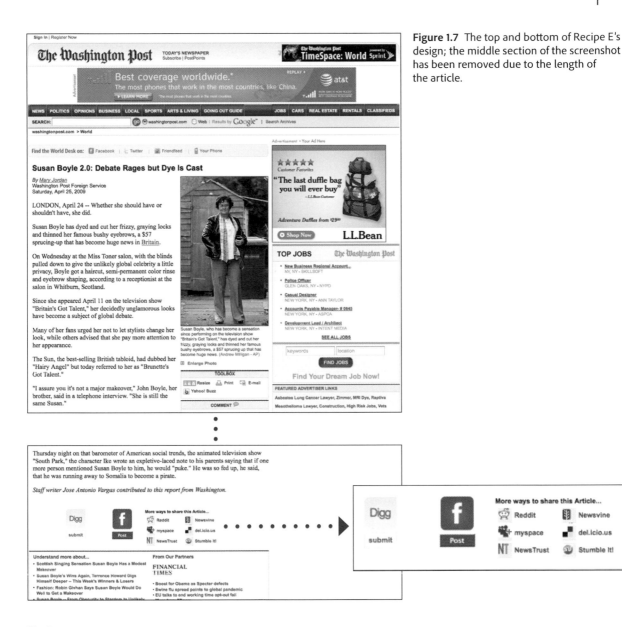

Figure 1.7 The top and bottom of Recipe E's design; the middle section of the screenshot has been removed due to the length of the article.

Design:

▶ The sharing links appear at the bottom of the article. Just like in Recipe C, the links for Digg and Facebook are more prominent than the others.

Risks:

▶ Observational research revealed that a lot of customers tend to scan articles quickly rather than read them in their entirety, and while some scanners reach the bottom of the page, not all do. If they don't make it to the bottom of the page, they won't see the links.

▶ The bottom of the page already has links to related articles. Placing the links to share on top of them will create competing calls to action.

Alternate design: Recipe F

The alternate design for Recipe F, pictured in **Figure 1.8**, was built based on the following analysis:

Figure 1.8 The top and bottom of Recipe F's design; the middle section of the screenshot has been removed due to the length of the article.

Hypothesis:

▶ The same as Recipe E, with the following additions: customers who click to share are more advanced users and will recognize the sharing sites from their icons alone. The less cluttered the page, the more likely customers will be to notice, rather than ignore, the different elements on the page. Therefore, placing the sharing icons at the bottom of the page using a minimal design will lead to increased clicks to share.

Design:

▶ The sharing links are exposed at the bottom of the article, all with equal prominence. The design includes the icons, but not the names of the sharing sites. This was a popular design for sharing links in 2009.

Risks:

▶ The same as Recipe E. Additionally, the set of customers who engage may be more limited, as even though some may click out of curiosity, it's more likely that only customers who recognize the social networks from their icons will click to share.

Results

The next task was to determine which designs, if any, would make customers more likely to share *The Washington Post*'s articles on social networks.

The testing process showed that Recipe E was the best-performing design and generated **188% more clicks to share** than the default—a statistically significant increase that strongly suggests the new design led to the rise in clicks, as **Figure 1.9** on the next page shows. The other recipes also dramatically boosted the number of clicks to share, with statistical significance, but not as much as Recipe E.

Note that test results are typically calculated as a percent of a percent. For example, if 2% of the visitors to the default page clicked to share an article (this figure is fictional; the actual number is confidential), then in Recipe E, 5.76% of the visitors clicked to share (5.76% is 188% larger than 2%). A 188% lift represents a very large increase in article sharing.

Overall, these results likely demonstrate that if a business wants customers to use a page element, it's best to expose it rather than hide it—and, while *how* best to expose it is difficult to determine, design testing can help. Exactly *why* Recipe E outperformed the other designs is a question that can't be answered from the test results alone. Human behavior is complex, and generally far from predictable. Testing is only one of several tools used in the Iterative Optimization Methodology to help create better customer experiences.

Later, the book will discuss subsequent steps, such as reporting and monetizing results, making actionable business recommendations based on testing, and launching iterative follow-up tests. For example, whether users who clicked to share in Recipe E were reading the article in its entirety, or scanning until the end, can't be determined from the test alone, but is one of many questions that future rounds of testing and observational customer research can seek to answer.

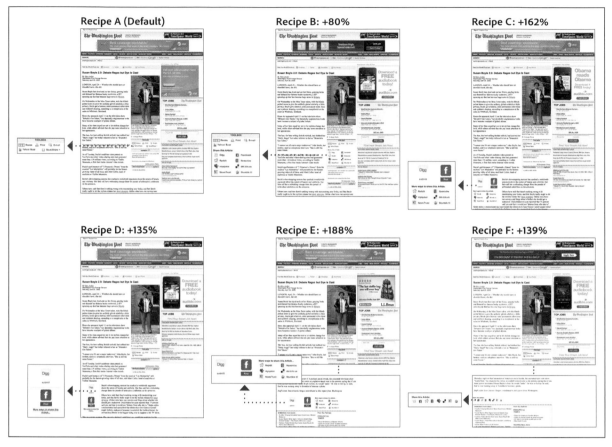

Figure 1.9 Results for the social networking test across all article pages.

2012 Presidential Election: Dinner with Barack Image Test

President Barack Obama's 2012 presidential campaign was known for making great use of data. Part 3 of the book includes a detailed interview with Kyle Rush, who ran the campaign website, Obama for America. Kyle and his team ran over 500 tests across the site—tests that are estimated to have raised the overall donation rate by 49% and the email acquisition rate by 161%.

The test described here was run on a page called Dinner with Barack, pictured in **Figure 1.10**. During the election, the page asked for a visitor's email address and zip code, after which they would be entered into the contest. People who submitted their email addresses were a top source of donations during the election, so collecting emails was one of the site's primary goals.

Figure 1.10 Test default version of the page, with a prominent picture of the President.

Figure 1.11 The alternate version of the page, picturing the President, the First Lady, and two previous contest winners together at dinner.

Kyle Rush explained, "We ran several of these contests. We would fly the winner, and one of their guests, out to Washington, D.C., and they would have dinner with the President. The contest sounded farfetched, so we wanted to see if testing could help people to see that it was a real, actual contest. All we did for this test was change the graphic at the top of the page.

"We found that there are many variables in photos that can affect performance, but possibly the biggest impact had to do with the context in which the photo was used. The default shows an image that is focused on the President [Figure 1.10]. Previous tests, elsewhere on the site, had shown that large photos with a focus on the President increased performance.

"The alternate image shows a photo of the President and the First Lady, at a dinner table with two people who previously won the Dinner with Barack contest [**Figure 1.11**]. We hoped that users would be more likely to convert if they could see just how close they would be sitting to the President of the United States during dinner."

The results are displayed in **Figure 1.12** on the next page. The alternate version of the page generated a 19% increase in email and zip code submissions—a huge lift. This is a great example of how a simple change, based on design instincts coming from a customer-centric point of view—hypothesizing that an image to help visitors imagine what dinner with the President and the First Lady was really like—can dramatically affect the performance of a site.

Business cases that appear in later chapters show how tools described in this book can help analyze a wide variety of success metrics, including pages viewed, accounts created, purchases completed, and revenue.

Figure 1.12 The image showing the President and First Lady, along with an actual winning couple, led to a 19% increase in email address and zip code submissions.

Recipe A (Control)   Recipe B: +19%

Building an Optimization Organization

The impact of the Iterative Optimization Methodology is not confined to improving a business's website. It can transform a company's culture, infusing it with a greater commitment to collaboration, creativity, and accountability as it begins to develop new strategies, structures, and skill sets for its team members.

The key to this process is the way in which the methodology marries creativity and data so that the influence of a design can be measured. This gives team members throughout the company the shared goal of driving customer and business value. Ideally, a company would then apply resources to changing the organization only in ways that can be validated through customer data in real-world situations.

Such culture changes don't happen overnight. Companies usually begin by running campaigns in an ad hoc manner, sometimes without even defining how success will be measured. They then start to plan individual campaigns in advance, document and share test results throughout the organization, and eventually begin to prioritize resources and ideas for testing.

Executives buy in, mandating that future investments in changing the business be measurable, and, as much as possible, be based on both data and innovative thinking. Team members begin to understand whether or not what they're working on is helping the business, and stop working on programs that aren't measurable. Real-time measurability can also offer early warning signs for projects that would otherwise be deemed too high-risk to attempt, opening up opportunities to experiment with more creative and ambitious ideas.

Embracing the principles of optimization can, then, be a long journey, and companies face a number of bumps along the road, from identifying essential roles and skill sets, to finding the best model of corporate governance. This book explores all of these issues, and more, in an effort to help companies embrace the potential of the digital age.

The Skill Set of the Future

The ability to acquire and nurture talent is one of the largest challenges when it comes to successfully running a business today. The current pace of innovation is so rapid that companies have to hire for roles that didn't exist a few years ago, and then quickly enable these employees to perform new skills. Few candidates have a solid foundation in both design and business, even though these fields are now deeply interconnected, and companies are still experimenting with ways to organize for the digital space.

Lying at the intersection of design, data, marketing, and technology, optimization is highly interdisciplinary and requires the ability to apply visual problem-solving skills in all of those areas. As more and more businesses are built online, the ability to combine these disciplines to create compelling interactive experiences will become increasingly important; indeed, it could even be called the skill set of the future.

Up Next

Refining design refers to the process through which a business continually redefines itself by experimenting with alternate designs. The framework outlined in this chapter helps companies achieve this goal by combining the art of creating powerful, effective designs that respond to changing customer and company needs, with the science of business, in which data analysis and experimentation are used to evaluate the effect of new designs.

Relatively new to the field of online design, this mix of art and science sometimes raises controversy: in particular, designers worry about the use of data inhibiting their creativity. The next chapter addresses this concern, discussing how data is used to guide, but not to dictate, business decisions. It also shows how, rather than stifling ideas, data and technology can assist in creating a space that allows even more room for creativity—creativity that, being more informed, delivers a more powerful impact.

References

1. How Long Do Users Stay on Web Pages? Neilson Norman Group: http://www.nngroup.com/articles/how-long-do-users-stay-on-web-pages/

2. Jeffrey Bezos, Washington Post's next owner, aims for a new 'golden era' at the newspaper: http://www.washingtonpost.com/lifestyle/style/jeffrey-bezos-washington-posts-next-owner-aims-for-a-new-golden-era-at-the-newspaper/2013/09/02/30c00b60-13f6-11e3-b182-1b3bb2eb474c_story.html

3. Facebook vs. MySpace: Tale of the Tape: https://blog.compete.com/2009/02/26/facebook-myspace/

CHAPTER 2

Using Data to Inform Design

There is a range of common misconceptions among designers and marketers about working with data. Some believe it will stifle creativity; others fear that data-driven decisions will trump common sense. Such concerns arise from the traditional design process, which is often shaped by bad or incomplete data, or by internal politics. This chapter reexamines the traditional design process, and shows how striking a balance between data and design actually enhances creativity as well as design effectiveness. It concludes with commentary from a host of business leaders, including influential people from some of the largest companies in the world, about how they use data as one of many ways to inform customer-centric design.

The Traditional Design Process

The conventional design process puts a business at risk by not testing new designs. No matter how large or small the scope of a new design—it might consist of whole pages, just a small element of one page, or an entire site—the traditional process differs from the method described in this book in two important ways:

▶ Only one version of the new design is created.

▶ The new design is not tested with customers in a controlled environment on the live site or in an app.

The traditional design process aims for perfection. Because only one version of the design is created, it needs to provide the ideal customer experience and to help the business reach its goals. When every pixel needs to be perfect, businesses often invest enormous amounts of time, money, and energy in building a single design. Yet even the most experienced and talented designers, marketers, and businesspeople are not able to predict with great accuracy how customers will engage with their designs. This overinvestment in reaching an unattainable goal may even demotivate team members who don't know whether they're helping or hurting the business when they launch a new design.

Most companies still follow this traditional process, which means they effectively make design decisions flying blind, basing their choices on either *bad data* or *internal politics*.

Design Decisions Based on Bad Data

Many businesses measure the performance of a page or website before and after a design change to evaluate its effectiveness. The trouble with this method is that without controlling for factors other than the design changes, it's impossible to know whether the change in performance is in fact due to the new design. A business's environment is always in flux and may be affected by such variables as the economy, seasonality, competitive dynamics, the quality of the traffic reaching the design, and more.

For example, the graph in **Figure 2.1** shows the conversion rate (percentage of visitors who bought something) for a major U.S. retail site over the course of a year. Notice how the conversion rate changes over time. It may vary not only because of design changes, but also because of other events, such as the business lowering prices, a competitor raising prices, the global economy picking up, weekday or weekend traffic patterns, a popular new product being released, and so on. If the retailer were to remake its homepage and try to measure the new design's effectiveness simply by monitoring the conversion rate over time, it would be unable to determine whether any changes were due to the new homepage or to other, completely unrelated reasons.

The same type of graph can be charted for any type of business—media, financial services, travel, and so on. No matter what sector of business is involved, any organization that attributes a change in site metrics to a design change that has been made outside of a controlled experiment risks assuming a cause-and-effect relationship where none may exist. For that reason, it is essential to control for variables through a randomized experiment.

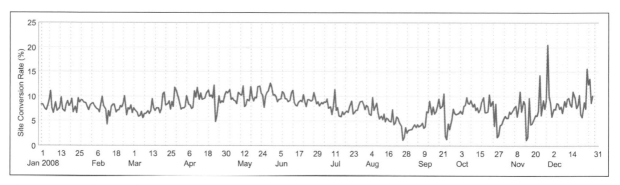

Figure 2.1 Many factors other than design impact the percentage of visitors who make a purchase from any online store; these factors are constantly changing, as this chart tracking a retailer's conversion rate shows.

The full-site redesign: Flipping a switch

A full-site redesign—changing an entire site at once—is sometimes referred to as *flipping a switch*: One second the old site exists intact, and in an instant it disappears and is replaced by an entirely new one.

Businesses typically put an enormous amount of time, effort, and money into redesigning an entire site. The process usually takes months and can even stretch into years. Every element of the existing site may be affected—pages, global navigation, overall aesthetics, multipage flows, and more. By changing everything at once, full-site redesigns follow the traditional design process, which focuses on building one perfect site.

Even when all involved are doing their best to redesign the site to provide customer and business value, chances are that some of the changes will be helpful, some will not, and some won't matter one way or the other. And because all of these changes are made at the same time, it's impossible to measure the impact of each one individually.

As a result, despite investing heavily in a full-site redesign, businesses may have little to show for the effort in terms of measurable customer and business value. All that effort and money could have been spent getting to know their customers better—a much more worthwhile pursuit.

Design Decisions Based on Pixel Politics

"Pixel politics" arise when people disagree about how to create or change designs; this is almost inevitable when companies try to work through multiple points of view in a quest for perfection. Even if the team members are extremely collaborative, conduct brainstorming sessions to give voice to all of their ideas, and sketch out several possible variations of the design, the traditional process allows only one version of the design to be chosen in the end. This means that all ideas need to be incorporated into the final design, dismissed altogether, or consolidated with other ideas through compromise. However, each of these options presents important pitfalls:

▶ **Incorporating alternate ideas.** It is difficult to create a simple customer experience when some ideas cannot be excluded. In order to settle debates, redesign teams sometimes resort to carving up the website into individual pages, or elements within pages, to give each stakeholder their own territory in which to deploy their ideas. Too often, the overall result is a cluttered, inconsistent, and confusing design.

▶ **Dismissing alternate ideas.** When a new concept is excluded, the business misses out on trying an idea that could delight its customers and bring in a lot of money. In addition, such choices don't reflect the customer's preferences, as determined by objective testing, but rather the unique balance of power that had developed to satisfy the business's internal politics: When one party *defers design* to another, the final say may go to the person with the most seniority, to whoever can best defend their design verbally, or, most often, to whoever claims to have the best design instincts.

▶ **Compromising on alternate ideas.** Although it may sound like a great idea, design through compromise may be the most dangerous approach of all. When competing ideas are modified to reach a middle ground, the core message risks becoming watered down so much that it is effectively lost altogether, creating a poorly focused design that may leave customers wondering why the business exists at all. For example, if there is disagreement over which of many different product benefits to promote, a design may in the end treat all benefits equally, relegating them to a low-key list of features rather than highlighting the most appealing one with a large headline. Similarly, rather than offering a few extremely distinct products in each category, a design by compromise may present an overwhelming number of similar products.

All three outcomes of "pixel politics"—incorporating alternate ideas, dismissing alternate ideas, and consolidating ideas through compromise—reflect a design process that addresses the need to resolve internal disputes within the business but does not necessarily satisfy the need to help customers or to make money.

Reexamining the Design Process

Over the last few years, the desire to understand whether new designs are effective has led to design testing, which allows businesses to determine objectively whether designs are driving customer and business value. Testing differs from the traditional design process in two important ways:

▶ Multiple new designs are created, with each representing a different idea.

▶ The new designs are tested with customers in a controlled environment, on the live site or in an app, to measure their impact.

The business no longer needs to make decisions based on bad data or internal politics because the new process provides a way to gauge the effect of the designs. Based on this knowledge, the business can make *better-informed* decisions. It is important to note that, although companies will generally use the best-performing designs, they don't have to: Test results are one of several pieces of data used to make decisions, and other priorities—like the desire to simplify an experience—can sometimes trump raw metrics. In addition, design testing not only provides a company with helpful data, but also has a largely positive effect on its internal culture, unlike the traditional design process.

Design Decisions Based on Good Data

The impact of a new concept can be measured by using technology to split traffic randomly between designs, establishing the original design as the control. As the environment around the business changes, all designs will be affected simultaneously. The graph in **Figure 2.2** shows a few weeks' results from a controlled experiment, and each line in the graph represents the performance of a different version of the design. Recipe A is the control, or default design, and Recipes B through F are alternate designs. (Design testing is also referred to as A/B testing, because the letters A, B, C, and so on, are sometimes used to refer to the various designs.)

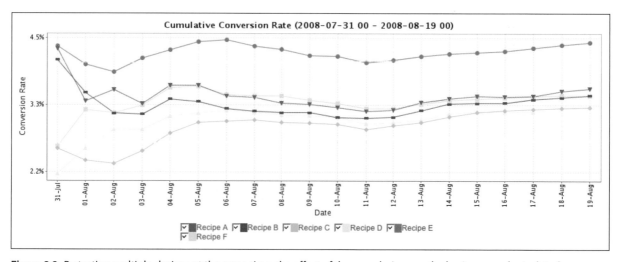

Figure 2.2 By testing multiple designs at the same time, the effect of the new designs on the business can be isolated.

The conversion rates for all designs rise from Aug. 3 to Aug. 4, fall from Aug. 7 to Aug. 10, and rise from Aug. 12 onward. Even though the conversion rates for all designs change over time, the difference in performance between the recipes can be measured: Version E, which is a new design, clearly leads to a higher conversion rate than the default design, version A.

The iterative design process isn't about being a genius whose every idea is guaranteed to drive customer and business value. Instead, it's about knowing whether or not changes to designs are constructive. Additional benefits of having good data to inform decision making include mitigating risk by "failing faster," encouraging innovation, responding quickly to change, and making good use of time and money:

▶ **Mitigating risk by failing faster.** In the traditional process, businesses replace old designs with new ones for all customers at once, but with no means of evaluating such changes, they don't even realize when a new design is losing them money every day. Testing allows a business to try out a new design on a percentage of its customers; if the design underperforms, it can be taken down quickly before any major damage is done. Mitigating risk in this way is called *failing faster*. The business can then quickly regroup, trying to understand why the new design didn't work and determining how to build one that will succeed.

▶ **Encouraging innovation.** Businesses that run design experiments can take much larger risks without having to commit to bad decisions for a long period of time. For example, if a news media business creates a special section during a presidential campaign news cycle, testing can help to determine whether adding features and funneling traffic to that section will lead to additional return visits, page views, and advertising revenue.

▶ **Responding quickly to change.** Optimization can help determine which levers, such as products, prices, and flows, businesses should exercise, based on their changing needs. For example, a retail site may find that, at the current moment, it needs to hit a certain revenue goal at the expense of profitability. Therefore, it may test lowering the threshold for how much a customer must spend before receiving free shipping or emphasizing popular but less profitable products more than usual. Testing these changes through design can help a business to determine how to achieve its goals as quickly as possible.

▶ **Making good use of time and money.** Some people think creating multiple versions of a new design is more time-consuming than building one new version. In reality, this is usually not the case. The traditional process squanders a lot of time and money while stakeholders try to decide which of several ideas is best, whereas with testing, multiple versions of a design can usually be created in the same, or even less, time. Not only is testing an efficient process, but it also saves money, because businesses using the traditional method can make decisions that cause them to lose customers and profits without knowing it. All in all, the iterative design process is time well spent and in almost all cases pays for itself very quickly.

Businesses can build all the financial models they want and ask customers their opinions, but until they take a risk and try out a concept they just won't know the outcome. Through testing designs, knowledge about what is and isn't helpful will grow iteratively over time, as will the business's understanding of its customers. At the same time, the optimization method allows for multiple ideas to be tested at once, thus expanding creative opportunities. In these ways, optimization not only improves the customer experience and increases revenue, but also positively affects company culture.

The Cultural Benefits of Testing Designs

There is no monopoly on good ideas, but in the traditional process, innovation is often the domain of only one person or one team. Rather than pitting one faction against another in a competition to select one good idea, the iterative design method is empowering for all involved, because companies can test two, three, four, or even more new designs at the same time.

The optimization process also helps unify organizations: Because ideas for testing can be suggested by anyone in the company, silos between different teams, such as analytics, marketing, and design, begin to break down. Everyone at the company can pursue the same set of goals: driving measurable business and customer value. Shared, measurable goals not only encourage people across departments to find new ways to collaborate, but they also lead to a culture of shared accountability.

Of course, not every idea will be tested: The business stakeholders will want to test only the designs they think have the most potential, but the bar should be set very low for this determination, because what customers find compelling can surprise even the most experienced businesspeople.

Without necessarily knowing it, customers will "vote" on which design they prefer. User behavior, as measured by a click of the mouse or a tap of the finger, can then inform a business's final decision on which design is the most valuable. The result is the "democratization" of both the creative process and the decision-making phase, because all people in the business can suggest ideas that can be tested, and all customers can participate in choosing which ideas win.

Online Design Is Not Fine Art

Some online designers incorrectly view their work as a form of fine art. They worry that measuring the impact of a design will compromise their artistic integrity and inhibit creativity. This all-or-nothing mind-set devalues data representing the customer perspective in favor of a "perfect design," as defined by subjective aesthetic opinion. This book advocates for a more balanced approach: Designs can be both pleasing to the eye *and* helpful to the customer.

What follows is an attempt to address some fears behind the concern that testing hinders creativity:

▶ **Data doesn't trump common sense.** Data on the performance of designs can only help *inform* decision making; ultimately, the decision about which design to use is still up to the business. For example, even though testing may occasionally show positive, short-term revenue results for non-user-centric designs—like checkout flows cluttered with up-sells, sites crowded with advertisements, confusing email opt-in selections, and intrusive pop-up windows—organizations need to apply sound judgment to create good long-term customer experiences. This is one of the many reasons why qualitative, not just quantitative, data is a key component of the Iterative Optimization Methodology.

▶ **There's no such thing as the perfect design.** Even when a business has optimized its designs to such a degree that any improvements may seem unnecessary, its customers' goals and the environment surrounding the business are always changing. As a result, the business's designs must evolve as well.

▶ **Iterative testing allows more opportunities for creativity.** Critics say testing stifles creativity, but in fact the opposite is true: By testing multiple versions of designs at once, and improving upon them in follow-up testing, the iterative method offers many chances to inject new ideas.

▶ **Value is generated from ideas; testing only helps quantify them.** Opponents sometimes point to tests that don't show a significant difference between new and original designs as proof that testing doesn't make a difference or that it can only lead to marginal improvements. If a new design gets less than stellar results in testing, it means the new design is having a negligible impact, not that the practice of testing isn't worthwhile.

▶ **Design changes don't need to be small.** Testing can help inform design decisions ranging from small copy and color changes to large redesigns of entire pages, flows, and sites. Although small changes can sometimes make a big difference in performance, design tests can be as ambitious as desired. Changing multiple design elements at once makes it difficult to know which of those changes had an impact, but there's absolutely nothing wrong with doing so and attempting to understand which of the individual changes was most influential during future rounds of testing.

▶ **Creating great designs is hard.** Without testing, people can easily assume that customers love all of their design ideas. However, companies that have been testing for years report that more than half of the designs they expect to provide positive lift do not. It is impossible to know how a design will perform in advance of testing it with real customers.

▶ **Computers are not replacing designers.** Common industry phrases like "data-driven design" or "designing by the numbers" may imply otherwise, but computers can't yet design businesses. Only designers can provide the creative spark needed to decide which ideas to test. At the far end of the spectrum of data-driven design, some "auto-optimizing" programs can determine which one, of multiple designs, to show to a customer, based on real-time test results; however, even in this process, it is still a designer who actually created all of the concepts being tested.

▶ **Industry awards are not as important as satisfied customers.** Designers and marketers are still often judged according to the "snazziness" of their work, and they strive for industry awards that reflect the opinion of the marketing and design communities. Although there's nothing inherently wrong with peer accolades, these are rarely based on business success or customer satisfaction. The latter can and should take priority now that the impact of designs is measurable. Norms for what constitutes "good" design, "catchy" headlines, and user experience "best practices" will change as designs are tailored to specific businesses based on real customer data.

Museum Pieces and Contrasting Colors

Designers accustomed to the traditional process often lose sight of their business role and create *museum pieces*—designs that might look beautiful framed and hung up on a wall but that rarely test well with customers.

People *use* and *interact* with webpages in almost the opposite way they engage with art. They view art for a wide range of reasons, such as the desire to learn about a new idea, to reflect on their feelings, or simply to absorb a visual experience. However, when people look at webpages, most are hunting for information or a place to click that will take them closer to their goal.

One way in which classical web designers wind up creating museum pieces is to layer colored text or navigational features on top of backgrounds of a very similar color (**Figure 2.3**). Aesthetically, this approach is appealing, because it makes the elements on a page harmonious. However, it also makes the text or navigational features hard for customers to see, undermining their ability to interact with the design.

An example of this phenomenon is gray text on a gray background: It's extremely difficult to read, yet it is one of the more popular design patterns on the web today. Although a stark black-and-white contrast may be jarring to the senses when it appears in fine art, a webpage is easy to read when black text is placed against a white background. This is especially true when the page is viewed on small mobile devices or the viewer has aging eyesight.

In summary, websites can look good, but if they look so good that they belong in an art museum, they most likely won't be easy for visitors to use.

Figure 2.3 Examples of paired text and background colors used in important headlines on leading websites. The text in the image says, "This is hard to read."

Advice from Business Leaders

Many business leaders from a wide variety of industries were generous enough to grant interviews for this book. In this section, key figures from Google, Facebook, and LinkedIn explain how they have found a way to address the issue at the center of this chapter—pairing data with design—in a balanced and highly effective way within their organization.

"There's a little bit of a tendency for people to pick sides. People may say, 'I want to go with my gut,' versus, 'I want to analyze this to death.' I don't think it's black and white. Clearly, there's a spectrum, and you can do too much of one thing, which is why we use a host of qualitative and quantitative methods. Design does not exist in and of itself. Design is not art. Design is about problem solving. That is design at its heart. As a designer, I could be doing a disservice to myself, and my users, if I was trying to solve a problem and then had no idea whether the design had solved the problem…. I would be designing in ignorance. That's not fair to the users we're designing for."

—**JON WILEY**
Lead Designer, Google Search

"I bet every single company struggles with these issues. For me, the key issue is how far the pendulum swings in one direction…. When people are completely dependent on metrics to make design decisions, they've gone too far in one direction; when people are adamant that metrics and feedback simply don't matter, they've gone too far in the other direction. In my day-to-day role this balance comes up constantly…. We want to empower our teams to be incredibly creative, take risks, and make bold decisions—but also, we want to be thoughtful about how the interfaces function, and we want to know how those decisions really impact people's lives."

—**NATE BOLT**
Design Research Manager, Facebook; Former CEO of Bolt|Peters
(acquired by Facebook)

"I would hate for designers to think that A/B testing doesn't allow them to try new things or go with their gut. We try to globally optimize. Sometimes, you need to take a hit on one metric for an overall better user experience. It's not always an exact 'this goes down, and this goes up' equation. As designers, we need to feel empowered to sometimes push back on a metric-driven business world. Yes, metrics matter, but you need to be willing to take risks in order to facilitate bigger design changes and bigger steps forward. We continually strive to simplify our products."

—**AMY PARNELL**
Principal Designer, LinkedIn

41 Shades of Blue

In February 2009, *The New York Times* published an article about how Google settled a debate over which tint of the color blue to use on its site's toolbar by testing 41 different shades. Less than one month later, Google's first self-described "classically trained designer" quit, publicly noting that although he understood the importance of testing, he was leaving because "data becomes a crutch for every decision, paralyzing the company."

The press ran with the story, publishing opinion pieces ranging from pieces praising Google's "refreshing and radical" approach to design, to scathing editorials claiming that Google's approach was "rigid," "tone-deaf on design," and even that it "assaults designers." Rather than trying to explain why Google may have run such a test in the first place, many stories framed the issue as a data-versus-a-designer debate, neglecting to mention that the data didn't represent a computer's opinion of the perfect shade of blue, but rather the preferences of millions of Google's users as expressed through their behavior, which Google measured not in order to hurt a designer's feelings but to improve its overall business and user experience.

Although choosing the correct shade of a color may seem unimportant to many businesses, it is essential to Google's business model. The world's most popular search engine, Google helps users find information by showing paid advertising links alongside the search results links and charging businesses when those paid links are clicked. It is a win-win-win scenario: Google's users have access to search results for free, its business customers pay to acquire valuable traffic, and Google makes more than enough money to continue to help its users find information. In 2012, approximately 95 percent of Google's $46 billion in revenues came from advertising. Both the paid and unpaid search links that Google offers its users are blue, so blue is an extremely important color—perhaps the most important color—for the company's business.

In an interview for this book, Jon Wiley, the Lead Designer for Google Search, noted that although the initial criticism highlighted the potential danger of "an over-reliance on one particular method of analysis," Google attempts to take an extremely balanced approach, incorporating design instincts as well as multiple methods that focus on the customer. He explained that testing comes into play in part because "very, very small variations in a design, which even to the trained eye are subtle, when multiplied across all of the times someone might use Google, can have an overall impact on their experience." (See Part 3 of the book for an in-depth interview.)

The Google story burned itself into the collective consciousness of the design community; almost five years after *The New York Times* article, this anecdote is still cited by those who fear data about customer behavior will take away creativity. It was brought up several times, unprompted, during interviews for this book.

It is a debate that doesn't need to exist—something this book aims to demonstrate. As Nate Bolt, Design Research Manager for Facebook, put it in an interview for this book, "I think the relationship between research and design is perhaps one of the most misunderstood in our industry," adding that "all the controversy around Google's 41 shades of blue experiment boils down to a little misunderstanding around how data can inform design decisions." It's simply a matter of striking the right balance, he explained: "Designers need to balance all the inputs. A lot of the best designers in the world understand the value of system (analytics) data, test data, qualitative data, and how they all fit together."

Up Next

This chapter set out to dispel some of the most common myths about the use of data to inform design, particularly the fear that testing will force creativity and good judgment to take a back seat to number-crunching exercises. It showed that, unlike the traditional process, with its quest for one perfect design, testing enhances creativity by allowing multiple concepts to be tried at once. It also eliminates the guesswork, bad data, and internal politics that often mar the traditional approach. Not having to be perfect is liberating: Business leaders can experiment more, learning about their business and their customers as they do, which is a win-win outcome for all concerned.

This chapter concludes Part 1 of the book, which defined the Iterative Optimization Methodology and explained the principal advantages of this highly effective approach to design. Part 2 walks the reader through the process, explaining step by step how the methodology is applied in practical terms and illustrating each step with real-life examples.

References

1. Putting a Bolder Face on Google: http://www.nytimes.com/2009/03/01/business/01marissa.html

2. Goodbye, Google: http://stopdesign.com/archive/2009/03/20/goodbye-google.html

3. Google's Marissa Mayer Assaults Designers with Data: http://www.fastcompany.com/1403230/googles-marissa-mayer-assaults-designers-data

4. Marissa Mayer Is Right 80 Percent of the Time: http://gawker.com/5189298/marissa-mayer-is-right-80-percent-of-the-time

5. Google Designer Leaves, Blaming Data-centrism: http://news.cnet.com/google-designer-leaves-blaming-data-centrism/

6. Google traffic: http://www.alexa.com

7. Google 2013 revenue (excluding revenues from 2012 Motorola acquisition): http://investor.google.com/financial/tables.html

8. Google Equates "Design" with Endless Testing. They're Wrong: http://www.fastcodesign.com/1662273/google-equates-design-with-endless-testing-theyre-wrong

9. Are Google's Nerds Destroying Design?: http://tech.fortune.cnn.com/2009/03/20/are-googles-nerds-destroying-design/

10. Google Instant or Google Stupid?:
http://www.zdnet.com/google-instant-or-google-stupid-4010018659/

11. Redesigning Google: How Larry Page Engineered a Beautiful Revolution:
http://www.theverge.com/2013/1/24/3904134/google-redesign-how-larry-page-engineered-beautiful-revolution

12. Testing times for Marissa Mayer as Yahoo's New Logo Falls Flat:
http://www.ft.com/cms/s/0/5c6239d8-163e-11e3-a57d-00144feabdc0.html#axzz2kqpEiD22

The Iterative Optimization Methodology

Part 2 provides an in-depth look at the Iterative Optimization Methodology, beginning with an overview of the process in Chapter 3. In subsequent chapters, this part presents a deep-dive analysis of each step, from the research and planning stages to the execution and analysis phases. Along with simple how-to instructions for each stage, Part 2 provides real-life examples, including visual illustrations, of how individual companies applied that step and how the process affected business and customer value in concrete terms for these organizations.

CHAPTER 3

Methodology Overview

This chapter takes a look under the hood of the Iterative Optimization Methodology, presenting a simple overview of each stage of the process. It then walks the reader through a real-life example of how each stage was applied by one of the hundreds of companies that now count on this straightforward and highly effective method to create designs that serve both the customer and the business in a constantly evolving market.

Step by Step

This chapter briefly sketches out the main stages of the methodology and then illustrates how they unfold from beginning to end, with a real-life example generously provided by PetCareRx, an online business that offers a variety of pet-care products.

Four key milestones mark the principal stages of the methodology:

1. **Optimization Roadmap.** Drawing on qualitative and quantitative research, companies generate a prioritized roadmap for testing across all areas of the business. Companies generally make minor changes to the roadmap after each test and consider major updates as part of their quarterly business reviews (QBRs).

2. **Optimization Plan.** Team members then create a plan for each test, including the objective, hypothesis, number of recipes, planned duration, wireframes, and final designs (sometimes called design composites, or "design comps").

3. **Optimization Launch.** The test is set up and double-checked during a round of quality assurance (QA) before it is launched.

4. **Optimization Results.** Team members analyze the test results, make recommendations based on those findings, and update the roadmap as needed. Results and next steps are communicated throughout the company, as the whole optimization process begins again, with updated goals.

The flowchart in **Figure 3.1** provides an overview of the most important components of the methodology; the numbered boxes mark the four milestones described in the preceding list. The roadmap, or planning, stage appears as a row at the top; the remaining stages are related to the execution of the process and appear in the circle below.

Ideally, businesses applying this approach will always have at least one optimization test running on their website; preferably, they will have tests running in multiple areas at once. In this way, they will discover where to focus future testing efforts based on what types of designs are and aren't working, and which sections of the site show the most need for improvement.

Finally, documentation is also a key, ongoing part of each stage in the process to facilitate communication across the company and to ensure team members can build on past experience and insights.

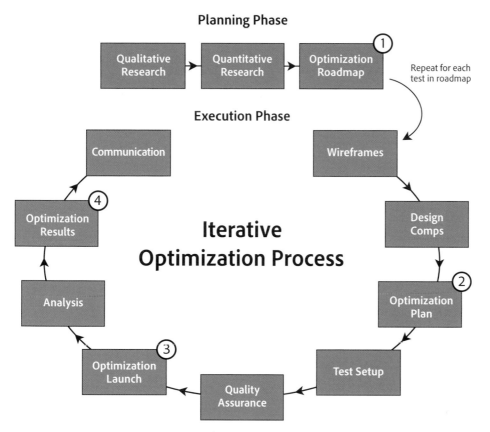

Figure 3.1 The step-by-step iterative optimization process. The top row shows the planning phase, culminating in the production of an Optimization Roadmap. The circle below this row will be repeated for each test prioritized in the roadmap.

The Paper Trail: Why It Matters and How to Do It

Documentation is an essential part of efficient communication and should ensure that actions, as well as the thought processes behind those actions, are captured for later reference. Many business cultures tend to go to extremes when it comes to documentation: They either create so much that almost nobody reads it, or they shy away from it altogether and risk wasting time repeating themselves as a result.

In the Iterative Optimization Methodology, documentation is designed to be:

▸ **Lightweight.** Documentation must allow others to grasp quickly what was done and why, as well as the result.

▶ **Standardized.** When team members communicate in a predictable way, it is much easier for everyone to stay on the same page, for hand-offs between new and existing teams to be smooth, and for feedback and approvals at any level to be obtained quickly. This also allows team members to spend more time thinking of creative test ideas rather than deciding how best to communicate their work.

▶ **Reusable.** Whenever possible, teams should reuse components of documentation to save time in writing up their work. For example, text explaining what test was launched and why would be recycled as part of the test results document.

▶ **Integrated into a library.** Teams should make the results from all campaigns easily accessible so that any member can reference what has and hasn't worked in the past. New actions will then build on past insights, making it easier to bring new team members onboard.

Documentation is built during each step of the process and plays an essential role in developing and communicating the successes of the iterative optimization program.

The Optimization Roadmap

The Optimization Roadmap is a strategic plan for testing across the business. The primary elements of this plan are:

▶ Data from qualitative and quantitative research, as well as results from previous tests

▶ Prioritized list of test areas (homepage, product page, etc.)

▶ Prioritized list of tests within each area (test new homepage layouts, test new product offering, and so on)

As noted in Chapter 1, the qualitative phase consists of gaining a better understanding of the customer's goals and determining how to align the business's objectives with them. This phase includes performing a heuristic review of the customer experience and comparing it with that offered by the business's competitors, using observational customer research, and other methods of inquiry. The quantitative phase consists of defining success metrics based on business and customer goals, as well as deriving insights from analytics data and other evidence-based inputs (see Chapters 4 and 5).

Finally, drawing on both of these kinds of data, the team identifies priority areas for improvements to the site and generates ideas for testing—a process that culminates in the creation of a blueprint for testing, which is called the Optimization Roadmap.

Campaigns are usually prioritized based on their perceived value and on ease of implementation, either technically or in terms of obtaining the required approvals. As noted, both individual tests and the entire testing program are reevaluated along the way and course adjustments made accordingly. These may include scaling up testing in some areas; scaling it down in others; launching larger, more ambitious tests in some areas; or launching smaller, more rapid-fire tests in others.

On top of these ongoing adjustments, many businesses also conduct a major review of the roadmap as a whole during their regular QBR cycle to ensure it reflects the strategic direction of the organization.

The Optimization Plan

The Optimization Plan contains all the information about an individual campaign prior to its approval for launch. Each plan includes an executive summary noting the objective of the test, the hypothesis being tested, the test methodology, and the estimated test length.

Most Optimization Plans follow the same basic structure, but depending on the tests they are supporting, these documents can scale from being assembled in just a few minutes—containing a few snippets of text and screen shots—to longer-term projects that take several hours or even days in the case of whole website redesigns, for example. Optimization Plans identify which metrics will be measured during the test and how they may be segmented for later analysis. They also include the specific designs being tested in the form of wireframes and design comps.

Wireframes

A *wireframe* is an illustration of a design—the place where an idea begins to be transformed into a visual experience. One of the most crucial elements in business design, wireframes (sometimes called user experience designs or recipe designs) can be as simple as a napkin sketch or as intricate as a final, pixel-perfect design.

Test ideas are often ambiguous when described in words. The wireframe provides a common language so everyone in the business can understand the concept being discussed without confusion. Wireframes usually include the specific layout, copy, and features to be tested. It is also during the wireframe phase that team members decide whether to test aesthetics such as colors and imagery, although such issues are usually finalized when the wireframe is translated into a design comp.

Design Comps

The *design composite*, or *design comp*, translates the wireframe into a fully developed design ready for testing. This stage presents a challenge in companies used to the traditional design process where one department, such as the marketing team, provides the wireframe, but another department—typically the design team—is responsible for translating that idea into an aesthetically pleasing design comp. Poor communication and competing priorities can easily derail the process at this stage. Businesses used to the traditional process may even skip the wireframing stage altogether and instead provide production designers with such vague directions that the objective of the test is unclear.

Translating a wireframe into a design comp should be a collaborative, back-and-forth process, not a firm hand-off between parties. In this way, the teams will build on one another's strengths, creating a final product that is greater than the sum of its parts. Once the design comp has been finalized, it is ready for testing.

Optimization Launch

Although the technical aspects of the Optimization Launch, including those related to using specific software for testing, are beyond the scope of this book, this stage will be discussed further in Chapter 6 from the point of view of business, analytics, marketing, and design stakeholders.

From that angle, the most important aspects of this step include ensuring that the final, interactive designs for testing look and function as intended; that all metrics for success, and segments, or different ways to group and view the data, are properly configured; and that screen shots of the final designs have been captured for posterity. Before the test is turned on, the details of these technical setup and Quality Assurance tasks will be added to the record of the Optimization Plan, iteratively transforming it into the Optimization Launch document.

Optimization Results

It is at the Optimization Results stage that testing reveals what matters to a business's customers, and the results can be surprising. This phase includes collecting and analyzing test data, making recommendations about the next steps, and communicating test results and any decisions across the company.

Analysis

Once the data has been analyzed, winning designs are usually implemented, replacing all other versions. As part of the analysis stage, team members learn what worked and what didn't, and often come up with new ideas about how to further improve both the customer experience and the business. These ideas will be added to the Optimization Roadmap, after which they'll be turned into hypotheses, which will in turn be translated into wireframes and designs, as the whole process repeats.

Communication

Like documentation, communication is not limited to summing up results at the end of a test; it is also a vital function that is integral to every stage of the process. Regular communication, through newsletters, a shared library, and other means, is critical not only as a way to keep team members and stakeholders informed about a testing program, but also as means of soliciting ideas for testing and of garnering support for the program throughout the corporate ecosystem.

Having described the optimization process, this chapter now turns to a real-life example of how one company used this methodology to achieve significant improvements in its revenue and in its overall customer experience. The case study walks the reader through each stage of the process, providing an overview of the optimization methodology in action, from start to finish.

Case Study: PetCareRx

One of many companies that have fully embraced the Iterative Optimization Methodology, PetCareRx graciously agreed to share an example of how this method has benefitted the company.

An online business focused on pet wellness, PetCareRx offers an array of prescription and nonprescription medications, toys, foods, and vitamins, as well as pharmaceutical services. The following example, from 2009, shows how this business applied the optimization methodology to improve its homepage. With visits to the homepage generating tens of millions of dollars in revenue each year, the resulting boost to homepage performance represented a significant lift in annual revenue.

Optimization Roadmap

As they set out to build their Optimization Roadmap, the PetCareRx team examined the following analytics data:

▶ Over 70 percent of visitors entered the site through the homepage, and the majority were first-time visitors, meaning this might have been their first exposure to the PetCareRx brand.

▶ The most common action visitors took after viewing the homepage was to exit the site.

For these reasons, as well as other insights from customer research, the homepage emerged as the top priority for testing. In an interview for this book, founder and COO Blake Brossman said he believes it is best to "start testing where you get the most traffic and where you lose the most customers, so you'll have the largest bang for your buck."

Although the homepage emerged as PetCareRx's top priority, customer research also revealed five other areas for improvement, as shown in **Figure 3.2**.

The example in this section focuses on the company's homepage testing. The default version of the homepage when the roadmap was being built appears in **Figure 3.3**. (Note that the homepage will not necessarily be the No. 1 priority for all companies: For many websites, it is not the primary point of entry, as visitors often arrive through pages deeper within sites, based on search engine results or bookmarked links.)

PetCareRx then conducted a deeper analysis of the homepage experience to identify areas to be tested.

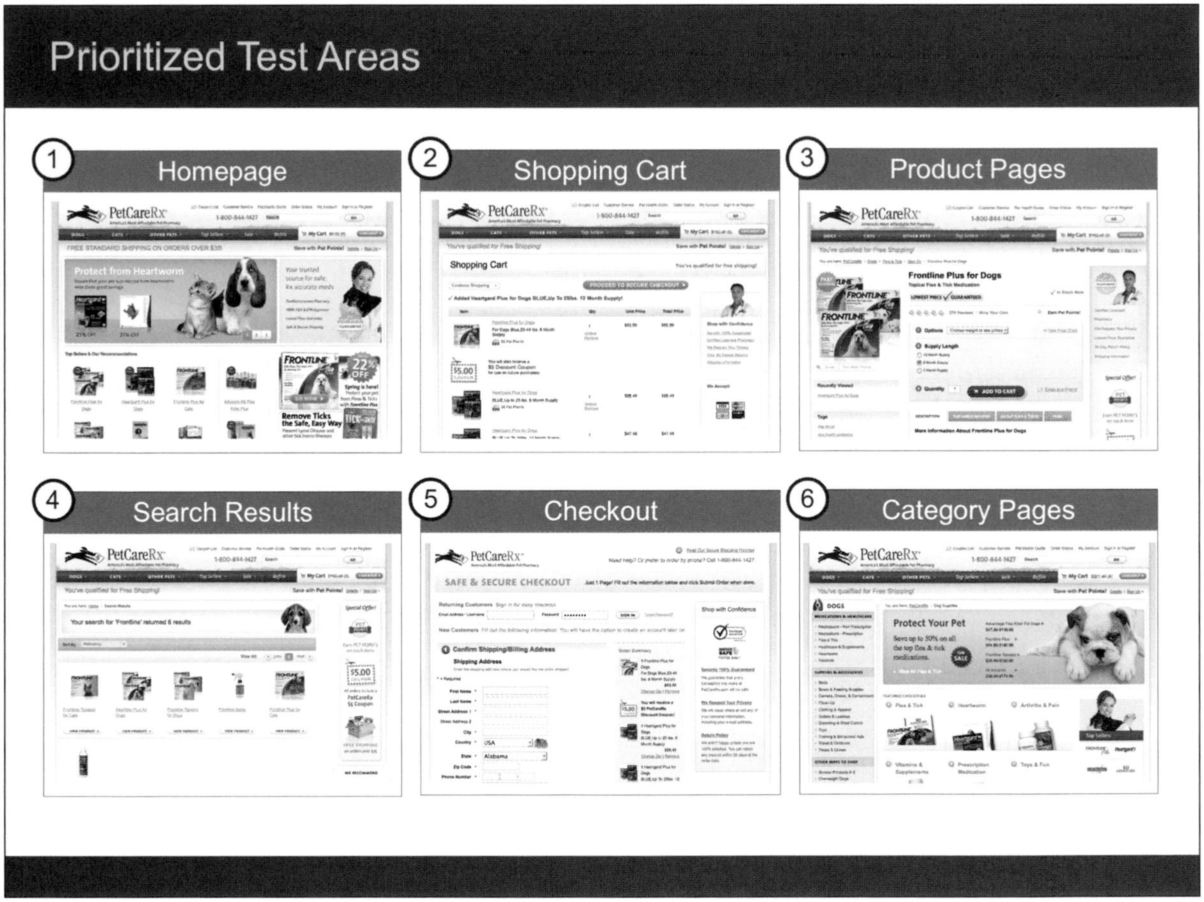

Figure 3.2 The top six prioritized test areas from an Optimization Roadmap for PetCareRx, based on qualitative and quantitative research.

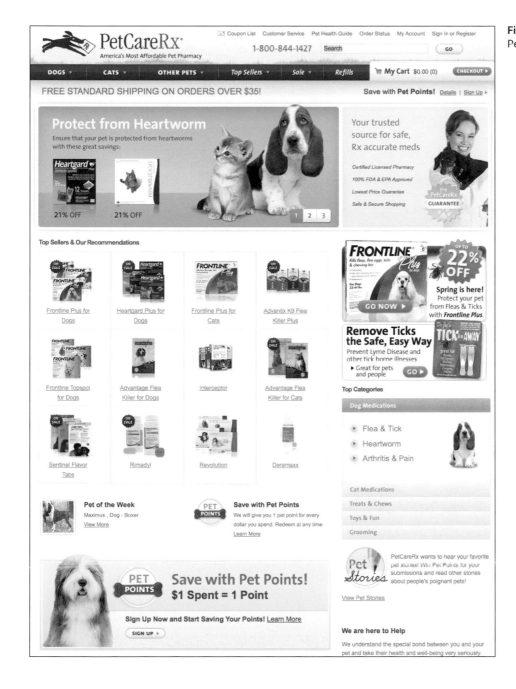

Figure 3.3 The default PetCareRx homepage.

This analysis, which drew on both qualitative and quantitative research, revealed the following:

▶ Of the homepage visitors who didn't abandon, many clicked on the 12 product tiles in the main area of the page, whereas the right column of the page received very few clicks.

▶ PetCareRx attracts more dog owners than cat owners as customers.

▶ The top categories of products sold were Flea & Tick and Heartworm remedies.

▶ Not all customers realized PetCareRx offers deep price discounts on store-brand products.

Incorporating this and other data, the PetCareRx team brainstormed and prioritized test ideas for the homepage, as shown in **Figure 3.4**. For example, because the homepage received so many first-time visitors, the first test idea was to experiment with different types of trust messaging, such as reassuring customers that PetCareRx is a reputable brand staffed with licensed pharmacists. This test fielded several different versions of trust messaging, but all yielded flat results.

The second test idea, highlighted in Figure 3.4, involved redesigning the area of the page below the hero and trust images to:

▶ Test emphasizing top-selling products and their prices, which are features that present a competitive advantage for PetCareRx.

▶ Test emphasizing the top product categories.

▶ Test emphasizing products for dogs over those for cats.

▶ Test de-emphasizing the right side of the page.

It is this second test idea that this part of the book will examine in detail, tracing how multiple versions yielded sharply different results when the optimization methodology was applied.

Prioritized Test List: Homepage

The test list has been prioritized by estimating the business value and difficulty to launch each test. Upcoming tests may be revised based on the results in each round of testing.

Test	Description	Type	Difficulty low→high	Value low→high
1.1	Value proposition (prices, trust messaging, dangers of offshore pharmacies, etc.)	A/B..N	low	high
1.2	**Redesign layout below hero to include sub-categories and price messaging**	**A/B..N**	**medium**	**high**
1.3	Messaging to SEM traffic about illegal offshore pharmacies	A/B..N	low	medium
1.4	Add a "Top Sellers" list	A/B..N	low	medium
1.5	Add coupon codes to homepage	MVT	low	medium
1.6	New hero banner (size, messaging, try removing altogether, etc.)	MVT	medium	medium
1.7	Allow customers to use Pet Points paired with other discounts	A/B..N	medium	medium
1.8	Make search tool more prominent	MVT	medium	medium
1.9	Add ability to buy products directly from homepage	A/B..N	high	high
1.10	Personalize homepage based on visitor pet preference (dog, cat, other, or none)	A/B..N	high	high
1.11	Note Pet Points earned for each product on page	A/B..N	low	low
1.12	Aesthetics for calls-to-action	MVT	low	low
1.13	Different forms of free shipping messaging and offers	A/B..N	low	low
1.14	Create and market product bundles	A/B..N	high	medium
1.15	Geo-target message and imagery by metro area	A/B..N	high	medium
1.16	Try competitors' layouts	A/B..N	high	low

☐ In Progress

Figure 3.4 This list shows the prioritized test ideas for the PetCareRx homepage. A similar list of ideas was built for each site area that appeared in the Optimization Roadmap.

Optimization Plan

As the first part of the Optimization Plan, the team created an Executive Summary, as shown in **Figure 3.5**. This figure refers to the industry term "RPV," or Revenue Per Visitor—the average amount of money visitors spend on the site. It is calculated by dividing the total number of visitors (whether they made a purchase or not) by the total amount of revenue made during the same time period. This figure is an indication of how successful a site is in generating revenue and helping customers.

Executive Summary – 1.2 Homepage Layout

Objective
Increase click-through traffic and RPV by testing different product presentations in the main area of the homepage.

Hypothesis
Including sub-category navigation and more prominent price messaging will drive customer engagement, and subsequently RPV.

Methodology
100% of homepage visitors will be included in this A/B test, which will consist of six recipes, including the default. Based on current traffic levels the test will run for two weeks.

Default Homepage

Figure 3.5 An Executive Summary slide from an Optimization Plan for PetCareRx.

Wireframes

For PetCareRx Test 1.2, all alternate designs highlighted PetCareRx's competitive pricing by adding specific product costs; product discounts; and prominent, red call-to-action buttons to the page. In order to clear space for these elements, all recipes removed the right column just below the hero imagery. Two very different layout concepts were built as wireframes:

▶ **Recipe B (Figure 3.6).** This version prominently featured the top three products—each getting its own row. Each product row offered multiple ways to purchase products (a 3-, 6-, or 12-month supply) and included detailed product value proposition bullets.

▶ **Recipe C (Figure 3.7).** The page was divided into three columns to allow more room to display large product images while still displaying the top 12 products. The products were placed in categories with Flea & Tick remedies on the left and Heartworm products on the right.

Recipe B

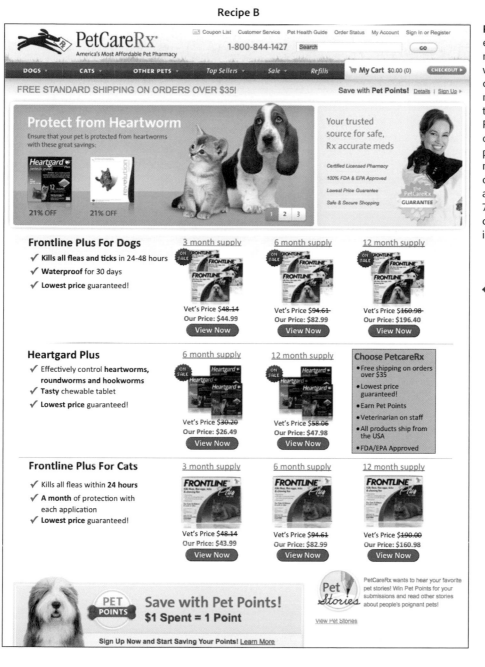

Figure 3.6 A visual expression of the marketing strategy, wireframes are used to communicate the information required to build the design comp. This is Recipe B, which focused on PetCareRx's top three products. The "768px" mark notes how much of the design was viewable at once on a screen 768 pixels high, the most common screen height in 2009.

◀ **768px**

Figure 3.7 This is Recipe C, which focuses on the top eight Flea & Tick products and the top four Heartworm products.

Recipe C

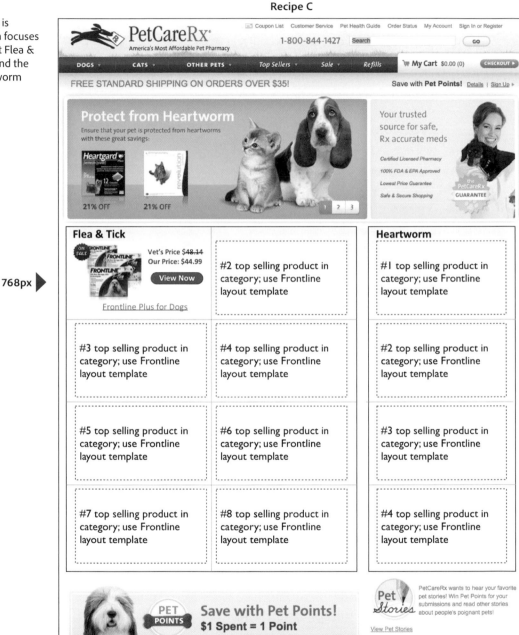

768px

Three additional wireframes were built as a variation on the themes introduced in Recipe C. Unsure whether customers preferred products to be categorized as Flea, Tick, and Heartworm remedies or simply as Dog and Cat products, team members tested both versions. Similarly, the team added another version of Recipe C using a horizontal rather than a vertical layout to find out whether this would help customers focus on the top category of products, and whether such a layout would be detrimental to the category on the bottom row. Here is how those three additional versions were mapped out:

▸ **Recipe D.** An alternate version of Recipe C, this version categorized the products as Top Products for Dogs on the left and as Top Products for Cats on the right. Dog products received twice as much space as cat products because PetCareRx has more dog owners than cat owners as customers.

▸ **Recipe E.** An alternate version of Recipe C, this version listed only the top nine products, placed in a horizontal layout. Flea & Tick remedies appeared on the top, and Heartworm products were placed on the bottom.

▸ **Recipe F.** A variation of Recipe D, this recipe showed only the top nine products, placed in a horizontal layout. Top Products for Dogs appeared on the top, and Top Products for Cats were listed on the bottom.

These wireframes aren't pictured here, but the design comps built from each appear in the next section.

Design comps

The design comps for all six recipes to be tested were prepared and launched, and the RPV for each one was measured over a two-week period. The design comps and each design's measured lift in RPV are pictured in **Figures 3.8** through **3.12**. The prices in the design comps for Figures 3.9 through 3.12 are all the same, because these are screen shots of the final design proofs before they were launched; of course, the real prices appeared on the website during the test. Also, note that the hero imagery changed after the wireframe was built, in a separate improvement initiative. Such changes are common as part of planned marketing calendars or promotions, and the same updated hero image was used in all tested recipes, including the default.

Optimization Launch

The Optimization Launch phase included setting up the test, checking the setup, and verifying that all key success metrics were measurable, as well as taking screen shots of the final recipes before the test was launched.

Figure 3.8 Recipe B: the three top-selling products with popular supply levels.

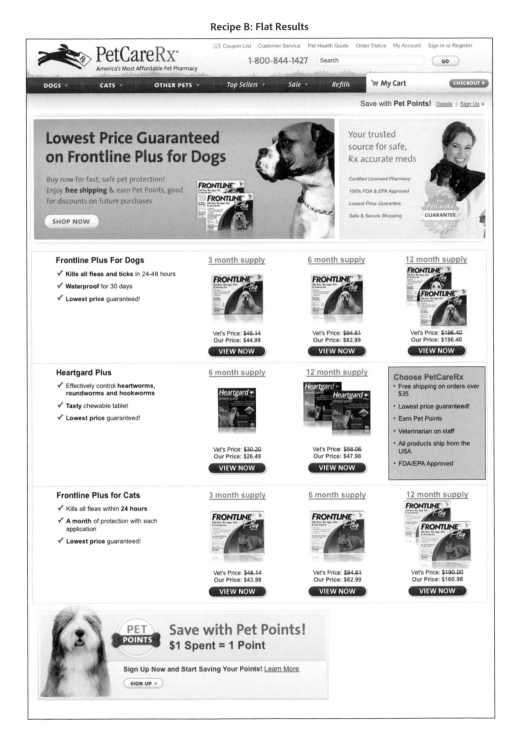

Recipe C: +7% lift in RPV

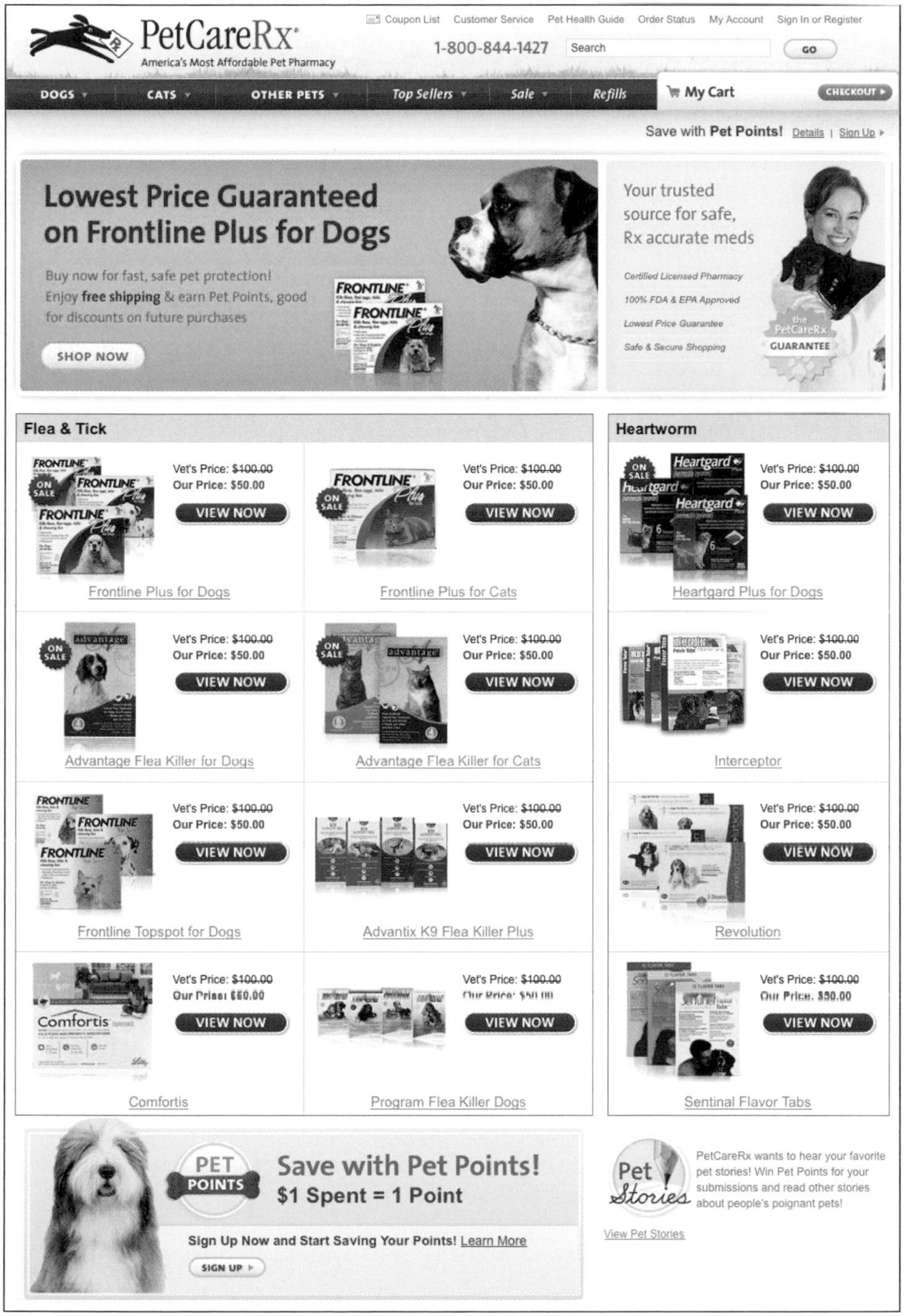

Figure 3.9 Recipe C: a vertical layout with Flea & Tick products on the left and Heartworm remedies on the right.

Figure 3.10 Recipe D: a vertical layout with Dogs on the left and Cats on the right.

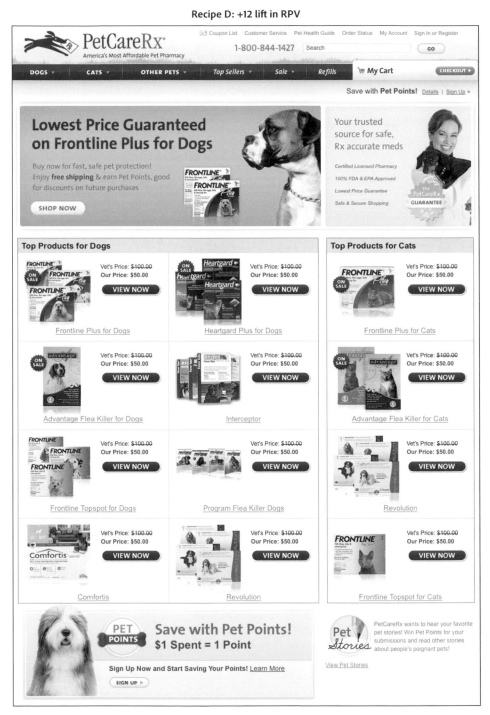

Recipe E: Flat Results

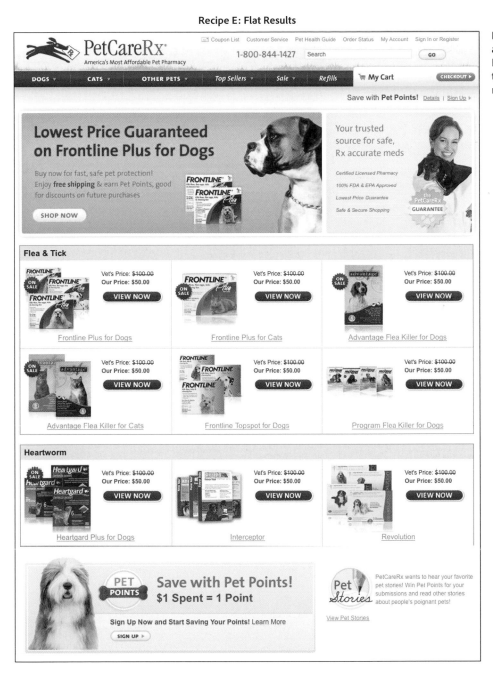

Figure 3.11 Recipe E: a horizontal layout with Flea & Tick products on the top and Heartworm remedies on the bottom.

Figure 3.12 Recipe F: a horizontal layout with Dogs on the top and Cats on the bottom.

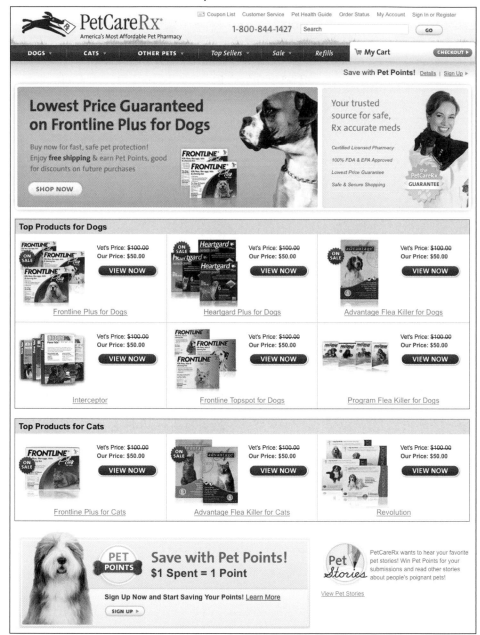

Optimization Results

Table 3.1 includes the results for each design, a key part of the Optimization Results document. Results for Recipes B and E were flat, whereas recipes C, D, and F provided 7 percent, 12 percent, and 23 percent lift in RPV, respectively. Recipe F was clearly the winner, indicating a customer preference to shop for Dog products over Cat products, with the categories stacked on top of one another. All recipes included better price messaging, but the difference in test results suggests that the horizontal layout, which gave clear prominence to the more popular Dog products, was the deciding factor. With the prospect of such a dramatic increase in revenue, this recipe was quickly pushed live to all visitors. The updated Executive Summary appears in **Figure 3.13**.

Table 3.1 RPV Lift Results

RECIPE	LIFT IN RPV
Recipe A: Default	Control
Recipe B: 3 top products	Flat
Recipe C: Flea & Tick and Heartworm (vertical)	7%
Recipe D: Dogs and Cats (vertical)	12%
Recipe E: Flea & Tick and Heartworm (horizontal)	Flat
Recipe F: Dogs and Cats (horizontal)	23%

The PetCareRx example shows how, by following the optimization methodology's steps, the company identified areas for improvement, developed hypotheses to address these issues, created several new designs based on that information, and then simultaneously tested all these potential solutions. Once the results were in, the business knew which solution worked best and was able to implement it quickly across the board. The results were: 1) a 23 percent boost in average revenue for all visitors to the homepage that could be worth millions of dollars a year to the company, and 2) a significant benefit to customers who were able to achieve their goals online more easily.

Executive Summary – 1.2 Homepage Layout

Objective
Increase click-through traffic and RPV by testing different product presentations in the main area of the homepage.

Hypothesis
Including sub-category navigation and more prominent price messaging will drive customer engagement, and subsequently RPV.

Methodology
100% of homepage visitors will be included in this A/B test, which will consist of six recipes, including the default. Based on current traffic levels the test will run for two weeks.

Results
• Recipe F increased RPV by an average of 23% across all visitor traffic. This could result in a dramatic increase in overall site revenue, should results hold in the long term.
• This winning recipe split the page into "Dog" and "Cat" categories with "Dogs" placed on top of "Cats." The right-hand column was eliminated to allow more room in which to feature top-selling products and emphasize the competitive pricing.

Recommendations
• Push Recipe F to all traffic.
• Test different versions of the product tiles (call-to-action, headline placement, imagery, etc.) within the new layout.
• Test which products should appear and in which order.
• Test targeted version of page for customers profiled as shopping for cat products.

Default Homepage

Recipe F

Figure 3.13 The Executive Summary of the Optimization Plan has been updated and included at the beginning of the Optimization Results document.

For PetCareRx, moving to the optimization methodology brought about a sea change that vastly improved the way the company created designs and its customers interacted online. COO Brossman said, "We're firm believers in testing being a staple for any company. Years ago we used to look at a design and say, 'We like that pretty picture,' so we would put it up on the website. Then if the sales went up we would say, 'It's because of the pretty picture,' and if they went down, we would say, 'It's because of something else.' Testing shows you what's actually going on."

Up Next

This chapter laid out the basics of the Iterative Optimization Methodology in practical terms, presenting an overview of the four main stages that constitute the optimization process. It then walked the reader through a real-life example, showing how one company applied the methodology to enhance its customer experience and boost business revenue.

The next chapter dives deeper into the method, examining in detail the first phase of the process in which qualitative data is analyzed and priorities are identified. Qualitative data plays a key role in the creation of the Optimization Roadmap—the blueprint that will guide the business as it launches wave after wave of iterative tests across each major site section simultaneously.

CHAPTER 4

Qualitative Research

Many businesspeople, even those responsible for the online experience, don't spend nearly enough time trying to see their business through the eyes of the customer. Qualitative research offers an invaluable way not only to get into the customer mind-set, but also to come up with ideas for innovation. This chapter discusses several types of qualitative research and shows how they can be used to generate test ideas while providing insights that will help guide the business in an evolving marketplace.

Benefits of Qualitative Research

Qualitative research is the art of capturing the customer's perspective on the online experience offered by a business and its competitors. Companies often neglect to do qualitative research and instead take the easy route by relying solely on analytics software to understand their customers' online behavior. However, quantitative research can only reveal how site users are *acting*; it can shed very little light on what they are thinking or feeling. In short, it is no substitute for truly seeing a company through the eyes of its users. This is not always a comfortable experience for business leaders, but it is key to helping them understand the customer perspective, adapt their business to evolving conditions, and generate ideas for new designs—tasks that metrics alone cannot fulfill.

In particular, qualitative research is critical to identifying:

▶ **Unmet customer needs.** If a business is failing to provide customers with what they're looking for, no analytics report can shed light on that gap. By watching and listening to customers, or by re-creating their online experience firsthand, researchers can discover users' expectations, unmet needs, and any sources of frustration.

▶ **The *why* behind the analytics data.** Sometimes metrics can generate more questions than answers. For example, an analytics report showing an increase in page views per visitor isn't always a good sign. Although it may indicate customers' satisfaction through deep engagement with the site, it may also indicate confusion about how to add products to their cart, or reveal unsuccessful attempts to locate information such as shipping rates or to find pages on the site that customers think should exist but do not.

Most qualitative research methods work with small, even statistically insignificant, sample sizes. As a result, this kind of research is best used for understanding broad questions—such as whether customers understand the basic business offering and whether it's something they need—as opposed to informing decisions about how to design every detail of a business. For the same reason, researchers often verify hypotheses based on qualitative data by referencing web analytics or testing to see if the hypotheses apply to a large number of customers.

Learning More About Customer Goals

The first step in qualitative research is to define realistic customer goals that explain why customers are choosing to interact with a business. This is not as easy as it sounds: Customers may access a site for very different reasons, and their goals can and do change over time. As Rob Blakeley, Senior Product Manager for WebMD, put it, "Our customers' goals are as different as there are blades of grass in New York City's Central Park."

However, most businesses can easily identify a preliminary list of the *most likely* customer goals and adapt this list as researchers gather further information. For example, a financial services company's customer goals may include opening or closing a deposit account, sending and depositing checks from a mobile device, getting a replacement credit card while traveling abroad, and so on.

If a businessperson is struggling with this task, it may help to ask the question: *If customers could come to the business looking for help with only one thing, what would it be?* It's much better to create a top-notch experience that can satisfy one important goal shared by many customers than to create several mediocre experiences in an attempt to address many different objectives.

Starting to Answer Qualitative Questions

The next step in qualitative research is to build a list of questions to explore. Like the customer goals, this list is preliminary and will change over time. The following is a list of potential questions that companies may use as a starting point in this process; of course, each business will tailor the list to its own priorities.

Fundamental questions:

▸ Why do customers come to the business?

▸ Why do they leave?

▸ Do customers understand what the business has to offer?

▸ Do customers want what the business has to offer?

▸ Is there anything customers want from the business that it is *not* providing?

▸ When analytics data shows areas of concern—for example, high drop-off rates, repeat page views, and so on—what are the reasons for the customers' actions?

▸ Which product or service is most important to customers?

▸ If the business could focus on only one product or service, what should it be?

On finding products, services, and content:

▸ Is the full breadth and depth of the product/services/content offering apparent?

▸ Are there too many or too few products/services/content to choose from?

▸ Do customers easily find products/services/content using site navigation and/or search?

On the customer's decision-making process:

▸ Are products/services/content easy to differentiate from one another, or are they too similar, leading to customer confusion over which to choose?

▸ Are the cross-sells, up-sells, and promotions clear? Do they interfere with the primary purchase?

▸ Is there enough information to make a purchase decision?

▸ Is it clear how to find related or popular content? Does it interfere with the primary content experience?

On conversion:

▸ Are there barriers to easily checking out?

▸ Are prices, taxes, shipping, returns, and security protections apparent? Are any of them barriers to checking out?

▸ Are there barriers to easily viewing additional content?

On the competition:

▸ Which competitors do customers go to, and how do the preceding questions apply to these competitors?

▸ Do competitors offer a product or service that would complement the business's offerings, such as accessories for a product the business sells? If so, should the business offer it as well?

Note that some of the preceding questions are based on quantitative research; however, it is not essential to have performed quantitative studies before tackling qualitative research. Most businesses already have a basic understanding of their data, and the iterative method means new insights, from both kinds of studies, will be added to the mix throughout the process, allowing team members to refine and add to their list of questions.

The next step in qualitative research is to try to answer these questions through firsthand experience, observing customers, and other methods, as described in the following sections.

User Experience Reviews

In *user experience reviews*, or *heuristic reviews*, researchers strive to experience the business firsthand in the same way customers do; then they do the same on competitors' websites for comparison. Before we examine user experience reviews in detail, it is helpful to explore some guidelines on customer behavior that can help the researcher, or reviewer, make their customer experience as authentic as possible.

Online Customer Behavior

Customers generally display the following tendencies when interacting with an online business:

▸ **Customers are goal-oriented.** They're looking for a place to click on the page or app that will take them to the specific product, service, or content that constitutes their objective.

▶ **Customers scan pages quickly.** They skip over details until they've found what they're looking for. For example, they may click through a business's homepage and several category and product pages rapidly, navigating with the help of images or keywords until they find a product they're interested in; only then are they likely to read details such as the price, feature list, reviews, and shipping policy. They are very good at ignoring anything that looks like advertising, a tendency that is sometimes called *banner blindness*.

▶ **Customers don't act like professionals.** They don't think about whether the navigation is consistent, which page they're on within the site, how individual page elements are working, what the business is trying to get them to do next, and so forth.

Experiential Business Review

Researchers first choose a realistic customer goal from the prepared list, and then follow a "customer scenario"—the actions a customer would take to pursue that objective. It is important here to step out of the professional mind-set and just experience the website as a customer would: If the reviewer can relate personally to the goal, all the better. For example, for a retail business the reviewers could go through the "browse and purchase" process for an item they're interested in buying or would like to get as a birthday gift for a friend; for a travel business, the reviewers could look into booking their next trip.

Taking notes along the way, reviewers should strive to do anything customers would do—call customer support, abandon the site when unable to attain their goal easily, and so on. If many customers visit the site from mobile devices, reviewers should try going through the scenarios using a phone or tablet.

After experiencing one scenario, the reviewers retrace each step of the experience to critique it as a professional, noting any opportunities for improvement. Was it easy to accomplish the goal? Were some elements especially difficult to navigate? Were there steps that confused the reviewers? The reviewers then repeat this process for the remaining customer goals.

Experiential Competitive Review

Because customers are also visiting competitors' websites, reviewers should do so, too. They follow the same procedure as before, exploring the same scenarios as customers, and then return to each step to critique the experience as professionals. To make the experience especially organic, reviewers may even start on their own business's site and then abandon it for a competing site based on their natural browsing behavior or on analytics data that shows where customers tend to abandon.

Documenting Experiential Reviews

It's important to document the heuristic reviews to share the findings and to prepare for the observation of real customer interactions. The documentation process should consist of screen shots showing the step-by-step interaction path, notes explaining the screen shots, and an updated list of qualitative questions based on the review. For example, researchers may ask whether customers also struggle or get confused where the reviewers did or whether users find it easy to navigate the same paths as the reviewers.

The following example illustrates how this process typically unfolds through a user experience review of the Gap, Inc. conducted in 2013. **Figure 4.1** encapsulates the main steps of the experiential review.

The accompanying notes for the steps in the figure include:

1. Reviewer visits Gap.com to look for a summer dress.

2. Reviewer sees red dress in middle right that looks cute and clicks on it. Reviewer is not taken to the dress but to a page listing many dresses that don't look like the one she clicked.

3. Reviewer sees a similar dress in a different color on the second row and clicks on it. Reviewer decides to purchase it. She tries to change the color to red by clicking on the large image of the dress in the middle of the screen, but doing so simply shows a zoomed-in view of the dress.

4. Just before abandoning, reviewer clicks on the small image of the dress in the middle of the screen.

5. Reviewer now sees the color palette and realizes that the dress is no longer available in red. She decides to buy it in coral as pictured. She clicks on "add to bag" but nothing happens, so she leaves to shop at a competitor's site. (The "add to bag" link failed because she first needed to select a size; there was no error message explaining this.)

Upon further critiquing the experience, the following questions were generated for the observational stage of the research:

▸ Do customers also struggle to find the product page for an item they liked on the homepage?

▸ Even though it was jarring to be taken to a page with hundreds of dresses after clicking on a single one, would it be a good customer experience to arrive on a page like that after clicking on the "Dresses" category in the Women's section of the site?

▸ Do customers also struggle to figure out what colors an item comes in and how to choose a different color?

▸ Do customers also find it difficult to add an item to their cart?

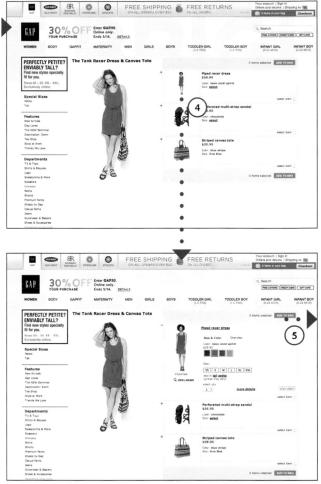

Figure 4.1 It's easy for customers to get confused or frustrated online. In this example of a user experience review, the customer would have abandoned the site after struggling to purchase the red dress she liked on the homepage.

▶ Do customers also try to buy before selecting a size and get confused when no message reminds them to pick a size or offers to help them do so?

Researchers seek to validate these questions by observing customers interacting with the site and by digging into the site analytics. Team members then create hypotheses, or proposed answers to these questions, and attempt to vet the hypotheses through test ideas, which are added to the Optimization Roadmap.

Don't Act Too Quickly

The purpose of the user experience review is to gain insights into the customers' experiences by stepping into their shoes for a moment. However, team members should resist making immediate changes to the site based solely on heuristic reviews unless clear technical errors are uncovered. Otherwise, the changes may reflect the perspective of online professionals, not the typical customer.

Conducting realistic user experience reviews is a skill that can be learned over time, but improvement requires an adequate feedback loop: Reviewers need to watch actual customers interact with the business and test new designs, not simply criticize the company's site in a vacuum.

Researchers must also exercise caution when exploring competitors' sites. All too often businesses assume a competitor's designs are effective and simply copy them without finding out whether these designs would work for their own business. As a result, not only do they risk adopting ineffective designs, but their sites also wind up looking very similar to those of their competitors.

One way to avoid this pitfall is to review sites outside of the business's circle of competitors when looking for new ideas; no matter where they find new concepts, companies must test them before pushing them live to all customers.

Observational Customer Research

Directly experiencing a site can be a great way to generate questions that lead to test ideas, but it's no substitute for spending time with real customers. As noted in Chapter 1, users aren't very good at articulating exactly what they need, so rather than asking customers for their opinions, observational research instead pays close attention to their behavior as a way of understanding their perspective. Team members strive to watch customers interacting naturally with the site; they provide them with opportunities to give open-ended feedback and avoid guiding them too much or prompting them with leading questions.

Customers are recruited in a variety of ways; although some volunteer, they're more often compensated through some form of payment, such as a check or gift card. Even though customers know they're being observed, the goal of this type of study is to create as natural a setting as possible, so it may take place not only in research facilities, but also in cafés, customer homes, and other venues. Sessions are conducted one-on-one, with additional researchers observing behind one-way glass or through a video feed.

Depending on the business, sessions can last anywhere from 10 to 60 minutes. High-level trends usually start to emerge after watching four or five customers, but to be on the safe side, researchers often observe eight to ten customers during each study. The frequency of observational studies varies according to the company, but most businesses should conduct them at least quarterly. Many sizable and successful companies conduct this type of research whenever they have pressing unanswered questions about their business, which could arise several times per month.

The following list outlines the basic framework for this type of research, as well as some best practices for observing customers online:

Recruitment

▶ The first few times a business conducts this type of research, it may be helpful to go through a recruitment agency and use an expert moderator to conduct the sessions. Later, the business can recruit by placing an ad online on a site like Craigslist or work with existing customers contacted through an internal email list.

▶ It is useful to recruit customers based on an experience they recently had or an upcoming experience that the business can help with. For example, a hospitality business might recruit customers who have recently booked a hotel room online or who need to book a room for an upcoming trip.

▶ If possible, the customers should not know the name of the business, because this information might influence their behavior. For example, recruiters can tell them the study is about online user behavior related to the general category of tasks the business is interested in observing (purchasing clothing, reading the news, searching for general information, and so on).

Setting scenarios

▶ When customers arrive, the researcher welcomes them and asks questions that prompt them to talk about a wide range of recent online experiences, such as "What have you recently shopped for online?" or "Have you planned any trips recently?"

▶ The researcher provides customers with a computer or mobile device that allows them to browse the web while recording their online session and facial expressions. (Of course, customers are informed in advance that their session will be recorded.)

▶ The researcher invites the customers to go through a scenario they had mentioned earlier that pertains to the business (e.g., booking a hotel room for an upcoming stay). Customers are asked to speak aloud while using the computer to let the researcher know what they're thinking.

Observations

▶ The researcher then sits back, pays close attention, and tries not to say anything. The key is to leave customers alone while carefully watching how they try to reach their goal—and what obstacles they face along the way—and paying close attention to shifts in body language, facial expressions, and so on.

▶ The researcher refrains from asking customers what they think about specific websites or designs. For example, the researcher does not ask whether certain sites are easy or helpful. Instead, the researcher focuses on what customers show through their actions; the more customers are prompted, the more likely they'll be to say or do something based on what they think the researcher wants to hear. If customers get confused and ask what to do, the researcher simply says something like, "Please do whatever you would normally do."

On prompting the customer

▶ Some customers have a tendency to remain silent throughout the session. If this is the case, the researcher will occasionally prompt them with a kind reminder to vocalize their thoughts.

▶ If, toward the end of the session, customers haven't used the online business, the researcher may prompt them by saying something like, "I'm interested in seeing you do the same thing with a few specific websites." The researcher will give the customers a list of sites that includes the business being studied as well as competitors not yet visited.

▶ The researcher should wait until the end of the session to ask any specific questions about the customer's behavior, and even then, they should avoid asking for any opinions. For example, a researcher can ask customers to explain what they were thinking at a specific moment rather than asking if they thought the experience was good or not. When listening to their answers, the researcher should be on the lookout for a mismatch between what customers say and their observed actions. People tend to jump around online from website to website very quickly and usually have difficulty remembering all the actions they took online, let alone why they took them.

▶ At the end of the session, the researcher should thank the customers for their time and pay them the agreed-upon fee.

After the session, the researcher reviews the video to capture any findings that provide insights into the list of qualitative research questions. These insights, in turn, may lead to the formulation of new questions for further exploration in the iterative process.

Other Research Methods

Although heuristic reviews and observational customer research are the most common methods, there are many other types of qualitative customer research. This section outlines some that are popular among online businesses.

It should be noted that two methods that remain popular today—focus groups and usability testing—do not figure in this section because they are not recommended. Focus groups tend to place customers in the role of product designer by explicitly asking them to give advice on design decisions, which is difficult for people to do when such decisions are not their area of expertise. Additionally, focus group participants tend to try to say the "right thing" to please the researcher or they succumb to groupthink.

Traditional usability testing asks customers to complete a predetermined list of online tasks based on actions the business would like to see completed rather than allowing customers to show the business their natural online behavior. Even though customers may be good at figuring out how to perform a task when asked, doing so takes them out of their typical frame of mind when interacting with websites.

Instead, the following are several tried-and-true methods for understanding customers through qualitative research.

Ethnographic Studies

Ethnographic studies are a special form of observational research that take place where the customer would normally interact with the company, such as at their home or office, or at the location of the business itself, so that they are more likely to behave the way they normally would. Just like observational customer research, these sessions are most effective when they are unguided and researchers focus on active watching and listening.

Kenyon Rogers, Director of Digital Experiments for Marriott International, said that his business regularly conducts ethnographic studies at select hotel properties. For example, in 2013 the company piloted a program that allows guests to "use their smartphones to check into the property and open their room door without needing to interact with a Marriott team member." Rogers added that very soon, "guests will be able to control their entire experience, including ordering room service, extending their stay, ordering transportation, and booking meeting rooms through their smartphones."

Look for the Post-its:
Pete Maher on Contextual Inquiry

Pete Maher is the Co-Founder and Chief Operating Officer of the LUMA Institute, an educational company that equips people to accelerate innovation. He is also the co-author of *Innovating for People: Handbook of Human-Centered Design Methods*, which has been adopted by the U.S. Office of Personnel Management's Innovation Lab as core training material for federal government employees. In this interview, he shares his thoughts on the importance of primary observational research.

Your book presents the "contextual inquiry" method, which is an ethnographic approach. Can you describe it here?

I've got a deep affinity for contextual inquiry research because it's a great way to get to insights that can ultimately uncover opportunities for innovation. Contextual inquiry takes place where the participants would normally conduct their tasks. The interviewer asks the participants to go about their tasks in a normal way, observes their actions in an unobtrusive manner, interjects questions at opportune moments, and records the sessions for later analysis.

Would you share an example?

When we don't deeply understand the context of the user, we sometimes assume that we're delivering against their needs. For example, it turns out digital products are incredibly difficult to use. From my days of doing research in the financial services industry, when we would go into people's homes to understand how they engage with financial products, we would commonly find things like Post-its stuck to monitors. It's no mystery that some of those Post-its contain usernames and passwords, or software instructions, because a lot of times companies with

great intentions—trying to protect a user's security—enact requirements that ultimately make it too difficult for people to achieve their goals.

So, when conducting contextual inquiry research, we'll advise teams to look for the Post-its or duct tape: What are the clever workarounds users come up with to make it possible for them to use the product? It's only when we ask people to show us how they actually use something that we're able to uncover really ripe opportunities for innovation. And, most important, close observation uncovers those gaps between what people do and what people say they do.

Would you tell us more about the gaps between what people do and what they say?

Margaret Mead, the famed anthropologist, really said it best: "What people say, what people do, and what they say they do are entirely different things." Anybody who has spent a lot of time doing research knows this to be the case. It's not because people are necessarily trying to lie or mislead. It turns out that we, as people, are simply not wired to be able to really articulate why we did that thing we just did.

For example, if you ask somebody to describe to you in detail how they completed a purchase on a website, you could imagine them describing the steps that they took and all the different things that they did along the way. But if you were to actually watch that scenario play out, you would see something very different. So contextual inquiry research, especially in the digital context, allows us to observe how somebody's moving through a digital experience to really know what they just did and to try to understand why.

Surveys

Businesses place surveys on their actual site or app, or email them to customers. Large surveys can have statistically significant sample sizes, but the researcher must be on the lookout for data not representative of the larger customer base due to self-selection bias. For example, not every customer wants to fill out a survey, and those who do may have the strongest positive or negative opinions.

As with all forms of qualitative research, the more open-ended the survey, the better. Surveys that ask customers about specific design decisions place the customer in the awkward position of being asked to provide advice outside of their area of expertise. Rather, understanding whether customers found their overall experience to be positive or negative and providing an open-form field for customers to write about any aspect of the experience they choose can often lead to actionable data.

Customer Panels

Customer panels are a subset of surveys: They typically consist of thousands of participants who have elected to give survey feedback on a regular basis. Panels may be run by a company's research team or by consulting firms on behalf of many businesses. Like surveys, customer panels can provide statistically significant sample sizes, but it's important to understand the segment of participants being queried. For example, although panels consisting entirely of self-selected users of one business might not be representative of the entire population, they can give the business insight into the behavior and opinions of their more loyal customers.

Eileen Krill, research manager at *The Washington Post*, oversees customer research for all of the business's print and digital brands. A panel of about 7,000 customers is included in the many types of qualitative and quantitative customer research she oversees. Krill will ask the panel "a wide range of closed and open-ended questions, depending on the objectives of the survey," including "satisfaction rating questions." She points out that "open-ended feedback is generally far more meaningful and actionable than the score itself" because it can help to "reveal the reasons behind the scores."

One question she often asks the panel is "whether a new product or feature will improve the customer's impression of *The Washington Post* brand." Although in most cases participants say such additions would have no impact, Krill still asks the question in case it provides an important insight. For example, she said, "We once tested the idea of starting an online dating service for *Post* readers, and that got a lot of people saying they would have a lower opinion of the company." Krill noted that "I think that research was one of the key things that may have killed the idea."

Diary Studies

Diary studies consist of a business asking customers to take notes and regularly send them back to the company, usually over an extended period of time. These studies may ask participants to take notes only on a specific topic area, like their regular interactions with a new site or app, or they may be more general and simply ask customers how they spent their day.

Google Search Lead Designer Jon Wiley shared an example of an ongoing diary study being run by the company. Through a mobile app, the study regularly asks participants to reply to the question: "What is the last bit of information you needed to know?" The information can be related to any aspect of their life, not only the material they were looking for online. Wiley and his team then "look at the needs that people have in their lives" and try to answer the question, "Is there a way that we, as Google, can find a solution for them?"

Card-sorting

A technique used to gain insight into how to organize content, such as ordering and grouping similar navigational links, card-sorting directly involves customers in the design process. Customers are provided with a stack of cards containing information and asked to perform a task, such as organizing them into logical categories. Although it is typically performed with index cards or sticky notes, card-sorting can also be performed online, and there is no limit to the number of participants.

Caution should be observed, because this technique is more guided than the aforementioned qualitative methods and may place customers in the position of being asked to act like a professional designer. However, if performed with minimal prompting, card-sorting can provide designers with a rare opportunity to gain insight into how customers think about information architecture and content hierarchies.

Nate Bolt, design research manager at Facebook, said the company used cart-sorting as one of many qualitative research methods to inform an ongoing redesign of users' Facebook News Feeds. After recruiting users, the Facebook Design Research team printed out each user's feed, up to the minute, on paper. Then, he explained, "they would cut out their feed stories, place them on a table, and group them into what they considered to be like-minded categories. That helped us reprioritize the ways that stories are grouped and organized within people's News Feeds in a real, human way. Obviously, this went hand in hand with all other data, including the system (analytics) data."

Feedback Forms

Feedback forms on websites, or email addresses for user feedback, can be a good source of information. Users who provide open-ended feedback in this way often have timely insights into customer frustrations, as well as positive comments on great experiences with the website or the business's team members.

John Williamson, the Senior Vice President and General Manager of Comcast.com, explained that "One of the best sources for information I have is the 'Website Feedback' link" that appears on the bottom of each page on the site. Williamson noted, "I was in banking in the mid-1990s, and I remember how excited we would get if we received a letter from a customer. We really would." Every day Comcast receives "hundreds of letters" from customers through the feedback link, and because they are a "huge benefit" that helps Williamson and his team understand their customers and their business, he added, "I read every one of them."

Acting on Qualitative Research

After the heuristic and other qualitative research sessions have been conducted, researchers summarize the insights they have garnered, as well as any remaining questions about customer behavior. For each insight, they write down possible ways of verifying the observations through analytics data, as well as any ideas for testing. This list will be used as a guide when crafting the Optimization Roadmap.

Case Study: Comcast

A leading provider of television, high-speed Internet, and digital voice services in the United States, Comcast uses qualitative and quantitative research to inform the iterative design process it applies to all aspects of its site.

Qualitative studies play a critical role in Comcast's design process. Williamson noted that in one redesign process during 2012, "We had over a thousand customers and prospective customers involved before we tested online....We had ethnographic research, customer panels, and online customer panels." The Comcast team also "went into the homes of over 20 customers and saw how they interacted with Comcast," which provided "critical" experiences that analytics "data cannot replace."

The following business case shows how insights gathered from qualitative studies triggered a redesign of the company's "TV Options" page, which customers use when purchasing television service online. This section walks the reader through the redesign process from beginning to end, showing how the qualitative study findings led to the formulation of hypotheses and redesign options, and finally to the first tests and the selection of highly effective new designs.

The goal of the "TV Options" page is to help customers choose their receiver type and to select service upgrades, such as premium channels. However, qualitative studies suggested three page elements were underperforming: receiver selection, premium channel logos, and other add-on options further down on the page. The default version of the page, with these three elements highlighted, appears in **Figure 4.2.**

Figure 4.2 The default page with three elements highlighted for testing.

Default

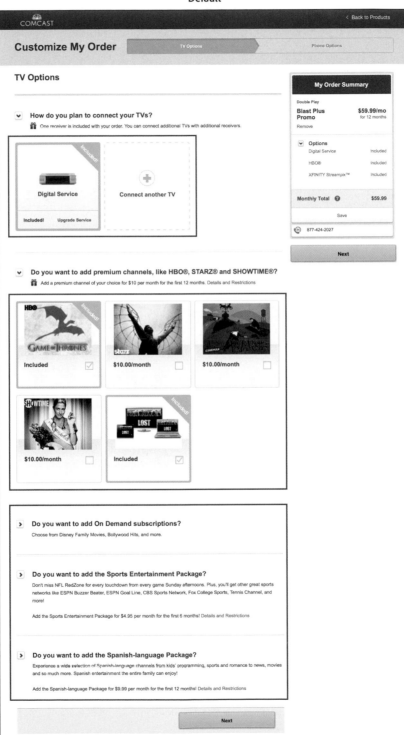

The qualitative study findings related to these three elements and the steps researchers took in response are summarized here.

Finding. Not all customers interacted with the first step of the process to learn more about upgrading to an HD or HD DVR receiver.

▸ **Hypothesis.** Customers do not notice the option to upgrade a receiver.

▸ **Validate with analytics.** Does the link to upgrade the receiver get very few clicks?

▸ **Test idea.** Find out whether more customers would upgrade if more information about the options to switch to an HD or HD DVR receiver appeared on the page without requiring additional clicks.

Finding. All customers understood how to select and deselect premium channels, so this function seems user friendly. However, the website highlighted specific shows carried on these channels rather than the actual channels, and several customers commented that they hadn't heard of these shows. Example: "I never heard of *Boss.* I never saw *Contagion.*"

▸ **Hypothesis.** Highlighting channel names rather than specific shows will clarify the process of adding premium channels.

▸ **Validate with analytics.** Do premium channel selections vary based on the featured shows?

▸ **Test idea.** To appeal to a wider audience, feature prominent channel names (HBO, Showtime, etc.) rather than specific shows.

Finding. Several customers commented that they didn't know what was included in the add-ons. Example: "What exactly is included in the Sports Package?"

▸ **Hypothesis.** Customers don't realize they can click on the toggle switches for more information. Because the switches are arranged in rows, followed by messaging for each add-on, customers may be mistaking them for bullet points.

▸ **Validate with analytics.** Do customers rarely click on these toggle switches?

▸ **Test Idea.** Replace individual offers with a one-line message reading "More customization options" to help customers understand that the image to the left is a toggle switch that, when clicked, will reveal the details of the offers.

As noted earlier, researchers targeted receiver selection, premium channel logos, and add-on content for design testing. An alternate version of each element was built and placed in a multivariable test (MVT). A *multivariable,* or *multivariate*, test is a special type of A/B test in which several page elements are tested across multiple recipes. Rather than simply testing two versions of the page—one with the original elements and one with the new ones—multiple versions of the page are tested, each including a different combination of the elements. In addition to determining which version of the page has the highest performance, this type of test measures the success of each element.

The default and alternate versions of each element are shown in **Figure 4.3**. This figure also includes which version of each element won and which out of all three elements most influenced the performance of the page:

▶ **Receiver section.** The default version has a blue link to upgrade. The alternate version adds a prominent message to upgrade to an HD or HD DVR receiver.

▶ **Premium channel logos.** The default version features a specific show for each premium channel. The alternate version features channel logos instead of shows.

▶ **Other add-ons.** The default version places content behind four toggle switches. The alternate version places content behind a single toggle switch, which, when clicked, expands to show all up-sell content at once.

The business goal was to increase the purchase conversion rate as well as the overall revenue per visitor (RPV). As Figure 4.3 shows, the winning version of the receiver selection element was not the new design but the original; however, the new versions emerged as winners for both the premium channel element and the add-ons further down on the page.

When Comcast integrated all three winning designs into the page and tested this revamped page against the original one, it found the changes drove a 4.6 percent lift in the purchase conversion rate and a 5.6 percent lift in RPV. The default and winning versions of the page are pictured in **Figure 4.4**.

Because the impact of each element had been isolated, Comcast was also able to measure how much each one influenced the performance of the final version of the page: The premium channel element was the most influential, accounting for over 60 percent of the increase in RPV, indicating that, of the three elements tested, it was the original version of this feature that had presented the largest obstacle to customers completing their goals.

The main recommendation was to push the winning version of the page to all visitors. Additional proposals included running follow-up design tests of each variable to further simplify the user experience, starting with the premium channel element, because it had emerged as the most important one overall.

Default Elements

Alternate Elements

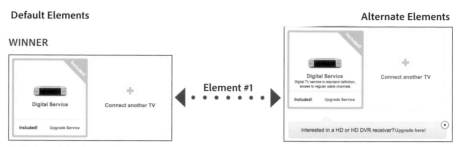

WINNER

Default: Minimal upgrade messaging

Element #1

Alternate: More prominent HD or DVR upgrade messaging

WINNER + MOST INFLUENTIAL ELEMENT

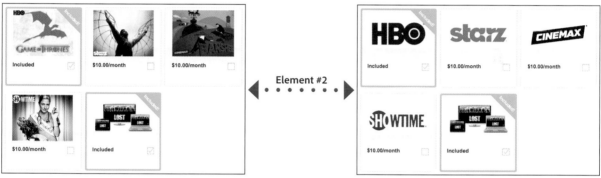

Default: Specific show for each channel

Element #2

Alternate: Channel name without shows listed

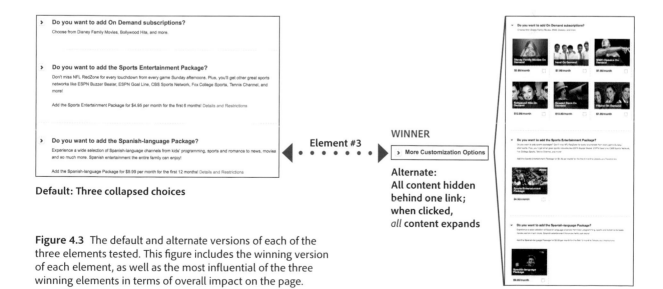

Default: Three collapsed choices

Element #3

WINNER

Alternate:
All content hidden behind one link; when clicked, *all* content expands

Figure 4.3 The default and alternate versions of each of the three elements tested. This figure includes the winning version of each element, as well as the most influential of the three winning elements in terms of overall impact on the page.

Default   **Winner**

+5.6% lift in RPV
+4.6% lift in purchase conversion rate

Figure 4.4 The default version of the page next to the redesigned page, which contains all the winning elements.

Take a Step Back

Although qualitative research is a key part of the ongoing design process, it can also play an invaluable role in helping to shape a company's overall direction. Grounded in the customer perspective, qualitative research helps businesspeople to shape long-term strategies by keeping their finger on the pulse of an evolving marketplace, a practice that helps them develop better ways of fulfilling their customers' needs in the present and in the future.

As businesspeople focus on the day-to-day activities related to delivering the same products and services, it's easy to lose sight of the *long-term* customer needs that are driving the demand for those same products—a phenomenon renowned marketing savant Theodore Levitt called "marketing myopia." Levitt argued that these companies tend to be "product-oriented instead of customer-oriented," and view their "marketing effort" as a "necessary consequence of the product, not vice versa, as it should be."

He cited the example of railroad companies: Once the titans of industry, they had fallen on hard times by the 1960s, all because they thought of themselves as being in the business of "railroads." Had they instead seen themselves as being in the business of "transportation," they would have begun to produce cars, trucks, airplanes, and even telephones—an expansion they were well positioned to tackle, given their extensive resources.

Levitt may have been writing in the 1960s, but his observations remain true: All too often, businesses focus on current successes instead of prioritizing their customers' present—and future—needs. In recent years, however, some companies have grown to recognize the importance of building for the future; a few examples of well-developed marketing strategies, or long-term game plans for providing customer value, appear in **Table 4.1**.

Each strategy conveys a straightforward understanding of why customers come to the business for help that goes beyond the current core product and service offerings. For example, Comcast's strategy to focus on entertainment and technology doesn't keep the company tied to current revenue sources, such as cable lines or set-top boxes, because these will likely be short-lived due to rapidly evolving technology; indeed, Comcast has expanded its product offerings to allow customers to watch movies and television shows from mobile devices even when offline. Similarly, IBM's online strategy is focused on work-related tasks for business customers; as such, IBM has expanded its services into cloud computing, "big data," and social technologies.

All these examples illustrate the importance of preparing a pathway for the future—a journey that, in many cases, begins with asking solid qualitative-research questions and paying close attention to the answers.

Table 4.1 Online Marketing Strategies

COMPANY	ONLINE MARKETING STRATEGY
Ally Bank	"We help our customers to achieve their savings goals." (Andrew Switzer)
Comcast	"Comcast helps our customers to enrich their lives through entertainment and technology." (John Williamson)
Foursquare	"We help our customers to make the most out of where they are." (Simon Favreau-Lessard)
IBM	"IBM helps enable our customers to do their jobs better." (Phil Corbett)
LinkedIn	"We help our customers to connect with new opportunities." (Amy Parnell)
PetCareRx	"PetCareRx helps to bring health and happiness to pet owners and their pets." (Blake Brossman)
Saks Fifth Avenue	"Our strategy is to inspire customer confidence and style with every Saks shopping experience." (Roger Scholl and Matt Curtis)
WebMD	"We help our customers to find health information." (Rob Blakeley)

Up Next

This chapter provided an overview of qualitative research techniques, which offer insights into customers' goals and the challenges they face when trying to accomplish those goals. These insights lead to test ideas that will be added to the Optimization Roadmap, as well as inform the overall direction for a company.

The next chapter outlines quantitative research methods that companies use to verify qualitative findings, as well as to identify which site areas need improvement the most and what test ideas to prioritize as part of assembling the Optimization Roadmap.

References

1. "Marketing Myopia," *Harvard Business Review*, Theodore Levitt (1960).

CHAPTER 5

Quantitative Research and Optimization Roadmap

This chapter outlines the quantitative research methods that, used in concert with qualitative studies, help shape the optimization process. It discusses the benefits of this type of research, including the kinds of questions it can answer and ways to focus organizations on using data to drive action rather than simply distributing analytics reports. It also includes an example of how one company used the iterative optimization approach to interpret analytics data in an effective, action-oriented way. The chapter concludes with instructions on how to assemble the Optimization Roadmap, drawing on qualitative and quantitative studies as well as other relevant insights.

Benefits of Quantitative Studies

Through quantitative research, a business is able to effectively spend time with *all of its customers at once* by measuring what user actions are taking place across the site. Quantitative research includes collecting data, drawing insights from that information, and recommending evidence-based actions to help the business and its customers achieve their respective goals.

All too often, businesses stop working with analytics after step one—collecting data. Because most analytics systems can automatically generate ready-made reports, it is easy for a researcher to export an analytics report, distribute it, and then consider the job of quantitative research complete. This is a shame because analytics data is representative of the entire customer population; therefore, it contains a wealth of information that may have implications for the business as a whole, and could, when used well, trigger collaborative efforts across the organization, leading to dramatic improvements in performance.

Two tips for avoiding the trap of simply issuing disjointed data reports are *to base quantitative research on answering questions, not simply referencing ready-made reports* and to apply the *insights and impact* method described later in this chapter to interpret the data.

This section opens with a brief discussion of these guiding principles and then provides an overview of several effective metrics available for quantitative analysis. Finally, the section concludes with a concrete example of how one company applied this approach to achieve a wide range of improvements in its website.

Starting with Quantitative Questions

With analytics systems automatically generating report after report, it is easy even for seasoned researchers to get lost in a sea of data that may or may not be significant, a dilemma sometimes called *analysis paralysis*. It is vital, then, for analysts to focus their research tightly on a few principal questions.

As mentioned in Chapter 4, they should use analytics software to validate any lines of inquiry identified by existing qualitative research.

They should also concentrate on finding answers to the two following questions:

1. In which site areas should the business start testing?

2. In each of these site areas, what should the business test?

As noted in Chapter 3, both qualitative and quantitative studies ultimately seek to answer these two fundamental questions; these guiding lines of inquiry in turn lead to more narrowly focused questions that researchers use as a springboard for testing ideas. The following list details the kinds of questions that quantitative studies can help to answer; of course, each company would tailor such a list to its own particular needs.

To answer: "*In which site areas should the business start testing?*" the researcher can ask:

▶ How do key metrics fluctuate over time?

▶ Which areas have the most overall traffic?

▶ Through which areas do most users enter the site?

▶ Through which areas do most users exit the site?

▶ Which site areas contribute the most to revenue?

▶ Which site areas contribute the most to conversions?

▶ Which products or services contribute the most to revenue?

▶ Which products or services contribute the most to conversions?

▶ How many times do customers visit the site before converting?

To answer: "*In each of these site areas, what should the business test?*" the researcher can ask:

▶ How did the customers get there?

▶ What actions do customers take once they're there?

Addressing these questions enables researchers to figure out which areas should be prioritized for redesign and testing. For example, site areas with high traffic or a lot of revenue flowing through them present ripe opportunities for testing, because they are clearly the areas of greatest interest to customers and the business; similarly, site areas showing high abandonment rates would be flagged as priorities for improvement.

Telling a Story Using Insights and Impact

The "insights and impact" method is a simple way of structuring data analysis to ensure that quantitative research leads to interpretation and action rather than the mere dissemination of automated reports. For each piece of data analyzed, researchers document the insights, or what the data means, as well as the impact, or how the business will act on the data.

For example, if an analytics report shows that a large percentage of users abandon the site immediately after adding a product to their cart, the "insight" could be that the cart page is causing customer attrition, which is surprising because customers reach that page right after presumably expressing an intent to purchase. The "impact" could be a decision to test alternate versions of the cart page, as well as any preceding pages, such as the product page, that may inform what customers expect to see on the cart page. Although some people may find the impact of data studies to be obvious or implied, reporting data without explaining what it means and what should be done about it leaves recipients—marketers, designers, and others—to interpret and act on the data in their own way rather than sharing ideas and collaborating across the company.

Before proceeding to a real-life example of the "insights and impact" method, the following section briefly outlines the main data analytics measures to which this method would be applied.

Online Success Metrics

This section summarizes the primary metrics, or units of measurement, accessible through popular analytics software packages. Although these metrics represent industry standards, some software may define the metrics in different ways; therefore, end users should verify all such definitions before implementation.

The following metrics are commonly used to answer quantitative research questions and to determine winning designs through testing:

▶ **Visitors.** This metric tracks the number of unique users who arrive on the site within a variable time period. For example, if a user goes to a site next Monday, Wednesday, and Friday, that user would be counted as *one visitor* during the Monday–Friday time period. This metric is also sometimes referred to as *unique visitors*, or *unique users*.

▶ **Visits.** This metric counts each time a visitor arrives on a site within a variable time period, which many analytics packages define as being 30 minutes or longer of visitor inactivity. For example, if a user arrives on a site, browses across several pages, leaves, and then returns 30 minutes later, that user will be counted as *one visitor* with *two visits*.

▶ **Page views.** This metric shows the number of times a webpage is viewed. For example, if a user arrives on the homepage, clicks to a product page, and then clicks the "back" button to return to the homepage, that will be counted as *two homepage page views* and *one product page view*.

▶ **Revenue and orders.** Revenue and orders are handled in a variety of ways by analytics systems. Of course, most systems produce reports showing the total number of orders placed and revenue generated during a variable amount of time. Some reports also track revenue and orders in one of two ways: *allocation* or *participation*. *Allocation* divides any online order evenly among all the pages viewed within the visit, and *participation* assigns the full order to each page viewed. For example, if a visitor viewed 10 pages and spent $10, then an allocation report would show each page as having led to $1 in revenue; a participation report would show each page as having led to $10 in revenue. Similarly, an allocation report would show each page contributing to 0.1, or one-tenth, of an order; a participation report would show each page contributing to one order.

▶ **Revenue per visitor (RPV).** RPV refers to the amount of money made during a variable time period divided by the number of visitors in that period. This is the best measure of whether a test recipe has resulted in more or less revenue, because it accounts for different designs receiving different volumes of traffic. For example, in the hypothetical case shown in **Table 5.1**, even though Recipe A brought in more money overall, this is because Recipe A received more visitors. Recipe B would likely be declared the winner, because it makes more money for each visitor it receives, on average.

Table 5.1 Revenue per Visitor Calculation

RECIPE	VISITORS	REVENUE	REVENUE PER VISITOR
Recipe A	200,000	$250,000	$1.25
Recipe B	150,000	$225,000	$1.50

RPV is especially important because even when setting up a 50/50 traffic split between recipes, it's rare for each design to receive the same number of visitors. In some cases, an optimization team will also choose not to split traffic evenly. For example, if researchers are concerned that an alternate design might be risky, they may start by splitting traffic 60/40 or 70/30.

RPV is a popular metric across all industries. Although it would seem at first glance to apply largely to retailers, businesses that derive revenue more indirectly also track RPV. For example, online media companies measure the value of advertisements viewed online as RPV, because ads are their principal source of revenue. Similarly, financial institutions measure the value of different accounts created; hotels measure the value of rooms reserved; and telecommunications businesses measure the value of subscription services, all using RPV. If the value of a transaction is not fully known during the test period (for example, customers can cancel hotel reservations made during the test), then an estimate is used to determine the winning design, and long-term results continue to be tracked even after the business has moved on to testing new designs.

▶ **Conversion rate.** This metric is the percentage of customers who take a specific action during a variable time period. This is the best measure of whether a test has resulted in a specific customer behavior. Although it can apply to any customer action, the conversion rate usually refers to the primary business goal—the percentage of customers who made a purchase at a retail store, for example, or the percentage of visitors who opened a deposit account at a financial services site. Many businesses create analytics reports for a "conversion funnel," the set of steps customers are expected to take. For example, a retail conversion funnel may consist of viewing a product page, adding a product to the cart, clicking to check out, filling out shipping information, giving billing information, and then checking out. Each step within that funnel can be represented by a different conversion rate (e.g., the percentage of customers who filled out shipping information, etc.).

▶ **Click-through rate (CTR) and bounce rate.** This metric counts the number of visitors who clicked a specific link divided by the number of visitors who viewed the page. For example, the CTR could be measured for customers clicking to "log in" to a site, "share" an article, or "check out." When people refer to the CTR without referring to a specific link, they usually mean the CTR of an entire page—the percentage of visitors who clicked on any link on the page. The opposite of the CTR for a page is the *bounce rate*, the percentage of customers who left the site from that page. The click-through and bounce rates are especially helpful in testing to see how design changes on a page affect customer behavior.

▶ **Average order value (AOV).** AOV is the amount of money made divided by the number of orders made during the test period. Unlike RPV, which accounts for all visitors, AOV counts only those who made a purchase. AOV can also be thought of as the average value of each cart at checkout. AOV is a great indicator of how new designs are affecting what customers spend.

▶ **Page views per visitor.** This metric is the average number of pages a visitor viewed during a variable time period. This metric is especially valuable for businesses such as media companies, where advertising in certain site sections is usually worth more than in others; by segmenting the page views per visitor according to site section, companies can determine whether readership within premium advertising sections has increased.

Thinking Big: The Template for Success

Analytics data allows researchers not only to zero in on the details of individual pages on a site, but also to pull back and see the big picture by tracking the performance of page templates. *Page templates*, sometimes called *page types* or *section types*, are the central framework applied to all pages within a particular category. For example, a retail company may have a product page template that sets out a common layout and color scheme for all of that company's product pages. In many businesses, hundreds of pages may conform to the specifications of a single template; for that reason, metrics that focus on templates can provide powerful, high-level insights into customer behavior.

Too often, companies focus only on individual pages, neglecting to aggregate their data by page templates. In fact, both points of view are essential. For example, an analyst for an online news site may track the number of visitors to an individual article to gain an understanding of the impact of that particular content. However, this research would not detect broader issues: For instance, if an obstacle on the homepage is making it difficult to access *any* articles, an article page template analysis would expose the problem, but an individual article page analysis would not.

► **Time on site (TOS).** Calculating the amount of time an average visit lasted, this metric helps to measure whether a particular user experience causes visitors to stay longer on the site or not. It can be a tricky metric from which to draw conclusions, because more time spent on a site isn't always a good sign. For example, on media sites a high TOS may indicate that the visitor is finding plenty of relevant content. However, it could also show that users can't figure out how to find what they want. Similarly, a short TOS is likely a *good* sign for a search engine site, signaling that visitors are finding what they're looking for quickly. Finally, researchers should keep in mind that some analytics software may register a visitor walking away from the computer as a higher TOS, though most advanced versions account for this possibility.

Analytics in Action: A Case Study

This section shows how companies can draw on the guidelines described earlier—starting with questions and focusing on insights and impact—to make the most of the resources that analytics software can provide. By walking the reader through a real-life example, generously provided by the technology firm Lenovo Group Ltd., it also shows how this approach fits into the iterative optimization process as a whole.

A multinational business specializing in the manufacture, sale, and service of computers and electronic devices, including laptops, tablets, servers, televisions, and smartphones, Lenovo was the largest computer vendor in the world in 2013, based on the number of PCs sold.

The following example is taken from research conducted in 2011, when Lenovo was building its first Optimization Roadmap, which the company used to iteratively redesign its entire website. (Note that this case is specific to the company cited. Analysts in other businesses may not find it necessary to pull all of the reports discussed or to pull them in exactly the same way. They may even consult a technical expert to customize their analytics software if necessary.)

In this diary-style excerpt from Lenovo's optimization program, the company's analytics team starts with the first of the two fundamental research questions described at the beginning of this chapter: *In which site areas should the business start testing?* To answer this question, the researchers use the list of more detailed questions listed earlier, narrowing the focus from the site to templates to individual pages along the way. In each case, they apply the "insights and impact" method when interpreting the data reports.

How do key metrics fluctuate over time?

Start with an overview of the entire site by *graphing the primary success metrics over time*. This can help analysts understand business dynamics, such as the amount of traffic available for testing, weekday versus weekend traffic, historical seasonality, and so on. For example, a report of the page views over time appears in **Figure 5.1**.

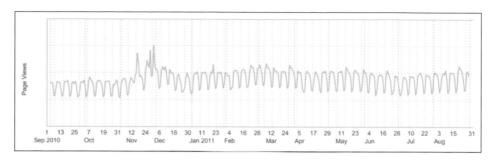

▶ **Insight.** Site traffic falls on most weekends. This might be due to the fact that Lenovo has a large audience shopping for computers for business use during weekdays.

Impact. This finding suggests several courses of action, including test featuring products, messaging, and promotions that will appeal to business users; segment test results by weekday and weekend traffic to understand whether customers behave differently depending on the day of the week; and test targeting experiences to specific consumer and business users.

▶ **Insight.** Although this insight is not apparent in the figure because the y-axis numbers have been redacted to preserve company confidentiality, there are consistently large volumes of traffic. Traffic levels also rise, and spike sharply, during the holiday season.

Impact. The high volume of traffic means the company can run multiple tests concurrently across the site all year round. The business should also ramp up testing just before and during the holiday season to take advantage of especially large traffic volumes.

A similar graph can be built for any metric: visitors, conversion rate, RPV, and so on. For example, a graph showing the conversion rate over time could be used to determine whether visitors are more or less likely to make a purchase during the holiday season.

Which areas have the most overall traffic?

Through which areas do most users enter the site?

Through which areas do most users exit the site?

Which site areas contribute the most to revenue?

Which site areas contribute the most to conversions?

One way to answer these questions is to build a *table listing all the site's pages ranked by key metrics over a set period of time.* The example in **Figure 5.2** shows Lenovo's top 15 pages ranked by the number of page views, alongside columns for visits, entries, exits, revenue, revenue participation, orders, and order participation. (Note that all raw data, such as the amount of revenue, the number of orders, and so on have been redacted for confidentiality reasons, leaving only percentage values. The same holds true for all subsequent figures in this chapter.)

	Page	Page Views ▼	Visits	Entries	Exits	Revenue	Revenue Participation	Orders	Orders Participation
1.	Select a country/region	19.9%	21.0%	26.9%	26.8%	0.0%	0.7%	0.0%	0.6%
2.	Homepage	19.8%	21.7%	27.3%	24.9%	2.5%	47.6%	1.7%	32.0%
3.	Laptops homepage (pre-loaded)	16.7%	17.4%	22.3%	22.2%	0.0%	0.4%	0.0%	0.4%
4.	Desktops homepage (pre-loaded)	11.0%	10.6%	13.6%	13.6%	0.0%	0.1%	0.0%	0.0%
5.	Shopping cart	1.2%	0.5%	0.0%	0.3%	14.0%	97.3%	20.2%	98.4%
6.	Search results	1.1%	0.7%	0.3%	0.5%	0.6%	8.8%	0.9%	10.1%
7.	Laptops homepage	0.9%	1.0%	0.4%	0.2%	1.4%	29.2%	0.9%	16.9%
8.	Professional laptops	0.8%	0.9%	0.2%	0.2%	1.0%	21.4%	0.5%	11.8%
9.	Sign-up	0.7%	0.2%	0.0%	0.1%	7.0%	46.7%	6.0%	39.5%
10.	Products: Laptops: ThinkPad homepage	0.6%	0.6%	0.2%	0.2%	1.0%	21.3%	0.5%	10.5%
11.	Learn: Laptops: ThinkPad homepage	0.5%	0.5%	0.0%	0.1%	0.5%	11.9%	0.2%	6.0%
12.	Products: Laptops: ThinkPad T homepage	0.5%	0.5%	0.2%	0.2%	0.8%	15.9%	0.4%	7.6%
13.	Products homepage	0.5%	0.5%	0.4%	0.3%	0.4%	10.3%	0.4%	8.3%
14.	Accessories homepage	0.4%	0.4%	0.2%	0.2%	0.3%	4.3%	0.8%	8.5%
15.	Customize your ThinkPad X220 laptop	0.4%	0.2%	0.0%	0.1%	2.2%	11.2%	1.1%	5.4%

Figure 5.2 Pages ranked by page views from July 1 to Aug. 31, 2011. The page with the highest number of page views appears at the top of the list.

▶ **Insight.** The five site areas with the most overall traffic are the "Select a Country/Region" page, the homepage, the "Laptops" page, the "Desktops" page, and the shopping cart.

Impact. Due to the large numbers of potential customers visiting these pages, all of these site areas are great candidates for testing.

▶ **Insight.** The shopping cart ranks among the top five for the number of page views—an unusual finding. This might indicate that very qualified traffic (i.e., customers who are highly likely to make a purchase) is visiting the site.

Impact. Look closely at cart-specific metrics to determine whether the cart is making good use of its high traffic levels by helping customers to check out easily. Also, because traffic is likely highly qualified, streamline access to the cart from areas throughout the site.

▶ **Insight.** The "Select a Country/Region" page has the most page views but also accounts for 26.8 percent of all exits from the site—an unusually high rate.

Impact. Test whether this page can be removed altogether, because it is leading to customer exits. Test using geo-location to determine a user's country from their IP address and then automatically sending them to the appropriate country site (this is also called *geo-targeting*). If this page must exist, try redesigning it to reduce the exit rate.

▶ **Insight.** The "Laptops" and "Desktops" category pages show very low revenue and order participation. It is unclear why, but a possible explanation is that customers are bypassing these pages when they place their order on a return visit. Perhaps these pages present an obstacle to customers who want to check out, causing them to abandon the site and come back later using a different path.

Impact. Conduct a detailed analysis of these category pages, as well as a path analysis for converting and nonconverting customers. Test different designs, including simplifying the number of product choices these pages present to all customers, in case an overwhelming array of choices is discouraging customers from making a decision. Test targeting customers who have a computer or other large item in their cart by showing them versions of these pages that encourage checkout. Test changing global navigation when a customer has a large item in their cart to encourage checkout.

This single analytics report can lead to many more insights with corresponding impacts. For example, by examining the data in the other columns researchers can seek answers to key questions such as: "Through which site areas do most users enter and exit?" and "Which site areas contribute the most to revenue and conversions?" This data report focuses on specific pages, but the same type of analysis can be built for templates, such as those for section pages, product pages, and so on.

Which products or services contribute the most to revenue?

Which products or services contribute the most to conversions?

An effective way to answer these questions is to build *a table listing all the business's products and services ranked by key metrics over a set period of time.* **Figure 5.3** shows an example of two such reports for the business laptops category. Each laptop model belongs to a subseries, or family of computers, that is in turn part of a larger series. These reports are ranked by revenue, although the actual dollar values have been redacted.

Figure 5.3 This figure shows Lenovo's top-selling business laptops listed by series and by subseries, and ranked by the amount of revenue generated.

	Series
1.	ThinkPad T Series
2.	ThinkPad X Series
3.	IdeaPad Y Series
4.	ThinkPad W Series
5.	ThinkPad Edge

	SubSeries
1.	X220
2.	T420
3.	W520
4.	T520
5.	T420s

▶ **Insight.** The ThinkPad T and X are the two most popular series of business laptops, and so should be prioritized for testing. Because these series offer a broad range of products, it is important to find out whether the wide variety of customization and pricing options is providing a competitive advantage or whether some customers feel overwhelmed by the number of choices.

Impact. Test removing certain lower-selling products (not shown in this report) from the site to simplify customers' choices, a move that could also save the business the cost of producing many different types of units. Start testing changes that can be made across all series pages at once, and segment the data by the individual series. Alternatively, start testing on the most popular series pages specifically.

▶ **Insight.** The ThinkPad X220 and T420 are the two most popular business laptops.

Impact. Conduct a deeper analysis to understand the purchase path for these and other top-selling models to determine whether points along these paths should be prioritized for testing. Test featuring these popular subseries on the homepage or other prominent pages.

How many times do customers visit the site before converting?

Start by compiling *a table listing the number of visits ranked by key metrics over a set period of time.* **Figure 5.4** shows one such report, which includes the number of visits a customer makes before making a purchase and the amount of revenue and orders received.

	Visit Number	Revenue ▼ ⑦	Orders ⑦
1.	1st Visit	32.6%	43.7%
2.	2nd Visit	17.0%	17.3%
3.	3rd Visit	11.6%	10.1%
4.	4th Visit	8.0%	6.3%
5.	5th Visit	6.3%	4.7%
6.	6th Visit	4.3%	3.3%
7.	7th Visit	3.1%	2.4%
8.	8th Visit	2.5%	1.8%
9.	9th Visit	1.8%	1.4%
10.	10th Visit	1.5%	1.2%

Figure 5.4 This Lenovo report shows the number of visits a customer makes before buying a product and the percentage of revenue and orders generated.

▶ **Insight.** The majority of customers visit the site more than once before making a purchase, which is not surprising, because computers are not an impulse buy. However, over 70 percent of all orders are placed, accounting for over 60 percent of the revenue, during the first three visits—a sign that these customers are extremely motivated to make a purchase. There is also a very long tail on this dataset, meaning that after the first three visits, the number of visits before converting varies widely, with some customers visiting hundreds of times.

Impact. Examine whether customers who purchase during the first three visits display common behaviors (for example, showing an interest in a specific type of product or discount) that can be emphasized to influence visitors who do not decide to purchase as quickly. Also, determine any barriers to checkout for visitors during their first three visits by examining the most common paths they take throughout the site, including their top entry and exit points. For visitors who visit more than three times before making a purchase, test ways to make it easy for them to save a cart or information on product configuration by emailing it to themselves. Additionally, test offering incentives on repeat visits, such as discounts, free shipping, free upgrades, and so on, to encourage customers to check out. Test more prominent placements for the company's online chat option and toll-free telephone number for those who visit repeatedly but do not make a purchase. Stage a future round of qualitative research to find out why some customers visit the site repeatedly but do not make a purchase.

When studying customers' behavior before converting, researchers often do a deep-dive analysis of the conversion funnel, creating what is known as a *funnel*, or *fall-out, report*. For sites with one-way conversion funnels, such as checkout processes or registration flows, this kind of report pinpoints where customers are entering and leaving the funnel, and helps to identify which areas of the funnel need the most attention. Although not all sites have enough traffic to test in multiple areas of the funnel simultaneously, any business can launch tests in different parts of the funnel one by one, using the results to determine in which other funnel areas to launch the next wave of tests. In the case study in question, Lenovo researchers analyzed several funnel reports, two of which are shown in **Figure 5.5**.

The first report shows whether customers who reached the shopping cart then progressed to the checkout, and the second shows the progression of users who visited the "Customize the Lenovo ThinkPad X220" page, which refers to the company's top-selling business laptop.

▶ **Insight.** Both reports show alarmingly high drop-off rates between the shopping cart and first step of the checkout process, with a 77 percent drop-off for all users, and an 80 percent drop-off for X220 customizers. Also, 74 percent of users leave the X220 configuration page before even reaching the shopping cart. Once customers make it past the cart, it is comparatively smooth progress to checkout, with a drop-off rate of 20–35 percent for each step. Although it would be worthwhile to reduce these numbers as well, the bottleneck is clearly at the top of the funnel.

Impact. The cart and configuration pages should be given a high priority for redesign. These pages draw some of the highest traffic on the site; all revenue flows through the cart, and any visitors who customize a computer use the configurator. Helping users through these two steps could not only increase customer satisfaction, but raise revenue for the business substantially.

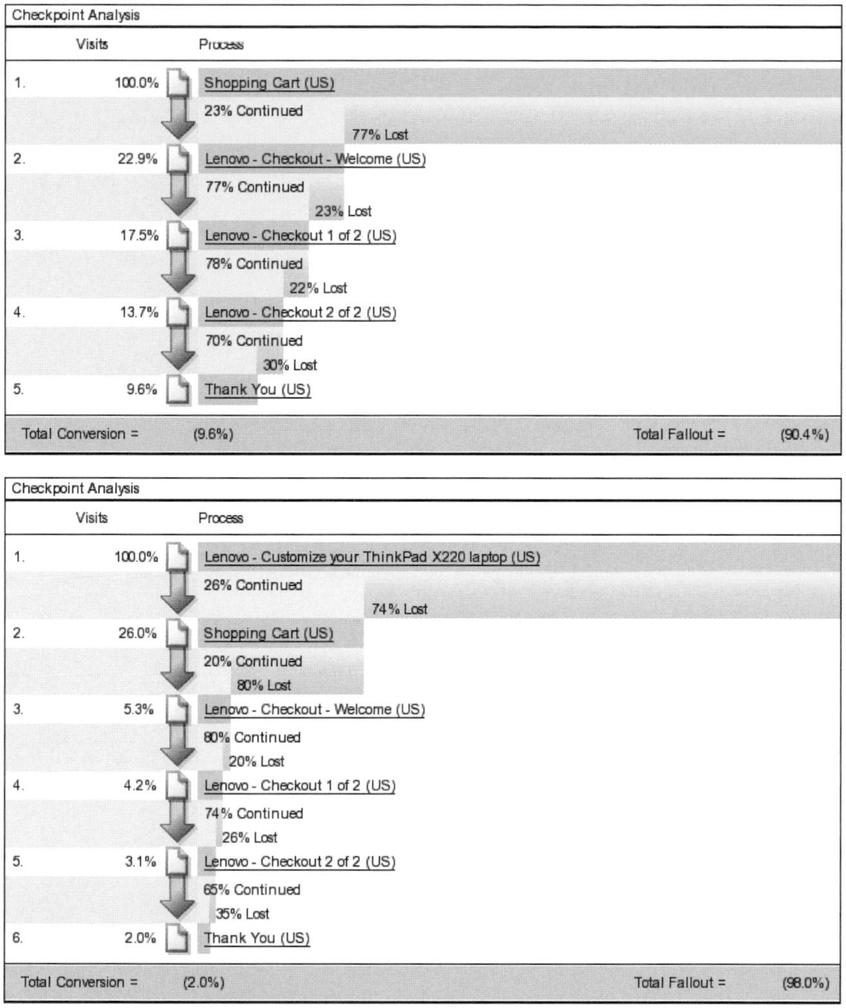

Figure 5.5 The first funnel report tracks the steps to checkout after entering the cart; the second traces the steps to checkout after visitors enter the "Customize Your Lenovo ThinkPad X220" page.

This analysis pinpoints the cart and configuration pages as top-priority areas for testing, which brings the Lenovo researchers to the second fundamental guiding question described at the beginning of this chapter: *"In each site area of interest, what should the business test?"* To help answer this question, they address the following two queries:

How did the customers get there?

What actions do customers take once they're there?

Path reports show how customers arrived on a page and their subsequent actions. An example of a path report for the cart page is shown in **Figure 5.6** on the next page. This report, which is a small subset of a much larger report, uses a tree diagram to show the top nine ways in which customers arrived on the cart page. Reports like this one can easily be expanded to show actions customers took two, three, or more steps before or after arriving on the cart page.

Figure 5.6 The path report for the Lenovo shopping cart.

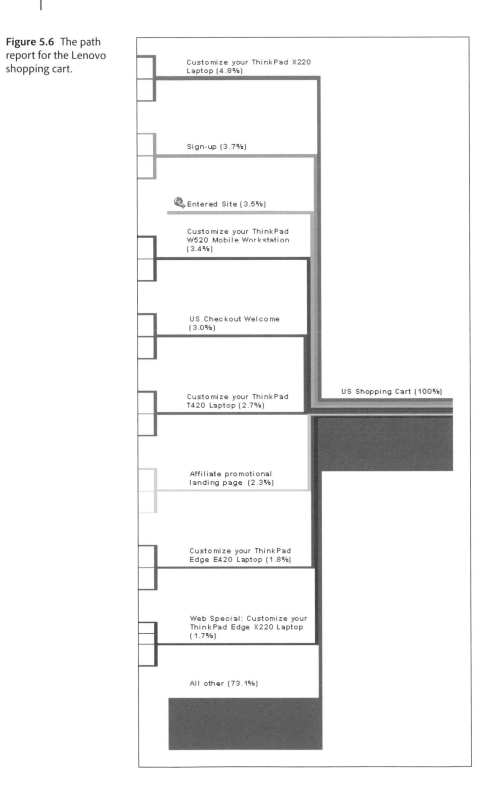

▶ **Insight.** Customization pages for the company's popular ThinkPad products make up five of the top nine ways in which customers arrive at the cart, which suggests that customization is an important point in the path toward the checkout page. However, it is not clear whether the majority of total cart visitors customize products beforehand, because 73.1 percent of the paths are not detailed.

Impact. Expand the path report to determine whether most customers customize products before going to the cart page. Test precustomized versions of products, or limiting customization options, in order to simplify or even eliminate this step. Conduct further quantitative and qualitative analyses of customization pages for all top products.

▶ **Insight.** The "sign-up" page is the second most popular way for a user to enter the cart.

Impact. After customers sign up, test sending them to the first page of checkout, bypassing the cart page altogether. Ensure that the checkout page displays a summary of cart contents and contains clear links to edit the cart.

▶ **Insight.** The third most popular way to view the cart is by entering the site directly, from a bookmark, for example.

Impact. This likely indicates that customers are successful in saving their cart and accessing it later. Build on this positive behavior by testing ways to make it easier for users to save or email cart information to themselves.

▶ **Insight.** The fifth most common way to view the cart is from the checkout page, an indication that users are backtracking in the checkout process. This probably indicates that the first step in that process is missing information and customers have to go backwards to retrieve it.

Impact. Test the prominence of existing information in the checkout flow, and test adding new types of information, such as cart contents, cart value, security messaging, shipping information, and so on. Conduct further quantitative research to identify the most common paths going backwards from the cart, and further qualitative research to understand customers' needs during checkout.

As the preceding examples of Lenovo's analyses show, quantitative research offers a powerful and highly versatile way to make sense of customer behavior. A few simple reports can yield a wealth of information, allowing even a relatively new analyst not only to validate qualitative research findings, but also to generate potentially impactful ideas for testing designs. It should be noted that these examples are by no means exhaustive: One can undoubtedly come up with more "insights and impacts" than are listed here.

Researchers can also pursue more questions using other data analyses, such as reports on page elements clicked, internal search terms, external search terms, referring-site URLs, marketing channel attribution, video engagement, and so on. Those with a keen interest in quantitative research may enjoy learning about predictive analytics, which incorporate statistical and machine learning techniques to model customer behavior; however, these topics are beyond the scope of this book.

Action Plan: Roadmap Assembly

The Optimization Roadmap pulls together the qualitative and quantitative research into an action plan for redesigning key areas of the business in an iterative and controlled fashion. The final stage in roadmap assembly requires some additional brainstorming and organizational work, as researchers focus on prioritizing what site areas to test and what to test within each area.

Accordingly, the roadmap document is typically divided into several parts: The first section includes research used to determine the prioritized site areas for testing; next, each prioritized site area has a section that details the qualitative and quantitative research used to build that site area's test list; finally, the prioritized test list is outlined for each area. The remainder of this chapter illustrates this assembly stage by outlining the process Lenovo used to arrive at its action plan.

Prioritizing Where to Test

As noted earlier, the main criteria for giving a site area high priority for testing are high volumes of traffic, unusually high or low conversion rates, high abandonment rates, or other factors identified by qualitative and quantitative studies. However, there is no hard-and-fast rule: The Iterative Optimization Methodology aims to get tests up and running in each area identified for redesign, so perfect prioritization is neither required nor possible. There will be opportunities to adjust the priority list throughout the process, as researchers respond to testing data along the way.

In order to keep it manageable, team members should limit the list of priority areas to 5–10. A list of more than 15 items suggests the site may be overly complicated, especially if the list includes templates, which can affect hundreds, even thousands, of pages.

Businesses that have gone through this process a few times often get creative with prioritization. For example, some companies create test areas that span multiple aspects of the customer experience, such as "Global Navigation" or "Social Interactions" (i.e., social-media features ranging from authentication processes, to sharing and comment options, to testing on social network pages).

In Lenovo's case, researchers drew on quantitative and qualitative studies to create a list of nine prioritized site areas, the first six of which are shown in **Figure 5.7**. Given the "insights and impact" analyses discussed earlier, it will come as no surprise that the cart, checkout funnel, and configurator were given top priority. (Although the "Choose a Country/Region" page had the most page views for Lenovo's international site, it does not appear on this list, which focused exclusively on the U.S. market.)

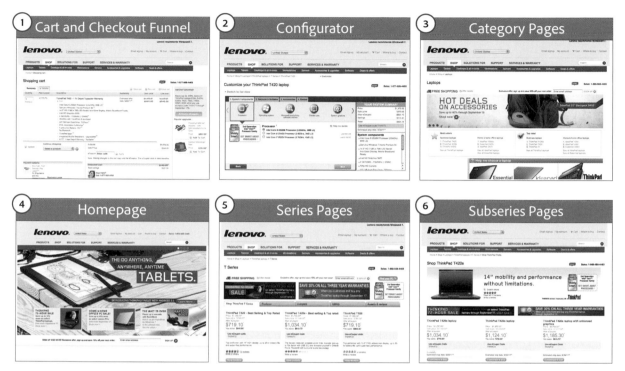

Figure 5.7 The first six prioritized site areas for Lenovo.

Prioritizing Test Ideas

For each of the site areas slated for testing, the Optimization Roadmap includes the relevant qualitative and quantitative research, and a prioritized list of test ideas. To generate test ideas, team members conduct a brainstorming session for each site area; the ideas are then prioritized according to the value they could bring to the business and to customers, as well as the perceived difficulty of implementation.

Brainstorming test ideas

This brainstorming step is sometimes called a *structured brainstorming session*, because rather than starting from a blank slate, team members draw on a range of research material and follow a structured process of idea generation, prioritization, and action for each site area. Team members first review the goals of the business and its customers, as well as the findings from qualitative and the quantitative research for the relevant area. Then they brainstorm test ideas, striving to come up with at least 10–15 ideas for each site area.

Here are a few tips when brainstorming test ideas:

- **Cast a wide net and get all ideas on the table.** Include as many stakeholders as possible from across the business to draw on diverse skills and to foster engagement throughout the company. No idea is a bad idea. Encourage people to get creative, and document all concepts.

- **Incorporate upcoming business plans.** If the business is working on new products, features, or other items, include those works-in-progress as test ideas for launch once the items are ready. The Optimization Roadmap should help drive the business, not exist outside of day-to-day operations. Early testing means the company can correct or stop making a flawed product or service before losing additional money.

- **Don't simply tweak what already exists.** Include full template redesigns as a test idea in each area.

- **Simplify.** Aim to simplify the user experience in every way possible—from the number of products, to the number of pages, to the way in which customers are asked to interact with the business. Examples of simplification include emphasizing important links and calls-to-action; making content easy to find and access; and removing extraneous page elements.

- **Embrace innovation while avoiding fads.** The best way to separate a fad from something truly innovative and helpful is to test it. Many online design trends of questionable customer benefit have emerged in recent years, including tag clouds, animated "splash" introduction pages, parallax scrolling, as well as skeuomorphic and flat design. There's a time and a place for most any technology or design style. What matters most is that technology and design be applied in a way that improves the customer experience and the business—and these improvements can usually be measured. Don't be afraid to take risks, but don't blindly follow the crowd.

Prioritizing based on value and difficulty

After brainstorming, team members arrange their test ideas in order of priority, based on how much value the new idea may bring to the business and its customers, as well as how difficult the test will be to launch.

Even though every test is based on research, predicting the value of a new design is a guessing game at the end of the day, even for the best businesspeople in the world. There's no way to really know the worth of a new design in advance: The whole reason for testing is to find out. Therefore, although value is a useful means of prioritizing ideas, it should not be rigidly applied.

To assess the difficulty of implementing a test, researchers weigh a variety of factors, including how many wireframes and creative comps will be needed, the process for building the new designs, timelines for internal legal reviews, and so on. Although many tests can be set up and launched in a matter of minutes in most organizations, the level

A Brainstorming Checklist

Some people find it helpful to brainstorm test ideas by systematically thinking through the options for each design element. The following checklist suggests some key design elements for brainstorming, followed by aspects of those elements that can be changed to improve performance.

- ▶ **Navigation** (global navigation, navigation within a section, etc.)
- ▶ **Calls-to-action** (anything clickable, such as links, buttons, images, etc.)
- ▶ **Imagery** (clickable or not)
- ▶ **Videos**
- ▶ **Text** (headlines, sub-headlines, value proposition bullets, product/service descriptions, trust messaging, phone numbers, etc.)
- ▶ **Products or services**
- ▶ **Features** (sharing and chat options, order status, recommended items, etc.)
- ▶ **Advertising** (internal advertising, third-party advertising, partners, etc.)
- ▶ **Flow** (checkout, registration, lead generation, application submission, etc.)

Test variables for these elements can include:

- ▶ **Redesign** (full redesign of page, template, email, etc.)
- ▶ **Layout** (element size, arrangement, surrounding whitespace, etc.)
- ▶ **Prominence** (emphasize, combine, remove, or alter an element)
- ▶ **Content** (copy, product or service name, button text, value proposition bullets, pictures and graphics, etc.)
- ▶ **Aesthetics** (color hue, saturation, luminance, etc.)
- ▶ **Function** (what happens when the customer clicks, etc.)
- ▶ **Pricing** (price, packages, sales, other special offers, etc.)
- ▶ **Alter flow** (rearrange steps, remove steps, etc.).
- ▶ **Algorithms** (internal search results, personalized offers, "people who bought this also bought," etc.)

Although such lists can be helpful, it is important to keep in mind that there's no magic formula for creating an innovative, customer-centric experience. Just let the creativity flow, and continue to generate new ideas as test results roll in.

---

of difficulty varies from company to company. A committee of stakeholders from different areas of the business should be involved in assessing test difficulty; this team should of course include members of the business's IT department.

Prioritization teams should assess value and difficulty simply as low, medium, or high, ranking tests with high potential value and low difficulty first. Team members should then stagger the remaining tests based on difficulty. For example, while easier tests are running, they can spend time preparing medium- or high-difficulty tests. They should also stagger tests that build on previous results. For instance, rather than placing two layout tests one after the other, team members should leave time to interpret the results of the first test before launching the second; in the interim, they can run an unrelated test to keep the optimization process going. After analyzing the results of each test, researchers should reevaluate the priority of upcoming tests.

Numbering tests to encourage iteration

As noted in Chapter 3, researchers assign numbers to site areas and tests to streamline communication. For example, for the Lenovo test labeled number 1.2, the "1" indicates that this is a test for the cart and checkout funnel, because this is site area 1 in Figure 5.7; the "2" indicates that this is the second test in that area. This numbering method facilitates iterative testing across the site, because team members can quickly determine where each test has run, how many iterative tests have run in each area, and sum up the total number of tests that have been conducted across the business.

This system also helps keep test results easy to find and retrieve when they are stored in a central location, such as a shared drive or library. As test lists are reprioritized, new test numbers may be added to the list, but once a test has run, no other test should have that number. Businesses often like to use descriptive names for tests, which is useful, but it's best to place the descriptive name *after* the number—as in "1.1 Homepage Hero Test," to aid in quick identification.

Up Next

This chapter showed how to harness the rich potential of analytics software without becoming overwhelmed by the volume of available data. It outlined how to keep a tight focus on business and customer value by applying the "insights and impact" method to data analysis. Finally, it showed how researchers decide what and where to test, as well as how they brainstorm and then prioritize test ideas, culminating in the assembly of the Optimization Roadmap.

The next chapter covers the last steps in the Iterative Optimization Methodology, from the planning and launch of design tests to the analysis of results and the launch of new tests, as the iterative cycle begins.

References

1. Lenovo Overtakes HP as the Top PC Vendor While U.S. Shipments Stabilize in the Second Quarter of 2013 (IDC Worldwide Quarterly PC Tracker; July 10, 2013). http://www.idc.com/getdoc.jsp?containerId=prUS24213513

CHAPTER 6

Optimization in Action

This chapter outlines each phase of test execution, from the planning stage, to test setup and launch, to the analysis and dissemination of results. It explains how to lay the groundwork for a successful design test by studying key factors, such as site traffic levels, available test types, and the number of recipes a company can test simultaneously. The chapter then outlines best practices for wireframing and design; test setup and quality assurance; and results analysis as well as communication.

Optimization Plan

An Optimization Plan lays out the details for each test in the roadmap. Because the roadmap will change over time, it is essential that each Optimization Plan stand as a self-contained document, recording any data that influenced specific test ideas so that the context of each test is available for future reference. An ever-changing roadmap is also a good reason not to build all the Optimization Plans at once, but instead to generate plans for each wave of tests in succession. For example, team members could focus on building plans for campaigns 1.1, 2.1, and 3.1 for the first wave of tests.

An Optimization Plan consists of the following:

▸ **Test methodology.** The first phase of planning includes the campaign objective, the hypothesis being tested, visitor entry criteria, the number of recipes to be created, test duration, and test type.

▸ **Supporting materials.** Additional information from the roadmap, such as the prioritized test list and the qualitative and quantitative research for the area being tested, helps establish the context for the campaign while keeping the Optimization Plan self-contained for future reference.

▸ **Metrics and segments.** Team members record the primary metrics and ways they plan to segment the data. This documentation is used as a reference guide during the test setup and quality assurance (QA) phases, and can help inform future test setups.

▸ **Wireframes.** Wireframes allow everyone to understand how the designs will look and function.

▸ **Design comps.** Once the final versions of the designs are complete, the test will be set up and launched.

Test Methodology

This section takes a closer look at the test methodology laid out in Optimization Plans. This methodology includes six components:

▸ **The test objective.** Usually stated as a one-line summary, the test objective outlines what team members hope to accomplish, including the metrics they are looking to affect. In most cases, this objective appears in the prioritized test list as well.

▸ **The hypothesis.** More specific than the objective, the hypothesis explains which elements will be altered, how they will be changed, and why. The hypothesis should be stated in a way that can be validated or invalidated through a controlled experiment.

▸ **Number of recipes.** The number of recipes is the number of different designs, including the control that will be tested.

▸ **Visitor entry criteria.** The percentage of visitors who will be included is known as the visitor entry criteria. For example, a campaign may target 100 percent of all shopping cart visitors or 25 percent of all homepage visitors profiled as female.

▸ **Test duration.** As best practice, tests should run for at least two weeks to incorporate both daytime and nighttime traffic, as well as weekday and weekend traffic; each of these periods can later be investigated to identify any differences in customer behavior. Of course, tests that target holiday or promotional periods may run for shorter amounts of time, in which case analysts launch several rapid-fire tests and make the best decisions they can in the available time.

▸ **Test type.** Researchers specify what kind of test they plan to launch: A/B, multivariable (MVT), auto-optimizing test, or other.

Having been discussed at length in previous chapters, the test objective and hypothesis require little further explanation; however, determining the number of recipes, entry criteria, test duration, and test type can be a complex process, which is outlined in greater detail in the following sections.

Number of Recipes

The number of recipes a site can accommodate for simultaneous testing depends on many factors, including the amount of traffic the business receives. Large online businesses with millions of monthly visitors generally don't need to worry about the number of designs they're testing at once; however, team members for sites with lower traffic levels must be careful to avoid testing too many designs simultaneously, so that their tests will yield accurate results.

Because different statistical software generate results using different methods, teams should include at least one member who understands the methodology behind the software, such as an analyst or engineer, when determining the optimal number of recipes.

An exhaustive review of the statistics of testing is beyond the scope of this book; instead, the following section offers a brief explanation of some of the concepts involved when determining the required sample size, or traffic volumes, for testing the difference between two or more recipes.

Type I and Type II errors

There are two types of errors, called Type I and Type II errors, that researchers can make when determining whether to accept the hypothesis that differences in performance exist between designs. A Type I error occurs when the researcher claims there is a difference in performance when in fact there isn't. The likelihood of a Type I error occurring is called the *significance level*. For example, if a test shows that the conversion rate for an alternate design is higher than that of the control design at the *5 percent significance level*, that means if the test is repeated thousands of times on independent data sets of the same size, then claiming that there is a difference in performance, when in fact there isn't, will happen only 5 percent of the time.

Type II errors occur when a researcher claims there is no difference in performance, when in fact there is. Based on the true performance of the designs, the test will be susceptible to either a Type I or a Type II error.

Two key factors affect the researcher's ability to detect differences in performance between the default and control designs:

▸ **Traffic volume.** The more visitors enter a test, the more confident the researcher can be that the observed difference in performance is not due to chance alone.

▸ **True difference in design performance.** The larger the true difference in performance between the designs, the more confident the researcher can be that the observed difference in performance is not due to chance alone.

Therefore, the more traffic a test has, or the greater the change a tested design elicits in customer behavior, the greater the degree of confidence researchers can have about their conclusions.

Of course, analysts don't know the traffic volume or differences in design performance until after testing; they need to estimate these factors to determine the number of recipes they will run at once. With millions of monthly visitors, many large businesses have such high traffic levels that instead of spending time on traffic and performance calculations, researchers simply dive into testing; however, businesses with smaller traffic volumes should assess the minimum number of visitors needed to avoid making Type I and Type II errors.

Minimum traffic levels

Most testing software provides the analyst with a calculator that can be used to estimate the minimum traffic levels needed to detect a hypothesized difference in performance between designs. This section shows an example of how minimum recommended traffic levels change due to different variables, in **Table 6.1** through **Table 6.3**.

The tables are based on a statistical formula, described in more detail to follow, that determines how many visitors one would need, under different specifications, such as desired lift in performance, for the threshold of making either a Type I or a Type II error to be 1 percent, 5 percent, and 10 percent, respectively for each table. It is up to the analyst which error threshold and lift in performance to aim for, with 5 percent being an extremely popular choice for the error threshold, and 10 percent being a common goal for the lift in performance.

The left-hand columns of the tables list the true conversion rate of the default recipe, and the top rows of the tables list the true lift of the alternate recipe. For any row, notice that as the lift in the alternate recipe's conversion rate rises, fewer visitors are needed to gain confidence in the result.

For example, if an analyst conducting a test on a shopping cart page assumes the current cart conversion rate of 15 percent will continue during the test period, he or she can make the following calculations:

▶ Referencing the row starting with 15 percent in Table 6.1 and reading across the first few columns: If the alternate version of the shopping cart provides an average lift of 20 percent over the default (meaning it reaches a conversion rate of 18 percent, which is 20 percent more than the 15 percent achieved by the original), then at least 13,351 visitors are required to each recipe for Type I and Type II errors to occur less than 1 percent of the time. If the alternate version of the shopping cart provides 15 percent lift (a conversion rate of 17.25 percent), then the difference in design performance is smaller, so at least 23,735 visitors to each recipe are needed to reach the same threshold for reliability.

▶ If the business analyst wishes for Type I and Type II errors to occur less than 5 percent of the time, with the default conversion rate of 15 percent, and an alternate recipe with a lift of 20 percent, then, referencing Table 6.2, each recipe only needs 7,220 visitors. Similarly, if the analyst wishes the threshold for Type I or Type II errors to be only 10 percent, only 4,758 visitors per recipe are needed, according to the figures in Table 6.3.

Table 6.1 Minimum Number of Visitors per Design (1% Threshold for Type I or Type II Errors)

		LIFT IN ALTERNATE CONVERSION RATE (E.G. 1% LIFT OVER 5% DEFAULT = 5% X 1.01 = 5.05% ALTERNATE CONVERSION RATE)					
		20% LIFT	**15% LIFT**	**10% LIFT**	**5% LIFT**	**2% LIFT**	**1% LIFT**
DEFAULT CONVERSION RATE	**20%**	7,510	13,351	30,040	120,157	750,980	3,003,918
	15%	13,351	23,735	53,403	213,612	1,335,075	5,340,299
	10%	30,040	53,403	120,157	480,627	3,003,918	12,015,671
	5%	120,157	213,612	480,627	1,922,508	12,015,671	48,062,683
	2%	750,980	1,335,075	3,003,918	12,015,671	75,097,941	300,391,764
	1%	3,003,918	5,340,299	12,015,671	48,062,683	300,391,764	1,201,567,055
	0.10%	300,391,764	534,029,802	1,201,567,055	4,806,268,217	30,039,176,351	120,156,705,403

Table 6.2 Minimum Number of Visitors per Design (5% Threshold for Type I or Type II Errors)

		LIFT IN ALTERNATE CONVERSION RATE (E.G. 1% LIFT OVER 5% DEFAULT = 5% X 1.01 = 5.05% ALTERNATE CONVERSION RATE)					
		20% LIFT	15% LIFT	10% LIFT	5% LIFT	2% LIFT	1% LIFT
DEFAULT CONVERSION RATE	20%	4,061	7,220	16,244	64,974	406,085	1,624,339
	15%	7,220	12,835	28,878	115,509	721,929	2,887,714
	10%	16,244	28,878	64,974	259,895	1,624,339	6,497,355
	5%	64,974	115,509	259,895	1,039,577	6,497,355	25,989,419
	2%	406,085	721,929	1,624,339	6,497,355	40,608,466	162,433,864
	1%	1,624,339	2,887,714	6,497,355	25,989,419	162,433,864	649,735,455
	0.10%	162,433,864	288,771,314	649,735,455	2,598,941,819	16,243,386,369	64,973,545,474

Table 6.3 Minimum Number of Visitors per Design (10% Threshold for Type I or Type II Errors)

		LIFT IN ALTERNATE CONVERSION RATE (E.G. 1% LIFT OVER 5% DEFAULT = 5% X 1.01 = 5.05% ALTERNATE CONVERSION RATE)					
		20% LIFT	15% LIFT	10% LIFT	5% LIFT	2% LIFT	1% LIFT
DEFAULT CONVERSION RATE	20%	2,677	4,758	10,705	42,819	267,618	1,070,471
	15%	4,758	8,459	19,031	76,123	475,765	1,903,060
	10%	10,705	19,031	42,819	171,276	1,070,471	4,281,884
	5%	42,819	76,123	171,276	685,102	4,281,884	17,127,534
	2%	267,618	475,765	1,070,471	4,281,884	26,761,771	107,047,082
	1%	1,070,471	1,903,060	4,281,884	17,127,534	107,047,082	428,188,326
	0.10%	107,047,082	190,305,923	428,188,326	1,712,753,302	10,704,708,133	42,818,832,531

These tables are populated numerically based on a statistical formula corresponding to the "two-sided Z-test," using the statistical software "R." The tables assume that only two designs, the control and the alternate, are being tested at once. They also assume that the metric being measured is binary, meaning that it has only two possible values: the visitor converted or they did not. By contrast, some metrics, such as revenue, can hold a wide range of values. If more than two designs are being tested at once, or non-binary metrics are being measured, different tables need to be generated.

Low volume sites or traffic areas

Not every business has enough traffic or conversions to support simultaneous testing across all major areas, but most sites can nevertheless support a testing program by making good use of their traffic. Similarly, some large websites have site sections that don't get heavy traffic but are still extremely important. Here are some tips for testing in areas with low traffic levels:

▸ **Test ambitious ideas.** To make the best use of traffic, test major changes to designs, test in site areas with large visitor volumes, or test global elements (e.g., a site header that appears on every page). Stop running tests that show little difference in performance; focus instead on tests that identify major potential improvements.

▸ **Make good use of traffic.** Analysts should use 100 percent of available traffic and limit the number of recipes in each test; they should also restrict the number of tests running at the same time.

▸ **Change the primary success metric.** Site areas further upstream in conversion funnels generally have larger traffic volumes, making it easier to avoid Type I and Type II errors. For example, results for a product page layout test may lift clicks to the "buy now" button on the page with a 1 percent error threshold but lift the final purchase conversion rate with only a 10 percent error threshold. Even when upper-funnel metrics are used to declare success, team members should monitor the health of the business by keeping an eye on its revenue numbers.

Test Results Do Not Predict the Future

Test results are a backward-looking measurement and cannot predict how the winning design will perform in the future because the exact conditions under which a test has been run cannot be duplicated. Factors that change between experiments include seasonality, competitive dynamics, the economy, and technological change, such as the advent of tablets, which means many desktop experiences must be redesigned for a smaller format.

There's no magic solution for predicting customer behavior. Team members should be prepared to make "good enough" decisions that will keep the business evolving rather than striving for perfection. That said, testing remains a highly effective way of gathering and interpreting customer data under real market conditions to inform business decisions.

Test Type

Different types of tests require different numbers of recipes, so an understanding of the number of designs that can be tested at once will inform how the test is structured. In this section, three of the more popular test types are discussed: A/B, multi-variable, and auto-optimizing. Researchers should choose the test type most likely to provide a clear answer to their hypothesis.

A/B tests

Straightforward and flexible, A/B tests, in which two or more designs are tested against each other, make up the vast majority of all campaigns; most other test types are simply a subset of this category. Because this kind of test has been discussed extensively in previous chapters, this section is limited to outlining a few additional best practices when planning A/B tests:

- **Enter visitors into one test at a time.** If visitors are being included in multiple experiments at once, the tests may interfere with one another. For example, running two pricing tests at the same time may cause customers to see different prices for the same item as they browse different areas of the site.

- **Tie the visitor to the design throughout the testing period.** Each visitor who enters a test experience in one site area should be shown the same version if they return to that area later in the testing period. This rule generally ensures consistency in tested data and avoids creating a disjointed customer experience, although there are some exceptions (see "Targeting and personalization tests" later in this chapter).

- **Isolate variables to understand their effect.** When many different elements in an experience change at once, the entire recipe is considered a single variable being tested. In such cases, researchers wanting to determine the impact of a particular element need to isolate it as a variable in a follow-up test. Businesspeople therefore need to strike a balance between improving the customer experience through ambitious testing and understanding which individual changes are making a difference.

Multi-variable tests

A multi-variable, or multivariate, test (MVT) is a specialized type of A/B campaign where more than one variable has been isolated.

The following is an example of an MVT:

- **Recipe A.** Default design
- **Recipe B.** Default design with a new call-to-action
- **Recipe C.** Default design with a new headline

Two variables are being tested in an isolated fashion: the call-to-action and the headline. The results of this test allow team members to learn:

▶ Which version of each element performs better: the old versus the new call-to-action, and the old versus the new headline

▶ How influential each element is compared with the other elements being tested: the call-to-action versus the headline

Understanding which elements are the most influential is a powerful insight that helps businesspeople decide where to focus future optimization efforts. For this reason, MVT tests are sometimes called *element discovery tests*.

Obviously, researchers are hoping that new elements outperform the original ones, but even if they lose badly, all is not lost: Such a result shows that the element is important to customers, and researchers can strive to build on the strengths of the original to create a new version that will ultimately outperform it.

Another form of MVT testing is called the *full-factorial multivariate test*. This type of testing includes all possible combinations of tested elements. For the preceding example, a Recipe D would need to be added to make it a full-factorial MVT:

▶ **Recipe A.** Default design

▶ **Recipe B.** Default design with a new call-to-action

▶ **Recipe C.** Default design with a new headline

▶ **Recipe D.** Default design with a new call-to-action and new headline

Testing in this way allows the businessperson to understand every possible combination of variables tested and which combination is the best-performing recipe. Tests like these are especially popular in cases where the elements being tested might interfere with one another if a customer is exposed to different combinations of them.

For full-factorial MVTs, researchers should be wary of adding too many new elements, because the number of recipes required grows exponentially. For example, testing five elements with three variations of each requires three to the power of five, or 243, recipes. Running a test with this many recipes could take months or even years for many businesses—time that would be much better spent on smaller, more rapid-fire tests. There are also shortcuts, such as *partial factorial multivariate testing*; these allow businesses to run otherwise large MVTs with a fraction of the number of recipes. This type of testing usually assumes that interaction effects between elements are extremely small or nonexistent. Although such tests can be very helpful in the right context, a full discussion of this category is beyond the scope of this book.

Targeting and personalization tests

A specific type of both A/B and multivariate tests, targeting and personalization campaigns are aimed at specific types of visitors. For example, on its homepage, a business may show specific categories of products to particular customers, based on products they've recently viewed. The terms "targeting" and "personalization" are often used as synonyms, although some people use "targeting" for the practice of showing content to specific customer groups and "personalization" for the practice of tailoring content to individual customers.

Although both approaches can be highly effective, businesspeople often overthink targeting and personalization. Customers are adept at self-segmenting. For example, a customer browsing for a laptop online should be able to find what they want easily by choosing from a list of navigation links on a homepage. By using personalization to focus the homepage narrowly on a presumed preference, a company might prevent the customer from seeing the full range of other products the business offers.

When they do choose to use targeting and personalization, optimization teams should keep such efforts simple and large scale. Otherwise, the rules that dictate which customers see what designs can quickly become complex and difficult to maintain. When targeting, it is often appropriate to expose the same customer to several alternate designs as their behavior changes (e.g., tailoring homepage designs based on the product category the customer has visited most recently). Because it requires manual effort to keep the rules up to date, it's usually best to run auto-optimizing tests if the rules do become numerous.

Auto-optimizing tests

Auto-optimizing tests incorporate a predictive model to determine which designs the campaign should show to which customers on the spot. These tests are normally seeded with the following: a variety of designs that may appeal to different types of customers; a list of business rules for the model (e.g., a rule against advertising checking accounts to customers who already have them); and thorough datasets such as demographic, environmental, and behavioral data that may be collected in real time throughout the test (e.g., visitor location, links the visitor has clicked on, time of day of visit, and so on).

Many auto-optimizing campaigns split traffic, cordoning off a portion for continuous testing; based on the real-time results of those tests, the campaign shows the winning designs to the appropriate customers. A simple version of an auto-optimizing campaign may enter more visitors into whichever recipe is performing the best during the test. Sophisticated versions include personalization algorithms for "recommended products" or "recommended articles" features.

More complex versions use advanced statistical methods, and incorporate all available data, to deliver specific offers to individual customers. A basic A/B test layered on top of an auto-optimizing campaign can help determine which of several algorithms is most effective, or how best to display the products or content suggested by those algorithms.

Advanced auto-optimizing campaigns are used in specific areas of sites with high traffic volumes, because this type of test shines at identifying which of many possible offers, such as products, articles, or discounts, the company should display to a particular customer. However, this kind of testing is rarely used to make major changes to the user experience, such as new layouts, functionality, and flows, because it is usually more efficient to choose a single winning design for all customers based on the results of straightforward A/B tests.

Success Metrics and Segments

Some analytics software automatically tracks metrics and segments broadly across tested designs, allowing the researcher to select any relevant reports for later analysis. Other software requires analysts to define which metrics and segments they want to measure before launching a test. In those situations, researchers should cast the net wide to capture data that may prove important in testing, even if that data did not seem so beforehand. Accordingly, analysts observe the following best practices:

▶ **Track all primary success metrics.** Popular success metrics include the RPV, AOV, and conversion rate. In situations where the campaign's primary success metric isn't directly related to revenue, but another indicator, such as the number of email sign-ups on a retail site, analysts should measure revenue anyway to ensure ancillary testing doesn't negatively affect the mainstay of the business.

▶ **Track several secondary metrics.** Although the primary metrics will likely be used to declare success, secondary metrics provide information on how customer behavior may have changed due to the test, and these insights can be used to generate follow-up tests. Popular secondary metrics include the click-through rate on various site elements, as well as traffic levels at each stage of a conversion funnel.

▶ **Set up segments representing large customer groups.** Rather than always viewing test results in aggregate, analysts can use segmentation to consider the results from different angles. For example, first-time customers may respond differently to tested designs than repeat customers do. If different groups of customers prefer particular designs, researchers should consider running follow-up targeting or auto-optimizing tests. Several popular segmentation categories appear in **Table 6.4**.

Many companies have strict privacy rules that prohibit the association of this data with any personally identifiable information (names, addresses, etc.). Used properly, this anonymous data can help create easier and more relevant customer experiences. However, team members must exercise caution when tracking and using customer attributes for segmentation. Lax privacy protection can jeopardize customers' trust, and decision makers who use this data unwisely probably won't have those customers—or their businesses—very long.

Table 6.4 Examples of Customer Attributes for Segmentation

SEGMENT TYPE	EXAMPLES
Behavioral	Visitor stage (new to site, repeat to site; new to test, etc.)
	Customer stage (prospect, customer, top customer, etc.)
	Account status (has account, has wish-list, has registry, etc.)
	Product or service affinity (visited dresses > 5 times, added shirt to cart, last viewed shoes, etc.)
	Purchases (last purchased a book, etc.)
	Marketing campaign responses (ads viewed, emails opened, etc.)
Environmental	IP address, country, time zone, season in country, type of device, screen resolution, browser type, operating system, etc.
Temporal	Time of day, day of week, month of year, etc.
Referrer	Referring domain, SEM or SEO search keyword, marketing campaign ID, affiliate ID, etc.
Offline	In-store purchases, in-store activity, etc.
Third-party data vendors	Gender, age range, income range, interests, company name, etc.

Wireframes

This section reviews the structure and assembly of wireframes, and includes some tips for creating wireframes. To foster a collaborative environment, many companies start the wireframing process by holding brainstorming sessions that include stakeholders from across the business.

Structure of a Wireframe

Wireframes include the following specifics:

- ▶ Layout
- ▶ Prominence of elements
- ▶ Copy
- ▶ Calls-to-action
- ▶ Functionality
- ▶ Colors
- ▶ Imagery

Wireframes should be as simple as possible and include written notes to explain any ambiguities. Most wireframes include the following structural elements to set the context for anyone who views them:

- ▶ **Border.** A dark outline defines the borders of a wireframe. Because designs often have white space at their edges, it can be difficult to distinguish where a wireframe starts and ends without a border.

- ▶ **Fold lines.** "The fold" is a newspaper term for the place where the paper is folded in half. Material placed "above the fold" is visible on newsstands, so important content is placed there to increase sales. Now the term is also used for the area of a screen that is visible without scrolling in devices such as desktops, smartphones, and tablets. Wireframes should indicate the fold lines so team members can see where the designs will appear on different devices and so they can set the scale of the designs.

- ▶ **Recipe name.** It may sound obvious, but it's important to label the design so people will know what they're looking at. The default should be listed as the first recipe, although instead of creating a wireframe, a screen shot will suffice for this because the template or page already exists.

Assembling Wireframes

Companies following the Iterative Optimization Methodology use a variety of wireframing tools, ranging from paper and pencil to basic presentation software. In order to make wireframes accessible to as many people as possible, companies should not use software requiring highly specialized skills to create wireframes. Chris

Kahle, Web Analytics Manager at Caesars Entertainment Corporation, says that at his company, "Wireframes can be built by almost anyone," adding that for basic wireframes, "We'll draw it out on the whiteboard during a team meeting, and the designer, who is sitting in the meeting, will build a comp from our whiteboard sketch."

To speed up the process, team members can make minor changes using screen shots and slide presentation software. For example, to change a headline, they can take a screen shot of the page, and then use the software to type in the new headline on top of the old one, making the original "disappear" by matching its background color to that of the page.

Creating Great Wireframes

This section offers a wide range of practical tips for generating customer-centric wire-frames. First, however, it describes the following principles, which will help inform the wireframing process as a whole:

▶ **Embrace simplicity.** There's no secret to producing great wireframes: If there's a consistent theme behind the creation of many winning designs, it is to *embrace simplicity*. This usually means stripping down each design to the bare minimum. For example, team members can help the customer make choices by limiting the number of calls-to-action. One primary call-to-action, even if it's repeated, is usually better than a hodge-podge of choices that will confuse or overwhelm the visitor.

▶ **Don't forget the blue-sky approach.** Although testing changes to individual page elements can provide large gains in performance, using the existing version of a page as a guide for the new wireframe can also lead to in-the-box-thinking. As an alternative, start with a blank screen and ask: "What business and customer goals must this page meet?" Then, aim to create only elements that help to satisfy those goals.

▶ **Take it to the wall.** Tape the wireframe to a wall, stand six or seven feet away, and determine whether the expected customer action is immediately obvious—it should be. Don't use arrows to point out what visitors should do next; the expected action should be intuitive. Also, check for design elements that might lead to misinterpreta-tion. For example, "45% off" could easily be mistaken for "$45" if the percentage sign is small, leading customers to abandon if the price is in reality much less than $45.

This section now turns to the nitty-gritty of wireframing, with practical tips on layout, messaging, and customer service. Although observing these practices should help team members create successful designs, it is important to keep in mind that only through testing can companies truly gauge the effectiveness of their designs and the strategies they used to create them.

Layout best practices include:

▶ **Design for the smallest screen size first.** Constraints can drive creativity, help the designer to see the customer experience in a completely different way, and force hard decisions about which elements are required and which are not. Currently, this technique is referred to as designing *for mobile first*, or *for touch first*. About a decade ago, when 1024x768 screen sizes were becoming popular, it was called designing for *800x600 first*.

▸ **Pay attention to fold lines.** While scanning, customers often scroll up and down webpages but will rarely scroll side to side—an important consideration when creating new layouts. Customers will scroll down if it's clear there is additional content, so make sure design elements peek above the fold to help customers realize that there's more to see.

▸ **Make strategic use of white space.** Customers are more likely to notice content if it's surrounded by lots of white space, as opposed to other content competing for their attention; similarly, customers are attracted to images they think will be helpful. Use imagery and white space to draw and then direct the customer's attention.

Messaging best practices include:

▸ **Optimize for scanning customers.** Incorporate elements that visitors can quickly scan, such as succinct and prominent headlines, concise value proposition bullets, and lists (e.g., best sellers, top-rated, most popular), instead of dense blocks of copy.

▸ **Clarify clickability.** Make sure customers can easily differentiate what's clickable from what's not. Calls-to-action that contrast with the rest of the page work well (colored buttons, colored and underlined text, etc.), as do images that aren't easily mistaken for advertising or for purely aesthetic elements.

▸ **Emphasize important elements.** Emphasize what matters: For example, if product images matter, try making them extremely large. Similarly, it's OK to repeat important design elements, such as key value propositions (e.g., "free shipping" for a retail site or "free gym facility" for a hotel chain) from page to page. It's better to have a simple message repeatedly reinforced than a dense message conveyed only once.

Customer service best practices include:

▸ **Build trust.** Customers need to know they can trust the business they're interacting with. Trust can be reinforced at every stage of interaction; examples include loading pages over HTTPS, placing security symbols near login fields, adding verified third-party trust logos in checkout flows, and making it easy for customers to find information about cancellation and return policies. Social proof, such as lists of recommended items, customer reviews and testimonials, and social network "shares" can also help.

▸ **Exercise caution with price tests.** Although price testing can be an extremely effective tool, researchers should approach it cautiously to avoid making customers feel confused or exploited. It is preferable to test discounts rather than different base prices and to test new product bundles and service levels rather than different prices for one product. Companies should never discriminate based on presumed gender, race, and so forth. In order to provide a good experience, some companies charge everyone the lowest tested price, including those customers who chose to pay a higher price, based on the recipe to which they had been directed in testing.

▶ **Meet contextually relevant expectations.** Qualitative research will reveal customers' expectations in each area of the site; it's then up to the business to meet and even exceed them. For example, customers may expect the search results page to return exactly what they're looking for in the top few results that are easily clickable; the story page to allow them to scan an article or watch a video and then quickly find something else engaging or easily exit the site; the checkout process to be quick and safe without requesting unnecessary personal information; and so on.

▶ **Don't get hung up on consistency.** Although consistency appeals to *online professionals*, customers rarely care because they are focused on scanning for a single link or piece of information to take them closer to their goal. For example, global navigation can appear and disappear, and logos and color schemes can change, but few customers will notice as long as they can easily find what they're looking for.

▶ **Don't focus on the advanced user.** Designers often worry that removing complex features will frustrate a small percentage of their "power users" who have become familiar with those designs. Although some naysayers will complain, the vast majority of customers, old and new alike, appreciate a simpler experience.

Although following the preceding guidelines can help, team members should keep in mind that wireframing is a creative and fluid process, during which there is usually some back and forth between crafting the hypothesis and creating the wireframes. For example, the wireframing process may generate new design ideas that will slightly alter the hypothesis or lead to prioritizing additional test ideas in the Optimization Roadmap.

Design Comps

Team members translate the completed wireframe into a design comp, also called a *production design* or *graphic design*, the polished final version of the new design. Some tips for a seamless process in creating design comps are as follows:

▶ **Don't introduce new variables.** As in the wireframing phase, pay close attention to which variables will be isolated for testing. For example, keep aesthetic treatments (fonts, colors, shadows, and so on) consistent unless they are being isolated as variables for testing.

▶ **Foster communication.** The wireframer and designer should have open and honest communication throughout the process. Start by talking about the wireframe, and share thoughts about the final look of the recipe. Great designers know how to take a wireframe concept and make it shine by adding an aesthetic layer that reinforces the most important page elements; however, they can't do this in a vacuum. The earlier the designer has been included in the process—including the definition of customer and business goals—the better equipped that person will be to create a successful design comp.

▸ **Get legal approvals in batches.** Businesses in some industries, such as finance, medicine, and dieting, often require their legal department to review designs before testing. This can slow down an optimization program. In order to expedite the reviews, request to have a large group of potential design elements approved in advance. For example, if different headlines and value propositions are on the Optimization Roadmap, ask the legal department to review a batch of 50–100 possible alternatives at once. Then there will be lots of approved alternate content to pull from when creating wave after wave of tests.

Optimization Launch

Once the designs have been finalized, the test will be set up, checked, and launched. Test setup techniques differ from company to company, and although the technical details of this process are beyond the scope of this book, this section discusses several high-level best practices.

Implementation

Implementation will vary based on the systems and software the business uses for testing, as well as the complexity of each test. Tests that are easy to implement, such as swapping images or changing copy, can usually be set up in a matter of minutes by anyone with basic computer skills. More complex tests, such as redesigning entire pages, rearranging steps in a flow, or adding new features, usually require IT involvement. The earlier IT is brought into the process to help scope out the level of effort required and create a project plan, the better.

The process of setting up tests is similar to launching any type of redesigned content, including those created as part of the traditional design process. Steps may include translating final designs into HTML, CSS, and JavaScript; uploading alternate elements to a content delivery network; backend coding; updating analytics reports to record new links, pages, and functionality; setting up campaign entry and exit conditions; and allocating site traffic among recipes. Some companies use third-party software to make testing easier, including JavaScript tagging solutions or content management systems.

Quality Assurance

Quality assurance (QA) is a process to ensure there aren't any bugs that might affect the testing process and that analytics data from the tests will accurately inform decision making. Thomas Lau, Senior Manager of Online Prospect Acquisition for American Express®, oversees the optimization program for the company. Lau advises, "If you can't record a metric, you're not going to be able to make the right calls. Make sure you understand any possible pitfalls of your technology platform, including whether special precautions need to be taken to transmit data across pages and sites."

Most businesses already have a QA checklist that team members use when launching new designs. When using the Optimization Method, QA teams should follow the same checklist, with the following additions:

▸ Default and alternate designs look and function as planned.

▸ Screen shots of all final designs have been taken.

▸ Campaign entry and exit conditions are working.

▸ Traffic is being split properly.

▸ All metrics and segments are being recorded for each design.

▸ Screen shots showing all metrics and segments have been taken.

▸ Verify that all of the preceding steps have been completed for all major browsers and operating systems.

QA is best conducted by professionals in that field who can help systematize and, in some cases, use tools to automate the process. The most important QA practices include:

▸ **Always check important metrics.** Bugs introduced in one area of a site can cause errors across the entire site and skew test results across the board. Be sure to check important metrics, even if they are not the ones being tested, to detect any malfunctions.

▸ **Define QA use cases.** Identify specific use cases, or common ways in which customers browse the site, that will be checked before starting QA. For example, if a checkout process differs based on whether a customer is logged in or not, the analyst should conduct a QA review of the experience both as a logged-in and as a logged-out customer across browsers.

▸ **Use consistent metric definitions across recipes.** Make sure metrics are defined in the same way for each recipe so that the results are comparable. For example, if the metric for Recipe A counts page clicks only once per customer but the one for Recipe B tallies every click a customer makes on that page, then those results can't be compared.

▶ **It's okay to exclude some web browsers.** Sometimes setting up a test for every browser is not cost-efficient, because coding for some browsers can be time-consuming. If a browser presents technical hurdles and is also used by few customers, companies often exclude those browsers from initial testing, waiting for the test results to see whether it is worthwhile to implement a new design on the less popular browsers.

▶ **Create QA links.** QA links allow stakeholders across the business to view a specific design easily without having to enter the test and be randomly assigned to a recipe. The QA links should be set up so that once the test has been launched, stakeholders can still interact with the links, but their activities won't be captured in the test results. IT specialists should set up QA links to allow easy entry by using URL parameters. For example, the QA links for a hypothetical test number 3.2 might look like this:

Recipe A: `http://www.website.com/category/?QA=3.2_recipeA`

Recipe B: `http://www.website.com/category/?QA=3.2_recipeB`

Recipe C: `http://www.website.com/category/?QA=3.2_recipeC`

▶ **Monitor test results in each recipe immediately after launch.** If any metrics don't increment as expected, this may be an indication that something is wrong with the test setup.

Once the test has passed the QA review, it is ready to be launched. The Optimization Plan should be updated to include screen shots of the final recipes along with their QA links. The plan can then be renamed as the Optimization Launch document and emailed to all stakeholders within the company to let them know the test has started. For example, a customer support representative may need to view a specific design in order to guide a customer through a purchase. Sharing the Optimization Launch document will also help to generate excitement about the test and let people know that it's time to place their bets on which recipe will win.

Optimization Results

As soon as a test ends, the optimization team immediately launches the next campaign in the roadmap. This ensures that site traffic is being put to good use while the team analyzes the data from the first test and writes recommendations as part of the Optimization Results document.

A single test won't necessarily save money or generate incremental revenue, but an iterative test-and-learn program almost always will. Each company has its own way of declaring whether a test has been successful or not, but for many organizations, simply learning something about the business or its customers is the measure of success.

To determine which design should become the new default, companies typically gauge the performance of one or two metrics, such as RPV and conversion rate. However, there are often trade-offs in deciding which designs are best for the overall customer experience and the company. For example, a design may cause the conversion rate to go up but the RPV and AOV to go down, indicating that more visitors are making purchases but less revenue is coming into the business. In such a case, decision makers may choose not to implement the winning design. When results are statistically insignificant, stakeholders often decide which design to use based on opinion or criteria such as perceived simplicity.

Additional techniques for analyzing data to better understand customer behavior include evaluating secondary metrics, segmenting results to reveal whether particular customer groups react differently to the designs, and graphing results to help expose patterns in performance over the test period.

When communicating results, analysts often quantify the possible annual revenue impact of a test. For example, one team might write, "Assuming all conditions remain equal, based on 1,000,000 visitors to the homepage over the course of a typical year, Recipe B could provide between $1,010,000 and $3,030,000 in annualized incremental revenue." A calculation like this helps stakeholders to compare the potential impact of different tests, because it accounts not only for the lift in the primary metric, but also for the number of visitors the new design might receive. For example, a design with a high lift in RPV but in a site area with very few visitors, might provide less additional revenue than a design with a smaller lift in RPV that appears on a prominent page; annualizing the test results is one way to make these differences clear. However, annualized incremental revenue numbers should not be used as assurances of future results (e.g., incorporated into P&L reporting), because they are based on a backward-looking metric, and many conditions can change between the time a test was run and 12 months down the road, as mentioned earlier.

Communication

It's important that communication take place through all stages of the optimization process. Keeping all stakeholders informed increases the likelihood of launching successful tests while building organizational support for the testing program. Communication can be fostered through a variety of means, from regular email newsletters, to adding campaign results documents to a shared library, to presenting roadmaps and test results at quarterly business reviews (QBRs). A few detailed examples include:

▶ **A results library.** Archiving test results in a central repository helps ensure a historical record will always be easily accessible. Results libraries range from shared drives to websites that allow the users to find results quickly, based on criteria such as site area and the primary success metric.

▶ **Email lists.** Regular email updates, usually in the form of a monthly newsletter, are a great way to keep stakeholders informed about the status of the optimization program. Such emails may include information on recent launches and results, upcoming campaigns, a schedule of team meetings, a link to the results library, and instructions on how to submit test ideas. Some businesses also send emails whenever new tests launch, or when test results have been written up, including the Optimization Launch and Optimization Results documents so everyone understands the context of the initiative.

▶ **Team meetings.** Teams working on the optimization program will likely hold regular meetings about how to act on the roadmap. Additionally, larger organizational or company-wide meetings are a good forum in which to highlight program successes, solicit test ideas, and acknowledge contributions from across the company.

Up Next

This chapter concludes the book's discussion of how to implement the Iterative Optimization Methodology in practical terms. It finishes with a description of the Optimization Results document, which tells the complete story of the test, from hypothesis and test setup through to results analysis and recommendations.

The next chapter shows how the Optimization Methodology can be applied in a wide variety of business settings. In particular, it explains how organizations of any size, from small startups to multinational enterprises, can successfully scale the techniques described in this book, gradually integrating the methodology according to a proven model that tailors the iterative optimization approach to the needs of individual businesses.

References

1. *Statistics* (4th Edition), 2007, by David Freedman, Robert Pisani, and Roger Purves (New York: W. W. Norton).

CHAPTER 7

Building an Optimization Organization

Adopting the optimization methodology can seem like a daunting task in today's business environment. Many companies are still experimenting with basics, such as how to organize for the digital space, and companies wanting to expand their testing programs have few existing models to follow in this nascent field. This chapter shows how companies of any size and sophistication level can gradually adopt the practice of optimization, adapting their organizational structure, collaborative approaches, and hiring practices over time.

Optimization Maturity Model

To apply the optimization method, most companies must adapt various aspects of their businesses, ranging from how they use data to how teams are organized and how collaboration works across the business. These changes do not happen overnight, and businesspeople who want to embrace optimization should ease their organizations into the process step by step.

After having worked with hundreds of companies to help them adopt the optimization method, the Adobe team has developed the following five-level system, and corresponding checklist, as guidelines. Based on the size and complexity of a business, it may take a few months, or even several years, to make the transition from one level to the next:

- ▶ **Level 1: Incidental Optimization.** The business begins to test designs in an ad hoc manner, and participation is limited to individuals or small teams.

- ▶ **Level 2: Planned Optimization.** The business builds Optimization Plans in advance, and small teams begin to test consistently in multiple site areas.

- ▶ **Level 3: Coordinated Optimization.** The company no longer conducts full-site redesigns using the traditional design process; instead, stakeholders prioritize high-value site areas in an Optimization Roadmap.

- ▶ **Level 4: Strategic Alignment.** Before this stage, optimization may have been implemented without buy-in at the highest levels within the company; during this stage, an executive sponsor helps ensure team members are able to dedicate time to optimization and that the roadmap aligns with the company's annual business goals.

- ▶ **Level 5: Embedded Optimization Culture.** Sometimes called "Best in Class" optimization organizations, these companies achieve success for themselves and for their customers by using data from qualitative and quantitative research to inform as many decisions as possible; all stakeholders view testing as an essential part of the company's strategy, and optimization is ingrained in the organization's culture.

Maturity Model Checklist

The checklist in **Table 7.1** can serve as a practical guide for companies as they advance from level to level, helping them track progression, prepare for change, and map out which elements of the program to work on next. The checklist contains six categories: culture, strategy, breadth, execution, communication, and organization. Each includes one or more goals that must be accomplished to advance to the next level. There are six categories and five levels—a total of 30 steps.

Table 7.1 Optimization Maturity Checklist

CATEGORY	LEVEL 1: INCIDENTAL	LEVEL 2: PLANNED	LEVEL 3: COORDINATED	LEVEL 4: STRATEGIC	LEVEL 5: EMBEDDED
Culture	Design decisions based mostly on opinion. Testing may or may not be supported by IT.	Winning designs are sometimes implemented, but opinion-based decisions often trump test results. IT supports testing.	Full site redesigns no longer conducted outside of testing; test results always trump internal pressures.	Optimization Roadmap developed to meet quarterly and annual corporate goals. IT requires testing of all major design changes.	Optimization is integral to company strategy. Site changes outside of testing, including behind-the-scenes changes to IT infrastructure, require a rigorous review and approval process.
Strategy	Tests run on ad hoc basis.	Tests planned in advance based on business and customer goals.	Roadmap prioritizes tests based on analytics and stakeholder input. Roles and responsibilities formally defined.	Qualitative research regularly conducted to inform roadmap. Follow-up tests are always run.	Roadmap used to plan iterative changes to all customer-facing designs online.
Breadth	Sporadic tests in one or more areas of site.	Consistent tests in multiple areas of site.	Testing in most high-value site areas.	Optimizing in onsite search, mobile, email, social, display, and SEM channels (if applicable).	No areas of user experience are off-limits to testing.
Execution	Program consists of basic A/B tests.	Program includes A/B and MVT tests. Results segmented to detect behavioral differences.	Targeting and personalization tests are aimed at select large customer groups.	Auto-optimizing campaigns make some design decisions using real-time data (e.g., recommendations or onsite search results).	Full range of test types used as appropriate. Online and offline data combined to build complete view of customer interactions.
Communication	Records may or may not be kept.	Plans made for all tests. Results communicated informally, if at all.	Results documented and shared for each test, and roadmap regularly refreshed	Documentation for each test stage is standardized across the organization.	Results regularly shared in company-wide meetings, emailed, and hosted in searchable central library.
Organization	Isolated tests driven by individuals or small teams outside of their day-to-day responsibilities.	Small team is driving regular testing in at least one site area.	Multiple teams coordinating to test in multiple site areas using company-wide roadmap.	Executive sponsor ensures team members can dedicate time to optimization; core optimization team formed.	Corporate mandate identifies optimization roadmap as the primary mechanism to make changes to customer experiences.

Stakeholders can score their company by checking off each box in the table as the goals within it have been accomplished. Then they would sum up the number of checked boxes and divide by six. For example, if they checked off nine boxes, the sum would be nine, and dividing by six would yield an overall score of 1.5, meaning that the company is between Level 1, Incidental Optimization, and Level 2, Planned Optimization.

Many companies update this, or a similar checklist, as part of quarterly business reviews, so stakeholders can plan how to progress to the next level. As the world of online business continues to advance, this checklist will undoubtedly evolve as well.

Core Optimization Team

As businesses progress from Level 3 to Level 4, many create a centralized team to oversee optimization efforts. This unit, sometimes called the core optimization team, ideally has executive sponsorship from the highest levels and includes representatives from all the teams that contribute to testing.

Most companies can create such a team regardless of their internal structure, including organizations where teams are siloed around different products and services (e.g., product teams have their own marketers, designers, and developers) and companies that use a shared-services model, under which larger departments such as marketing, design, and IT, support the entire company.

The mandate of the core team is to drive significant, measurable improvement in the business while making the culture of the company more customer-centric. This mission includes:

▶ Encouraging different units within the company to start testing

▶ Standardizing the testing process to make it easy to implement

▶ Training team members in the skills required for optimization

▶ Leading the creation of a single, centralized Optimization Roadmap for the business

▶ Sharing test results and optimization best practices across the company

In some companies, the core team starts as just one person who is curious about optimization and explores it in his or her spare time. For small businesses, it rarely takes more than a couple of people to reach Level 5. For larger businesses, as more people gradually join the core team the adoption of optimization accelerates.

As a business reaches Level 2 in the maturity of its optimization program, more people in the organization begin to spend time on testing. By Level 3, although there may not yet be sponsorship from the C-Level, members of the central team will have formal approval from their managers to dedicate time and resources to optimization. In most organizations, this team is virtual until Level 4, meaning that people participate on the committee as representatives of their unit but still report to their departmental managers.

Many companies create a dedicated team to help their business vault from Level 3 to Level 4. This is usually accomplished by appointing business and technical leads to oversee the committee alongside an executive stakeholder. However, dedicated optimization teams should not be allowed to grow too large, because they can then present an obstacle when a business tries to advance from Level 4 to Level 5. It is not the remit of the core team to take on the task of handling daily, company-wide optimization efforts itself; rather, the team should focus on changing the culture of the company so that everyone whose work affects the customer experience makes optimization part of their day-to-day activities. Keeping the dedicated team lean will also help to reduce the risk that it will wind up competing with other departments over design initiatives. By Level 5, the culture change is complete as the executive team mandates that the optimization method drive changes to all customer-facing designs.

Hiring and Nurturing Talent

From data analysts and marketing experts to designers and copywriters, the Iterative Optimization Methodology draws on a wide range of skill sets spanning multiple disciplines within a company. Because it is rare for one person to possess all the necessary skills to run an optimization program, people with different specialties must work closely together to create customer-centric designs. This section discusses how to assign roles and responsibilities in advance of each test, the duties of the core optimization team, and some best practices when hiring optimization team members.

Roles and Responsibilities

Assigning clear responsibilities in advance for each step of the optimization process helps ensure efficient execution. Most organizations are able to identify who is responsible for each step based on the type of test being launched or the area of the business in which it is run.

The following are a few tips when assigning roles and responsibilities:

▶ **Be inclusive.** All critical stakeholders, from marketing and design members to IT representatives, must be included from beginning to end. For example, companies fluent in testing often report that including IT in each stage of the process has been a recipe for success: The engineers help suggest test ideas that, for example, reduce page load time or display device-specific content for mobile versus desktop browsers; they also streamline testing by making small changes to the new designs that significantly decrease the time it takes to set up the test.

▶ **Assign a primary point of contact for each test.** In addition to having primary points of contact for each step in the process, one person should be responsible for the overall success of the effort, steering the test from beginning to end. In smaller organizations, or companies new to testing, this person may be part of the analytics, marketing, product, or design teams; in larger organizations, this may be a member of the core optimization team.

An example of a responsibility assignment matrix for each step in the process appears in **Table 7.2**. In this example, the marketing department is largely steering the test; however, the main drivers of optimization will vary by company and by the area being tested. Some businesses add an "Approver" role to the matrix to make it clear which person or team needs to sign off on a step before completion.

Table 7.2 A Marketing-Driven Roles-and-Responsibilities Matrix

	ANALYTICS	MARKETING	DESIGN	ENGINEERING
Optimization Roadmap	Contributor	Driver	Contributor	Contributor
Qualitative research	Contributor	Driver	Contributor	Contributor
Quantitative research	Contributor	Driver	Contributor	Contributor
Optimization Plan	Contributor	Driver	Contributor	Contributor
Wireframes	Contributor	Driver	Contributor	Contributor
Design comps	Informed	Contributor	Driver	Informed
Optimization Launch	Contributor	Informed	Informed	Driver
Implementation	Contributor	Informed	Informed	Driver
Quality assurance	Contributor	Informed	Informed	Driver
Optimization Results	Contributor	Driver	Contributor	Contributor
Analysis	Contributor	Driver	Contributor	Informed
Communication	Informed	Driver	Informed	Informed

Although it's important to keep roles and responsibilities well defined to "divide and conquer" the testing process, overspecialization can lead team members to lose sight of the big picture.

Several business leaders from companies interviewed for this book spoke about the need to find creative ways to balance collaboration and specialization. Steven Webster, Senior Director of Experience Design for Microsoft, noted that his team believes in "handshakes, not handovers." Amy Parnell, Principal Designer for LinkedIn, agreed, noting that members of different teams, like Design and Development, sit together when working on the same project in order to create a "strong sense of teamwork" and to ensure that "hand-off is not a 'throw it over the wall' behavior."

Core Optimization Team Roles

To advance large businesses beyond Level 3, the core team usually requires at least three people: an executive sponsor, an optimization lead, and a technical lead, as mentioned earlier. Team members with expertise in project or program management are sometimes also added to the core team. Although each business has its own needs, the structure of the team should be kept as simple, lean, and nonhierarchical as possible—just like any organization. The following sections discuss the responsibilities of each of these three roles and the amount of time they allocate to optimization.

Executive sponsor

One of the most important factors in the success of an optimization program is its executive sponsor. Most optimization programs start from the ground up, as individuals use testing to make better-informed decisions; however, moving large organizations away from the traditional design process usually requires an executive sponsor to champion optimization.

The responsibilities of an executive sponsor include:

▶ Promoting optimization at all levels of the organization, including at executive board meetings

▶ Providing an understanding of enterprise-wide goals and initiatives, as well as their priorities, to the core optimization team

▶ Aligning resources across the company to support optimization efforts

▶ Holding the optimization team accountable for meeting business and customer goals

Optimization lead

The optimization lead, or business lead, is responsible for the success of the overall program. By overseeing the core optimization team and working closely with the executive sponsor, this person uses the Iterative Optimization Methodology to ensure that the customer and business goals align. This multifaceted role may include duties ranging from generating actionable insights from qualitative and quantitative customer research, to creating wireframes and overseeing design, to partnering with statisticians to improve auto-optimizing solutions.

The responsibilities of an optimization lead include:

▶ Driving the company's progression along the optimization maturity model

▶ Acting as the primary liaison between the core optimization team and business stakeholders within the company (e.g., analytics, marketing, product and/or design team members)

▶ Ensuring nontechnical team members have the skills they need for optimization

▶ Overseeing knowledge-sharing, the application of methodology, and documentation and communication practices across the company; this responsibility includes prioritizing a global roadmap that is in line with corporate objectives

Technical lead

The technical lead ensures that any changes to the online experience are seamless and their effects are measurable. These aspects include the implementation of analytics, optimization systems, custom development, and quality assurance.

The responsibilities of a technical lead include:

▶ Acting as the primary liaison between the core optimization team and technical stakeholders (e.g., IT, Engineering, Development, and/or QA team members)

▶ Ensuring technical team members have the skills required for optimization efforts

▶ Ensuring that team members throughout the business have access to web analytics and optimization data as needed, including real-time test results

▶ Overseeing measurement standards, including defining metrics across software systems and techniques for tracking new designs

▶ Supervising quality assurance, including troubleshooting problems in test implementation or data collection as they arise

▶ Partnering with technical stakeholders to make testing a required step before implementing new designs

Time allocation

As a company's program matures, the people in each of the three roles just described will need to dedicate more time to optimization duties. Using a large retail company as an example, **Table 7.3** shows what proportion of their full-time job the three leaders will likely devote to optimization at each stage of the process. For example, prior to Level 4 the optimization and technical leads can still perform duties unrelated to optimization, but by Level 4 they will most likely need to devote all of their time to the test-and-learn program.

Table 7.3 Time Commitments for Sponsor and Leads

	LEVEL 1	LEVEL 2	LEVEL 3	LEVEL 4	LEVEL 5
Executive sponsor	0%	0%	10%	15%	20%
Optimization lead	10%	15%	50%	100%	100%
Technical lead	10%	15%	50%	100%	100%

Hiring for Optimization

This section discusses how to hire and nurture talent for optimization teams, for both junior- and senior-level roles. It includes the typical educational backgrounds for most qualified candidates, a sample senior-level job description, and interviewing tips.

The importance of the liberal arts

Although optimization spans a range of skill sets, many of these can be learned on the job; at the junior level, the field of online business mainly needs team members who know how to learn and experiment with new ideas rather than people with formal training in the area. A manager looking to fill junior- or entry-level positions should consider candidates from a range of backgrounds, especially those with liberal arts degrees.

Although many people with formal training in design or business are innovative, and some are inarguably the best in their fields, employers should be wary of hiring candidates who treat their own design, marketing, and business instincts as dogma as opposed to hypotheses.

On the other hand, people with backgrounds in the humanities and sciences tend to do well at business optimization. Many are comfortable with open-ended problem solving and focus on asking the right questions rather than assuming they need to have all the answers. Degrees in Art History, English, Architecture, Psychology, and Computer Science tend to serve candidates very well.

For example, art historians are trained to compare and contrast visual experiences, and then articulate the differences verbally or in writing—skills that translate well to optimization. For their part, English majors understand the power of the written word and of storytelling; interactive designs must tell customers a sequential story (e.g., what the business can offer to help the customer and where to click next) using visuals and language, and small differences in word choice can make a significant difference. Architects study how form follows function; like buildings, websites need to be designed to solve a particular customer need while being aesthetically pleasing. Psychologists analyze perception, behavior, and motivation, all of which play an important part in online business. Team members with training in other sciences, such as Computer Science, Physics, Chemistry, or Biology are also valuable because they know how to work with data and technology, and understand how to run controlled experiments.

Senior optimization hires

A liberal arts background is desirable even for senior-level positions, although companies usually seek candidates who also have a business background and at least some experience in optimization. It used to be difficult to find candidates with the hands-on experience required to build optimization programs. Fortunately, due to rapid growth in the field many people's résumés now list "conversion optimization" and "A/B testing" as skills, or "Optimization Manager" as a job title. To help companies seeking to hire optimization managers, the sidebar on the next page shows a sample job description for an optimization lead.

When it comes to hiring talent for an optimization team, Kenyon Rogers, Director of Digital Experiments at Marriott International, advises, "Optimization roles require a jack-of-all-trades. A good optimization lead understands business, user experience, analytics, development, design, and project management, and has experience with customer research. They need to see the bigger picture of ingesting data and acting on insights, which is part of the art and science of optimization."

Interview tips

Interviewing candidates is hard work, and it's important to get it right, because companies succeed or fail based on the abilities of their employees. Well-run interviews have much in common with qualitative research: The interviewer attempts to create as natural a work environment as possible and closely observes the candidate's responses and body language while assessing answers for authenticity and motivation.

Heuristic techniques can often provide a more accurate impression of the candidate's skill set than the usual verbal exchange of questions and answers. For example, heuristic approaches can be used to assess the following key attributes:

▶ **Online business acumen.** The interviewer asks candidates to pull up a few websites from different industries, to identify the business and customer goals, to guess what the analytics might reveal, and to identify which success metrics the business might measure and what those metrics might look like and why. For example, the candidates may be asked to guess where customers click on the page, and then explain why. Based on this hypothetical data, they are then asked how they would redesign the experience to improve the customer experience while helping the business make more money. The goal of this exercise isn't to have candidates magically guess analytics data, but to appraise their ability to apply logic based on their understanding of a user experience.

Optimization Lead

JOB DESCRIPTION

The Optimization Lead is responsible for improving the customer experience and top-line revenue through conversion rate optimization, and the redesign of high-visibility sites, pages, and experiences. The Optimization Lead is a senior role requiring an advanced marketing, technical, and managerial skill set.

Optimization specialists gain a deep understanding of the customer and business goals to create an Optimization Roadmap designed to significantly increase conversion rates. They lead a team of analysts, marketers, designers, and developers to help execute the Optimization Roadmap. Optimization leads must be comfortable building, defending, and driving a business case in front of C-level executives on the marketing, technical, and design sides of a business.

METHODOLOGIES

▸ A/B testing, multivariate testing, segment-based targeting, behavioral targeting, display ad targeting, and landing page optimization.

RESPONSIBILITIES

▸ Gain an in-depth knowledge of the site architecture, online business model, and customer goals.

▸ Build Optimization Plans using A/B testing, multivariate testing, rules-based targeting, and auto-optimizing software.

▸ Analyze large and detailed data sets in order to make recommendations on follow-up tests.

▸ Build detailed wireframes and manage their creative production in order to accomplish testing goals.

▸ Mentor analysts, marketers, and designers to provide constructive criticism around data analysis, wireframing, design comps, test setup, results analysis, documentation, and communication skills.

▸ Partner with analyst, development, and quality assurance teams to troubleshoot technical issues, ensure proper content display, and properly manipulate JavaScript, HTML, and CSS.

▸ Deduce and present results, lessons learned, and recommendations from tests.

▸ Manage multiple projects, with multiple remote teams, at one time.

▸ Work with leadership teams to achieve company goals through optimization program growth.

QUALIFICATIONS

▸ Bachelor's degree required.

▸ Experience presenting in front of large groups. Must be very comfortable in a public role.

▸ 5+ years' experience in online marketing, user experience, and/or user interface design.

▸ 5+ years using online analytics and/or A/B testing systems.

▸ 2+ years creating wireframes and managing design comp creation.

▸ 2+ years crafting online marketing strategies across multiple industry verticals (retailers, financial services, media, travel, lead generation, etc.).

▸ Experience running A/B, multivariate, and behavioral targeting tests.

▸ Experience with observational customer research.

▸ Must have a passion for the web and creating engaging user experiences.

▸ Intermediate JavaScript, CSS, and HTML.

▸ Must be self-motivated, responsive, and dedicated to customer success.

▸ Exceptional organizational, presentation, and communication skills (verbal and written).

▸ Demonstrated ability to learn quickly, be a team player, and manage change effectively.

SPECIAL CONSIDERATION GIVEN FOR

▸ Management experience.

▸ Undergraduate degree in Art History, English, Architecture, or Science (Computer Science, Psychology, etc.).

▶ **Wireframing.** The ideal candidate for an optimization role isn't intimidated when asked to sketch out ideas; instead, strong candidates get excited about wireframing several ideas, and then not only defending them, but also considering alternate hypotheses when asked and creating different versions on the spot. Interviewers can simply offer candidates a pencil and paper or a whiteboard and marker to sketch out their wireframes. Many professional marketers and designers are great at selling their clients on ideas verbally but decline to even pick up a pencil or marker, because they're used to relying on someone else to turn their ideas into sketches or wireframes. Once the candidate has sketched a few different ideas, the interviewer can suggest a new set of hypothetical data and repeat the exercise. This scenario is sometimes repeated for several types of pages, or for online businesses in a range of industries. The goal is not to have candidates build picture-perfect wireframes, but to assess their curiosity, versatility, and ability to apply creative thinking to visual problem solving.

Up Next

This chapter concludes the book's practical guide to the Iterative Optimization Methodology with a model showing how businesses can progress step by step in integrating optimization. The chapter also explains how to organize for optimization and outlines hiring practices that will help employers find the creative and versatile team members they need to make the most of the optimization approach.

Moving on to Part 3, "Visual Business Cases," the book explores examples of companies that practice customer-centric design. In the following pages, leaders in the fields of design, marketing, and analytics from a wide range of companies share their unique approaches to building test-and-learn cultures while talking about some of their favorite design tests.

PART 3

Visual Business Cases

In this part, more than 20 business leaders from a range of industries discuss their favorite design campaigns, which are illustrated visually where possible. These candid interviews, citing more than 60 test cases, offer rare insights into practical ways in which companies have used the optimization method to address a variety of business problems and provide inspiration for those who are interested in design testing.

Some of the test results are intuitive, and others are difficult to explain, illustrating the point that only by putting new designs to the test can companies know for sure whether they are effective. Several companies not only provided the details of their test campaigns, but also generously shared the projected financial impact of particular design ideas—both for those that led to a drop in revenue during testing, and for successful versions that were expected to bring in hundreds of millions of dollars.

Customer-centric design has permeated all major online industries. The examples that follow extend from fashion, to banking, to social networking, and more; the businesses range in size from corporations with hundreds of thousands of employees to small start-ups. Similarly, the test cases cited span all areas of online business, from homepages and product pages to mobile checkout flows. Most of the examples highlight general interactive design or business ideas that can be applied beyond the industry in which they are featured.

The diverse backgrounds of the interviewees reflect the interdisciplinary nature of optimization. Their fields of expertise include design, marketing, and engineering, among others, and their roles range from individual contributors, to managers, to senior executives.

One by one, design tests like those described in this book are helping to shape the future of how people spend their time online, including what it means to "go shopping," "check the news," "play a game," or "plan a date." Hopefully, the examples that follow will help the reader to think big about the possibilities for their company and embrace optimization as a way to emerge as an innovative and powerful presence in an ever-changing marketplace.

Mikel Chertudi, Senior Director, Media & Digital Marketing

Mikel Chertudi is responsible for increasing brand awareness and driving demand across Adobe's Marketing Cloud, Creative Cloud, and document offerings.

Jeff Fuhriman, Senior Optimization Program Manager

Jeff Fuhriman is Senior Manager of Conversion Optimization at Adobe and is responsible for personalization, testing, and targeting for search engine marketing (SEM) and digital marketing properties on Adobe.com.

Adobe

Adobe is the global leader in digital marketing and digital media solutions. Adobe helps its customers make, manage, measure, and monetize their content across every channel and screen.

What are your business's goals?

Adobe.com generates awareness of our leadership in the Creative, Marketing, and document spaces. We also help to source and influence recurring revenue across our products in these categories.

What are your customers' goals?

Creative and Marketing Cloud customers create groundbreaking digital content, deploy it across media and devices, measure and optimize it over time, and achieve greater business success. Our Acrobat, Acrobat.com, and Adobe EchoSign customers are trying to create, protect, and distribute documents through digital workflows.

Visual Example

Illustrator Product Page A/B Test: Simplify Layout

This test was to determine whether a simplified product page template would increase revenue per visitor (RPV). We've seen the layout we tested across the web, as it has grown in popularity among designers, over the last year.

The default version of the page uses a standard multicolumn layout (**Figure 1**). There are two major columns, with product content on the left and product images with multiple call-to-action buttons on the right. A lot of content is squeezed above the fold within the main column, including elements labeled "See the top new features," "Touch Type tool," and "Part of Creative Cloud." The alternate version of the page, in **Figure 2**, uses a single-column layout, includes only one call-to-action button, and makes more use of whitespace to ease the customer into learning about the product by focusing their attention on only one element at a time. The alternate design increased RPV by 56.30 percent and the conversion rate by 13.75 percent. We quickly made it the new default, and then tested a similar design across all our product pages.

RECIPE A (DEFAULT)

Figure 1 The default product page.

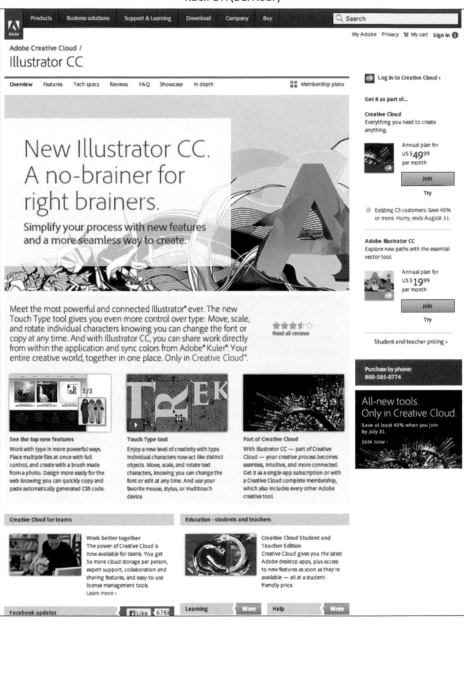

RECIPE B: +56% RPV

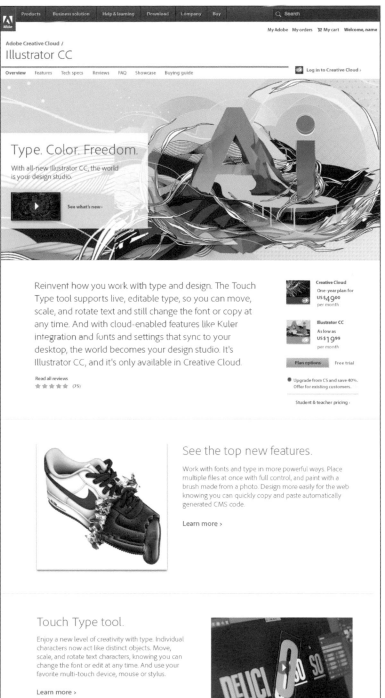

Figure 2 The alternate product page.

Andrew Switzer, Director of Online Sales and Marketing

As the Director of Online Sales and Marketing , Andrew leads a team responsible for converting site traffic through a consistent series of tests, site improvements, and visitor personalization while also supporting the marketing and product development teams to deliver compelling campaigns and product innovations.

Ally Bank

Ally Bank, founded in 2008, is a subsidiary of The General Motors Acceptance Corporation. Ally Bank has been ranked the "Best Online Bank" by *MONEY Magazine* in 2011, 2012, and 2013.

What are your business's goals?

To drive account creation and deposits through website conversions, and to encourage customer engagement and utilization of our online account services.

What are your customers' goals?

To achieve a high yield on their savings. This includes longer-term savings, like retirement liquidity, as well as shorter-term savings goals, such as for a vacation, college, and so on.

How is your business organized for optimization?

We have moved from being a start-up focused on branding to more of a mature marketing organization. Throughout the evolution, our Chief Marketing Officer (CMO) supported a culture of test and learn. As long as the tests align with business objectives and are impactful, we have a lot of program flexibility.

For execution, we have a dedicated designer, developer, and channel manager that partner across the different lines of business. Each line of business has objectives that may include account growth, retention, and engagement.

Design experiments aren't always well received by designers. What is your point of view?

In the past, I have found that great designers have a good eye for what the user expects. However, there is always opportunity for error in judgment or observation bias. We have evolved as an organization to appreciate both perspectives and tend to balance measurement with experience or talent-based decisions. We let creative expertise act as a filter to minimize choices, and then use a blend of data and qualitative research to create the testing scenarios. This approach has allowed our creative teams to feel empowered but ultimately leaves decisions to be based in data. When debating opinions objectively, it's hard for a couple of people to argue against the results of millions of visitors.

Visual Examples

Homepage A/B Test: Focus on Product Categories vs. Specific Product Rates

This was one of a series of tests we ran on our homepage. We had seen success with a similar test when we ran it on the Canadian homepage, so we decided to try it on the U.S. homepage. The default page, shown in **Figure 1**, regularly featured specific products, along with the annual percentage yield (APY) for those products, in three tiles on the bottom half of the homepage.

Ally offers great products across the categories of checking, savings, and CDs. The hypothesis behind this test was that prominently featuring our top product categories on the homepage, with details around why they're so great, would help users better understand the value we provide. For example, since Ally is a relatively new online bank, customers may wonder whether they can withdraw money from ATMs without a fee or whether our checking accounts pay interest. As an online bank, we're able to refund ATM fees and provide relatively high interest rates, because we can pass our savings from not operating physical branches along to our customers. Both of those messages, and more, appear on the homepage in the new design, displayed in **Figure 2**.

Another change between the designs is that the first design features rates in the tiles, and the second design does not. The reason is that the new design focuses on product categories rather than specific products within those categories, and customers can already get detailed rate comparisons on the product details pages, like the one displayed in **Figure 3**. The other reason we removed rates was because even though Ally regularly pays the highest, or among

RECIPE B: +37% new account creation rate, +22% money deposited

Figure 2 The alternate homepage.

Figure 3 The compare rates page.

RECIPE A (DEFAULT)

Figure 1 The default homepage.

the highest interest rates from banks, rates across the overall industry are low due to the economy, so featuring them in comparison to other banks rather than on their own may make them more compelling in the current economic environment.

The performance of the new design, featured in Figure 2, was fantastic. Measured results showed it led to record or near-record increases in all of our key metrics. Results included a 7 percent lift in the click-through rate to the homepage, a 140 percent lift in the click-through rate to the homepage tiles, a 78 percent lift in application starts, a 37 percent lift in new accounts created, and a 22 percent lift in money deposited into accounts. This winning design became our new default homepage, and we've been iterating on it ever since.

Log-off Portal A/B Test: Promoting Social Links

This test was geared around improving our social marketing efforts. Following Ally Bank in the social spaces gives customers and prospects a direct and open outlet for two-way communication. It's a source for customers to learn about our brand, products, smarter financial decisions, and personalized topics. Our social marketing efforts are key to improving our natural search performance through content creation and popularity building. They create a sizable and engaged population of social followers that can help drive user-generated content and build loyalty with existing customers.

The hypothesis behind this test was that we could increase clicks to social experiences by targeting our customers who actively engage in online banking. This test was run on the log-off portal, which is a page customers see once they log out of online banking. The default version of the page is shown in **Figure 4** and includes prominent messaging to

Figure 4 The default log-off portal.

RECIPE A (DEFAULT

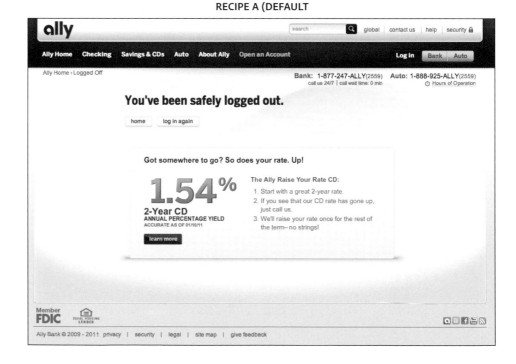

encourage existing customers to sign up for a complimentary account. It included small icons linking to social sites only at the very bottom-right side of the page. The alternate design, in **Figure 5**, removed the messaging about signing up for another account and replaced it with several links to our social presence across Facebook, Twitter, YouTube, and our blog.

The results, pictured in Figure 5, showed a 382 percent lift in clicks to social sites on Recipe B versus Recipe A. We also measured activity across our social sites during the test period, which showed unique views of our Facebook page rose 45%, daily Facebook comments rose 15%, Facebook Newsfeed impressions rose 68%, Twitter mentions rose 28%, and visits

to our blog rose 7%. It's important to note that for this data we didn't track whether visitors arrived from Recipe A or B, so the increased numbers likely include visitors from both recipes.

However, all this increased social activity came at a cost, which was a 6% loss in the conversion rate for new account creations. This is likely because the link to open a new account was removed from the alternate design and replaced with social links. This loss was too large to justify using the alternate design in the future. Instead, we proposed a series of follow-up tests to try balancing both messaging around opening a new account with links to the social sites.

RECIPE B: +382% CTR to social sites, -6% new account creation rate

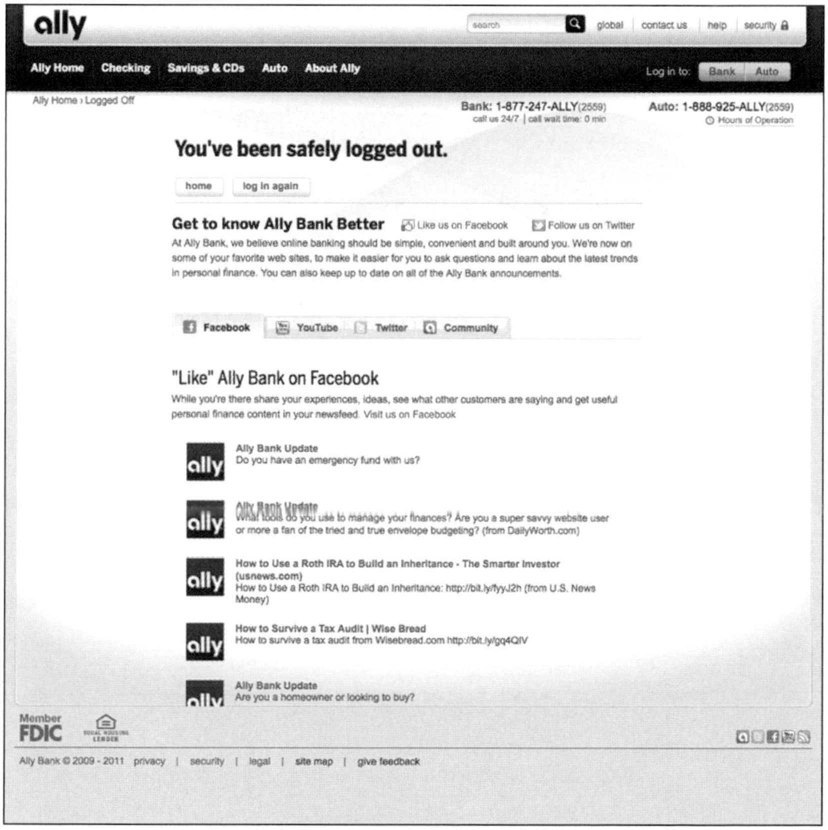

Figure 5 The alternate log-off portal.

Thomas Lau, Senior Manager, Online Prospect Acquisition

Tom manages the American Express® customer experience for the onsite and offsite prospect acquisition channels. As part of his role, Tom oversees the central optimization program, including A/B and multivariate testing, web analytics, acquisition marketing, project management, process management, and digital capability development.

American Express®

American Express® is a global financial services company. For the seventh year in a row, consumers have rated American Express® highest in customer satisfaction among U.S. credit card companies, according to the annual nationwide study by J.D. Power. American Express® remains the only credit card to receive the study's top ranking since it was first conducted in 2007.

What are your business's goals?

There are several business units within American Express®. My department is tasked with acquiring creditworthy customers who spend money using our products. Like many other companies, we generate revenue through product usage and fees.

What are your customers' goals?

We want our customers to use the products in a way that works for them. Customers choose products based on value, ease of use, and because American Express® has been a trusted brand for over 160 years. Although many of our products have similar core benefits, each also has its own unique features. For example, the Platinum Card® from American Express® provides complimentary access to participating airport clubs, which can enhance the travel experience.

Can you tell us a bit about your organization's optimization program?

We optimize the digital experience to make it easier for our prospects to explore and discover the right products based on their needs. The optimization program has evolved over the past couple of years. It's gotten more complex as we've gone from testing copy to testing product mixes, offers, site features, and conversion funnels.

As the centralized optimization team supporting the company, we try to make it as simple as possible for business partners to submit test ideas, especially if they don't have a background in A/B testing. We've standardized the testing and data collection processes, including the definition of key performance indicators. This helps us to clearly document what we're testing and why.

Have you seen testing impact the overall business strategy?

All the time. That is why businesses need test-and-learn programs. I look at a website as an ecosystem. Each page does not exist solely on its own: Each affects the customer as they go through a conversion path, and testing helps us learn more about the optimal path to provide for our customers. Websites used to have one flavor; now there are many flavors as companies personalize and target experiences to customers.

Visual Examples

If users clear their cookies and reload a page several times, they can tell we are running tests, and although I can't share specific results, the figures note which design became the new default experience.

Offers: Points

Many companies test different levels of incentives to maximize conversion. The tricky part here is striking the right balance. You want to present an offer so that customers convert, but if you can get similar results with a lower offer, then you need to rethink your strategy. Like any business decision, it's about optimizing to find the sweet spot where the customers are happy and the business is happy as well. For example, **Figure 1** shows screen shots of a card detail page for the American Express® Green Card. Version B is the same as version A except it includes 10,000 bonus points as an incentive to apply.

Content: Products and Imagery

When there are multiple products on a page, there is competition for the customer's attention, and products may cannibalize each other. The display of multiple products on one page should help customers to better understand the benefits of one product over another and lead them to apply for the product that best fits their lifestyle. That's a win-win: Customers will get a product that suits them, and they'll hopefully make good use of it, which will provide more value to the company.

It's also important to segment test results. For example, if a high-value customer enters the page and products don't feature specific services that have been built for their segment, the customer may select a product that is not right for them.

As an example, **Figure 2** shows changes for the Blue Cash landing page. The Blue Cash Everyday® Card is an extremely popular card because it provides cash back with no annual fee. Alternatively, the Blue Cash Preferred Card® provides even more cash back, but it has an annual fee. The Blue Cash Preferred Card® was added to the page to provide a side-by-side comparison.

VERSION A: NEW DEFAULT

VERSION B

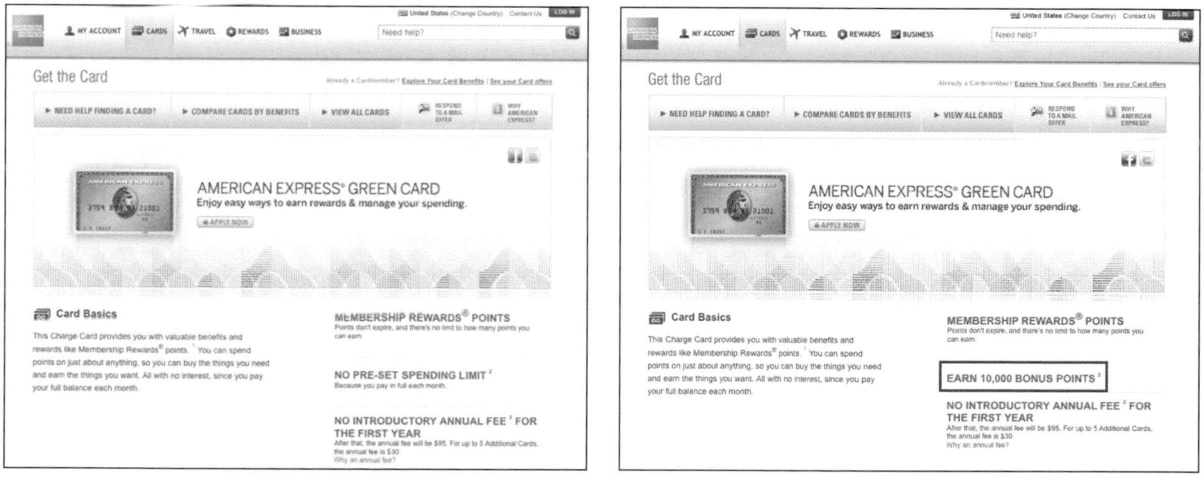

Figure 1 Versions of designs with and without a bonus point offer.

Another example is the Delta SkyMiles® Credit Card page that was redesigned in **Figure 3**. Version A has different tabs for personal and business cards, whereas version B includes additional imagery and features only personal cards. In the end, version A became the new default. This could have been for any number of reasons, including version B moving the cards too far down the page, or removing the option to view business cards.

VERSION A

VERSION B: NEW DEFAULT

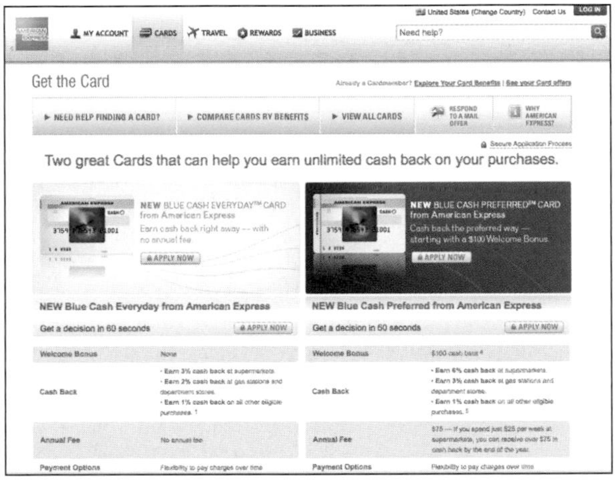

Figure 2 Alternate designs for the Blue Cash Preferred Card® landing page.

VERSION A: NEW DEFAULT

VERSION B

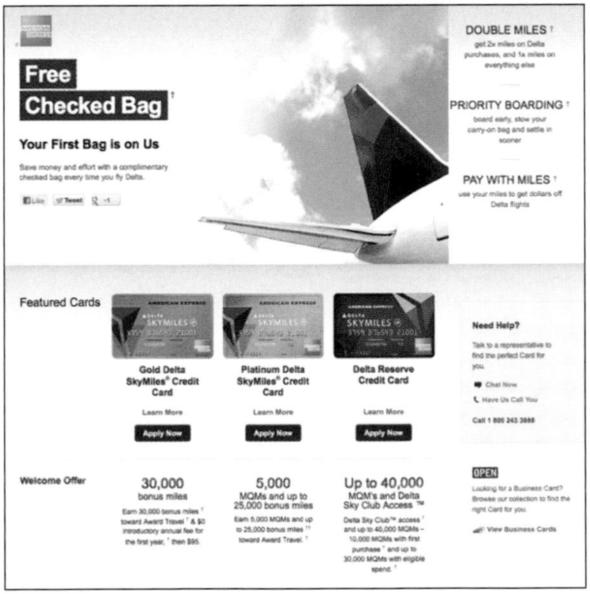

Figure 3 Two versions of the same Delta SkyMiles® Credit Card page.

Chris Kahle, Web Analytics Manager

Chris oversees the analytics, testing, and optimization programs for all of the Caesars Entertainment brands online. Chris's responsibilities include setting the strategic direction as well as the day-to-day management of those programs.

Caesars Entertainment

Caesars Entertainment Corporation is the world's most geographically diversified casino-entertainment company. Since its beginning in Reno, Nevada, more than 75 years ago, Caesars has grown through development of new resorts, expansions, and acquisitions, and now operates casinos on four continents.

Would you please tell us a bit about your role?

The testing and optimization program aims to raise our conversion rate and has launched well over 100 tests based on the data provided by the analytics program. We've tested everything from simple button tests, to different landing pages, to entirely new booking flows.

What are your business's goals?

The business goals are to improve our key performance indicators (KPIs), which are revenue and conversion rates related to booking room nights and total rewards sign-ups. We try to build loyalty with our customers through great products and great customer service, and by being leaders in operations and technology. We want our customers to stay with us on their second and third trips, and to build up points with us through our Total Rewards program so we can give them incentives to come stay with us.

What are your customers' goals?

We divide our customers into two different segments: We have Frequent Independent Travelers (FIT) and Total Rewards customers.

FITs aren't necessarily loyal and are most likely customers who are coming to the website to become familiar with our franchise and the amenities we offer. But most important, they come to compare prices for hotel rooms with our competitors or across comparison and booking engines like Expedia.

Total Rewards customers are our loyal customers. They belong to our Total Rewards loyalty program, which you can sign up for online or at any of our properties. The more you stay and play, the more points you earn, and the more offers you will receive. The power of our loyalty program is that it extends across all our properties, from Caesars Palace in Las Vegas to Caesars Atlantic City. Total Rewards customers come to the site to log in and view their offers, which are personalized based on their level of play to incentivize them to come stay with us. Some Total Rewards customers visit once a year, and some visit seven times a year. A personalized offer could range from a $15 dinner credit to five nights at Caesars Palace, totally complimentary.

So we're going after two very different types of customers: rates and amenities versus offers.

Can you tell us a bit about your organization's optimization program?

We've had an active optimization program for four years. It started out small. The impetus for the program was that the business, information technology, and design teams would regularly "get into it" and disagree about what our site should look like. They would argue about everything: colors, layouts, copy, and so on.

Testing and optimization changed our culture. We started to test which image, copy, or layout worked better. We were able to say, "Your opinion does matter, but now we're going to test it out. Which ever opinion wins, will win, and we'll start developing our best practices off of that." We have to work together as a team to accomplish the tests on our Optimization Roadmap and to continuously improve our optimization program.

How do you keep track of results?

At the conclusion of a test, we develop a presentation to capture the test objective and results because we don't want to get six months down the line and make the same mistakes. We'll also communicate what we learned from the different customer segments. For example, East Coast customers may have acted differently than West Coast customers, new customers may have behaved differently versus returning customers, and so on. I place the presentation on a shared network drive so that everyone can access it.

People throughout the organization view our test results, and not everyone is familiar with analytics and optimization. We found that people were interpreting the numbers differently, in ways that were wrong, so I record myself talking through the presentation, slide by slide, and post that file to our shared network drive.

Visual Examples

Semi-annual Sale Landing Page A/B Test: More Prominent Booking Module (Summer Sale)

We run semi-annual sales across all of our properties in all markets. The sale aims to incentivize customers to book by offering them a percentage off their stay, based on the property. During these sales, we drive a lot of traffic to the sale landing page from our paid search and email channels. The default landing page appears in **Figure 1**, and due to previous testing on our Winter Sale page, it features an extremely prominent booking module. We built two alternate versions of this page. Recipe B, pictured in **Figure 2**, included imagery and strong calls-to-action to our top properties, and Recipe C, pictured in **Figure 3**, included text links to more top properties. Each image contained the same booking module and headline but slightly different lifestyle imagery. Recipe B provided a 5 percent lift in the booking conversion rate, and Recipe C provided a massive 30 percent lift in the booking conversion rate, indicating that customers responded to the list of text links. Because this campaign was using a new default recipe, we looked at the previous years' summer sale results and observed an overall 45 percent lift in the conversion rate from one year to the next. Of course, that lift wasn't measured in a controlled fashion; we were just comparing performance across two years. A lot of effort went into that year-over-year lift, including optimizing across email, display advertising, SEM, our landing pages, and the booking funnel.

RECIPE A (DEFAULT)

Figure 1 The default version of the Summer Sale landing page.

RECIPE B: +5% booking conversion rate

Figure 2 The tested Recipe B of the Summer Sale landing page.

Figure 3 The tested Recipe C of the Summer Sale landing page.

RECIPE C: +30% booking conversion rate

My Offers A/B Test: Full Redesign

Our Total Rewards customers are our most loyal customers, accounting for 65 percent of our bookings. These customers earn special offers based on their level of play, and go to the "My Offers" section of the site to learn about and act on their offers. The old user interface (UI), in **Figure 4**, was not very clean. In addition to having multiple calls-to-action, it was difficult to use and also sort of ugly. The new interface, in **Figure 5**, used an interface we borrowed from Microsoft Outlook's three-pane layout. The middle pane lists all the offers, grouped by property, and allows users to highlight offers as favorites by clicking on the star icon. When the customer clicks on an offer, its details show up on the right, and they include a room picture, a detailed description of the offer, and a large call-to-action to check offer availability.

Because this redesign was on such an important part of our business, we started the test with an 85/12/3 split, where 85 percent of users were sent to the default recipe, 12 percent were sent to the new design, and 3 percent were sent to the new design with a survey asking them for feedback. In some cases, we would ask people who submitted feedback to hop on a screen-share with a developer who could see what they were seeing and quickly fix any bugs. Even with some early bugs, the results from this new design were amazing: It led to a 74 percent lift in the booking conversion rate. It didn't take us long to push this new design live to all customers.

RECIPE A (DEFAULT)

Figure 4 The default version of the My Offers tool.

RECIPE B: +74% booking conversion rate

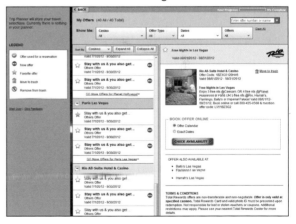

Figure 5 The alternate version of the My Offers tool.

John Williamson, Senior Vice President and General Manager of Comcast.com

John is responsible for the company's digital sales and service activities. John joined Comcast from Verizon where he was Vice President, e-Commerce & Digital CRM, and responsible for managing online sales and customer support for the company, including driving new customer acquisition, increased utilization of the company's digital self-service tools, and cross-selling of services through the company's digital platforms. Prior to Verizon, he was with J.P. Morgan following its acquisition of Bear, Stearns & Co.

Comcast

Comcast is one of the leading providers of entertainment, information and communications products and services in the United States. Comcast is the largest high-speed Internet provider in the United States and as of 2012 had over 50.4 million video, high-speed Internet, and digital voice customers.

What are your business's goals?

They're pretty simple. The primary goal is to drive revenue growth for the company. Like a lot of Fortune 50 companies, we have a significant push to move more to digital. We look to increase overall customer adoption of our digital experiences. I'm responsible for driving that effort.

What are your customers' goals?

Customers want to really enhance their lives through TV and the Internet, for both the utility and entertainment value. They want to be able to consume content easily without having to think about it and to be able to leverage the technology in their day-to-day lives. We're the largest Internet Service Provider (ISP) in the country. If you think of what we do as a company, it's not just delivering cable to our customers.

We spend a lot of time in the lab with real customers getting their feedback on where we have opportunities. We're testing in a big way because I know we're never going to hit the target out of the gate. If we reach a point where we've plateaued, we'll see how we can rethink the experience with our customers.

Can you tell us about your online strategy?

If you think about the future of where we really want to be, it's the entertainment operating system of not just our customers' households, but of their lives. We're approaching this goal in three ways:

1. The vision for the business is to make digital the preferred, as well as the primary, interaction point for all our current and prospective customers.

2. We achieve that by spending a great deal of time delivering dynamic customer-centric experiences. A lot of what we do is across the television, desktop, and mobile experiences.

3. We aim to deliver experiences that are human. The person you've historically most interacted with at the cable company has probably been the technician, at home when you're getting set up or if you had an issue. We're looking to replicate in a digital way the experience of a human touch.

Can you tell us a bit about your organization's optimization program?

I believe in embedding data, analytics, and optimization across every role in the organizations. I spent most of my career in financial services and a component of that on Wall Street. I actually have a patent on how to model portfolios. We run the business like a hedge fund.

Could you please share some examples of how you apply your experience on Wall Street to managing Comcast.com?

Every morning I run a call similar to one any Wall Street bank would: The Tale of the Tape. We look through everything that happened. And we try to make real-time decisions in the meeting to try to optimize on anything that's not performing the way we want it to. We embed data into the design efforts, and then we measure the results and make changes based on the data. We hold a weekly Investment Committee meeting similar to any asset management company. We go through investments we're currently making, or looking to make, and try to prioritize those.

One of the big gaps for a lot of online businesses today, especially in Fortune 50 companies, is that they don't embrace data in the right way. They aren't structured to—they have a user experience (UX) team that sits here, an analytics team that sits there, and in many cases aren't part of the same organization; data from analytics isn't leveraged by UX for customer-centric design. I got to build something from scratch at Comcast.

The ultimate results-driven cultures have been Wall Street, asset management, and hedge funds. If you could foster that culture in a very large company, with a group that is empowered like ours is to make decisions, then you can drive significant results relative to an organization that isn't empowered and results-driven. We think it's a competitive advantage. We're going to move faster and more decisively, and always have our eye on the end game.

Is your optimization program ROI positive?

The return on our investment has been huge, and quite frankly, like many businesses, we're in early innings and there are much bigger returns to come. We're a significant portion of the overall business for a Fortune 50 company. Any misstep could be meaningful in terms of impact to company results. We want to test into things. Even today, when we make changes to promotions on the site, we're trying to test into those, and not all of them work, which is fine.

Can you tell us more about the self-service aspects of the program?

Self-service is a very important component of what we do. The majority of customers don't want to have to call us to the extent they have a question about their service or are looking to resolve some issue they have with their service. They would rather very quickly answer or resolve that question themselves.

We offer a digital product, and there's no better place to get service, or answer questions, or buy that product than online. We are focused on giving our customers choice and control. Some customers will still want to call, but we want to give them the choice of using an online experience to resolve issues. There's been a big impact on customer satisfaction from these new experiences.

What advice would you give to someone in your position at another company about starting and scaling an optimization program?

In many cases it starts with the culture and the folks that you have within the organization. I'll be honest, it's not a culture that's for everyone, and that's okay. We run a very results-driven entrepreneurial business. It's very fluid. We all wear a lot of hats. Data and optimization is part of everyone's role.

A lot of UX folks don't have as much comfort around it. The future of design and UX will have a very heavy data component. If you want to be the rock star in the future, from a design perspective you'll need the ability to bridge the creative aspects and the ability to understand customer wants and needs—which is really critical—but then the ability to take as an input the actual test results. The speed of change we were making 10 to 15 years ago is nowhere near today's levels.

Visual Examples

Mobile Product Page A/B Test: Calls-to-Action (CTA)

The mobile version of the site allows customers to purchase TV, Internet, and digital voice products and services. Customers can complete their purchase online or over the phone. When customers complete their purchase online, it's generally a faster and better experience for them. Placing an order online versus over the phone also provides a cost savings to the business; however, we are committed to giving our customers a choice in how they complete their purchase. The goal of this test was to determine whether we could increase clicks to make a purchase online. The default version of the site, along with three variations, are shown in **Figure 1**:

▶ **Default.** Equally prominent CTAs reading "Add to Cart" and "Call to Order." The first CTA would allow customers to complete their purchase on their mobile device.

Figure 1 Different mobile product page designs and their results.

- **Recipe B.** The "Call to Order" button has been turned into a text link.

- **Recipe C.** The "Add to Cart" button's copy has been changed to read "Checkout Online," and the "Call to Order" button's copy has been changed to read "Checkout by Phone." We thought this might make it clearer that customers could complete their purchase using either option.

- **Recipe D.** The "Add to Cart" button's copy has been changed to read "Buy Online Now," and the "Call to Order" button's copy has been changed to read "Call to Buy." We thought this more direct language might help customers understand that they could quickly complete their purchase with either option.

The results displayed in Figure 1 show the measured lift of clicks to make a purchase online. Although all recipes provided lift, Recipe C was clearly the winner with a 35.43 percent lift in clicks to check out online. As an added bonus, Recipe C also increased the overall number of orders placed over the web or by phone. Our recommendation was to push Recipe C to all visitors and to run tests to improve the downstream mobile purchase process.

Global Navigation A/B Test: Minimize in Buyflow

Purchasing TV can be an intricate process, and we've been iteratively working on making it simpler by redesigning the configuration funnel. However, our analytics showed that many customers were abandoning the TV buyflow by clicking on the top navigation to browse for products. Our hypothesis was that the top navigation had too many competing calls-to-action on it, which made customers unsure whether they should select bundles through the navigation or through the buyflow. Once customers reached the buyflow, they were in the right place to select any products or bundles they desired. The default and alternate versions of the site were:

- **Default (Figure 2).** The two-tier global navigation, including the search box, is exposed.

- **Recipe B (Figure 3).** The navigation has been removed and replaced with the logo, and a single link to go "Back to Products."

This was a very simple test to run, and the results were wonderful. We tested the cart across all our products: TV, Internet, voice as well as add-on options. Recipe B's design led to a 29.71 percent increase in RPV and a 32.62 percent lift in the conversion rate, which could lead to hundreds of millions of dollars in annual incremental revenue should the results hold over time. Our recommendation was to immediately push Recipe B to all visitors.

Buyflow Customer Information A/B Test: Social Security Number Explanation

Part of the purchase funnel requests that users enter their date of birth and social security number. These are required fields so that we can protect our customers against identity theft. Observational research revealed that a majority of customers didn't understand why this information was needed and were wary of entering it. **Figure 4** shows the default and two alternate versions of the page, including the alternate messaging explaining to our customers why we needed this information:

- **Default.** No explanatory messaging.

- **Recipe B.** Explanatory message emphasizing, "We're looking out for you."

- **Recipe C.** Explanatory message emphasizing, "We need your Social Security Number to verify your identity."

Recipe B was the clear winner, providing a 4.15 percent lift in RPV and a 4.80 percent lift in the purchase conversion rate. This could lead to over $50 million in annual incremental revenue should the results hold over time. Our recommendation was to push Recipe B to all visitors, and to continue testing ways to improve messaging for security-related topics.

Figure 2 The default cart experience with two-tier global navigation.

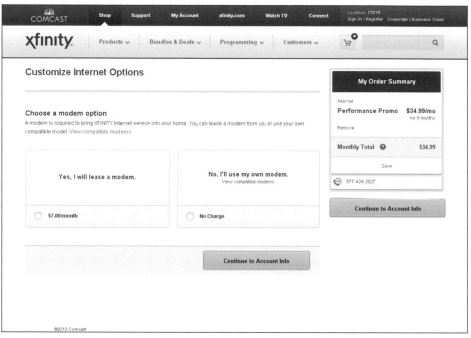

RECIPE A (DEFAULT)

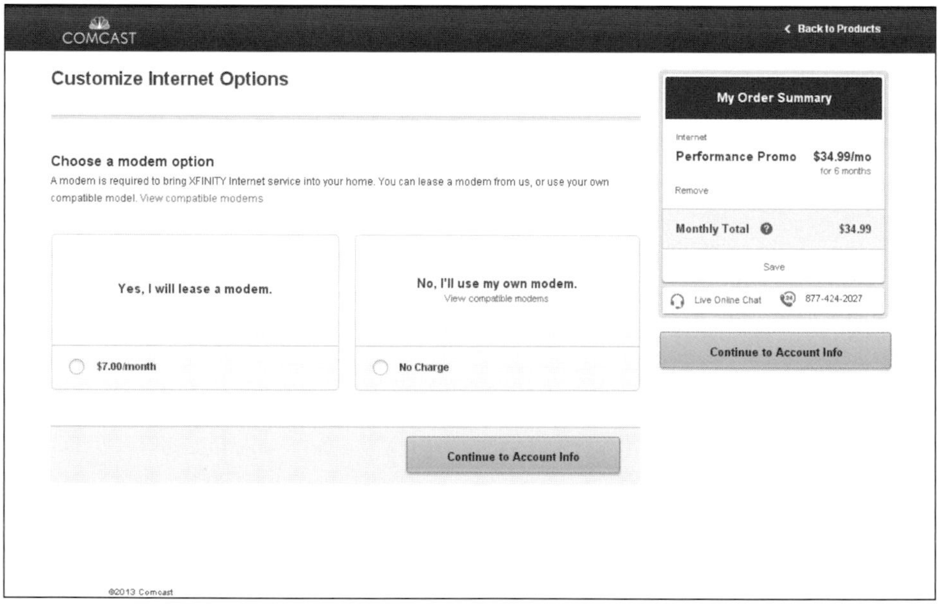

Figure 3 The tested experience where the navigation has been removed throughout the cart, no matter the product or products being purchased.

RECIPE B: +29.71% RPV, +32.62% conversion rate

RECIPE A (DEFAULT)

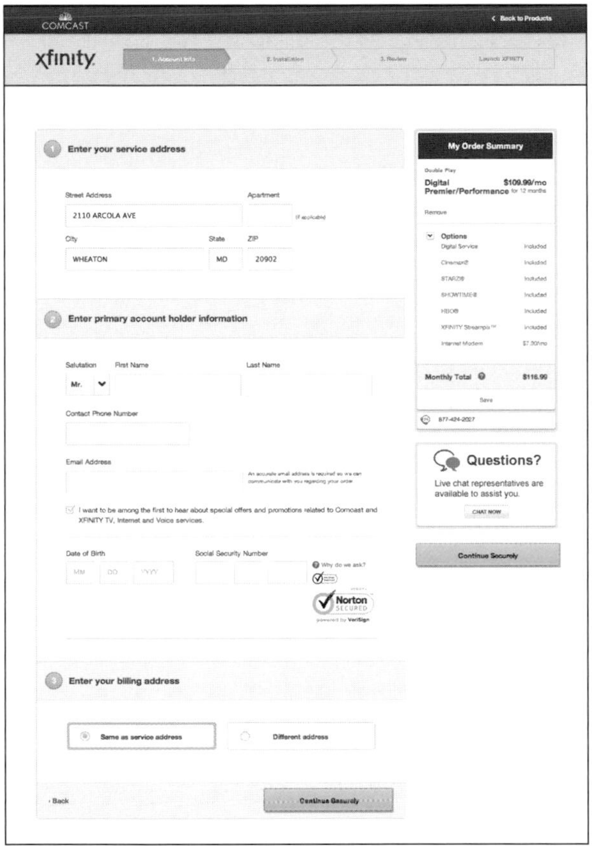

RECIPE A (DEFAULT)

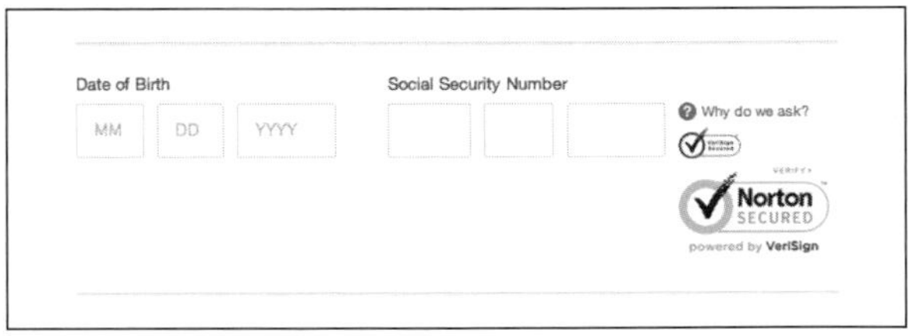

RECIPE B: +4.80% RPV, +4.15% purchase conversion rate

RECIPE C: +1.4% RPV, +1.30% purchase conversion rat

Figure 4 The default and alternate versions of the Social Security messaging.

Payment Completion Page Personalization Test: Self-service Messaging

Self-service is a very important part of our business, because customers have a better experience when they can quickly and successfully help themselves online. The hypothesis behind this test is that customers would be receptive to self-service messaging after completing a payment.

The default version of the page, in **Figure 5**, thanked customers for their payment and provided them with a receipt. Each alternate version of the page did the same while including additional messaging and a call-to-action, in the form of a blue link, to sign up for one self-service program (Figure 5). We created business rules to determine which self-service programs to message to each customer. Examples of the designs appear in **Figure 6**.

Results from this test were fantastic. We were able to increase self-service sign-ups for the following programs:

▸ **Auto-payments.** 6.62 percent lift in program sign-ups.

▸ **Payment reminders.** 102.39 percent lift in program sign-ups.

▸ **On-demand alerts.** 30.34 percent lift in program sign-ups.

▸ **Appointment reminders.** 21.03 percent lift in program sign-ups.

▸ **Support.** 28.62 percent lift in program sign-ups.

DEFAULT

ALTERNATE WITH ADDITIONAL MESSAGING

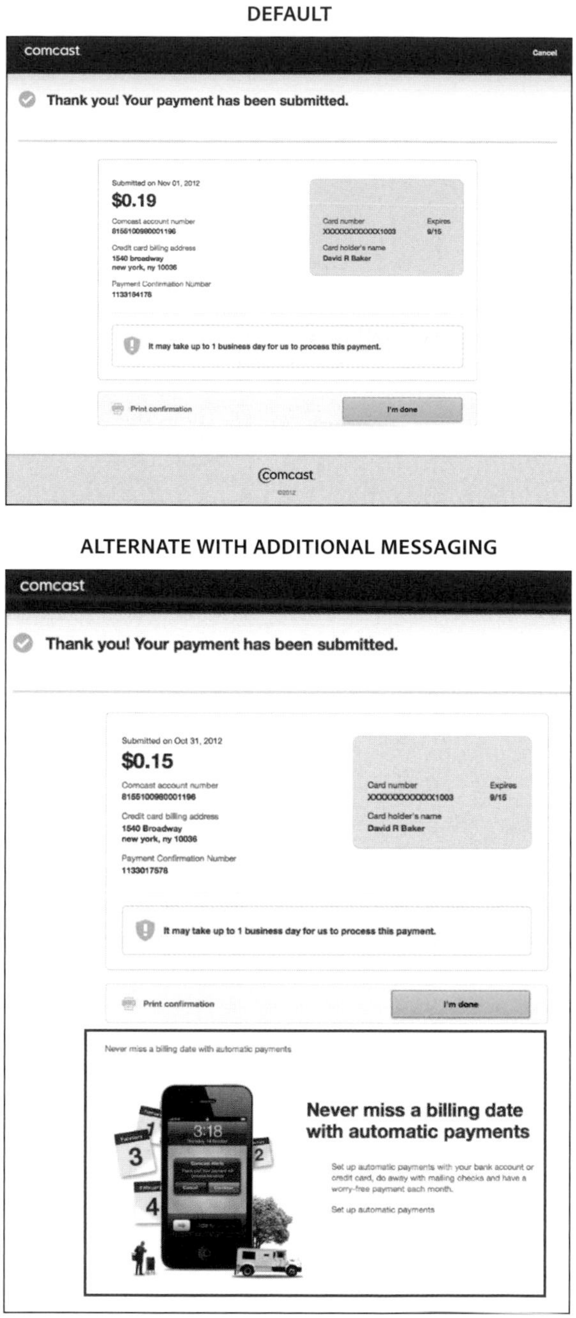

Figure 5 The default version of the payment completion page with an alternate version including additional promotional messaging outlined in blue.

AUTO-PAYMENTS: +6.62% program sign-ups

PAYMENT REMINDERS: +102.39% program sign-ups

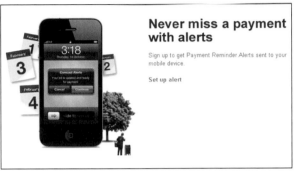

ON-DEMAND ALERTS: +30.34% program sign-ups

APPOINTMENT REMINDERS: +21.03% program sign-ups

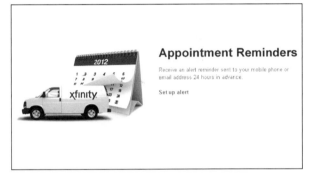

SUPPORT: +28.62% program sign-ups

Figure 6 Versions of the additional promotional messaging along with the lift in each respective program measured during controlled tests.

Emily Campbell, Executive Director of Global E-commerce

Emily leads Dell's Global E-commerce Marketing Team. Emily's responsibilities for Dell's online business include online consumer and enterprise sales; the desktop, mobile, tablet, and app experiences including required technology deployments; the acquisition, conversion, optimization, personalization, social, customer relationship management, and the overall go-to-market strategies.

Dell

Dell provides end-to-end solutions ranging from consumer PCs to enterprise IT solutions, including networking, servers, software, cloud applications, and professional services.

What are your business's goals?

Our business goals are twofold: First, we have very standard goals: Revenue, margin, site traffic, conversion, average order value (AOV), up-sell, cross-sell, and so on are all metrics that we track. We also look at the types of sales online: client sales, consumer sales, enterprise sales, and others. We look to understand what percentage each is of the mix. We have some key initiatives that we focus on as well. For example, at the moment we have specific sales goals around laptops. For all these goals, we compare ourselves to industry averages, if we have those available, as well as offline sales. We try to make sure we're looking outward and being externally focused when it comes to our goals.

Second, we have customer experience goals. We use standard Net Promoter Score (NPS) and Customer Satisfaction (CSAT) surveys on our website to get a short-term view of customer pain points and to put action plans around them.

What are your customers' goals?

That's a huge challenge for us. Our customers span across several segments. Customers range from individual consumers who are buying products that may be as small as ink, to large corporate customers that may be working on a deployment of a thousand Blade Servers over three different locations. Many companies have global websites, but very few companies transact in over 100 countries like we do. Also, a significant portion of our focus is on improving the e-support experience. Customers may be coming to download a driver, check on order status, or diagnose a problem with their PC.

Would you please share a bit about Dell's current online strategy?

Dell.com helps our customers by delivering a simple, reliable, and effective online experience:

▶ **Simple.** This is about moving from a "more is better" approach to having a "less is better" approach. Asking, "Can we simplify the message?" "Can we take something out and make it more effective as a result?" and, "Can we tighten up the content to make it easier and more streamlined?" This reminds me of a Coco Chanel quote that goes something like, "Before leaving the house, stop, look in the mirror, and remove one piece of jewelry." Simplification is a huge initiative for us.

▶ **Reliable.** This is about more than just a website technology reliability metric like 99 percent uptime, because that may not reflect the customer perspective. We may pat ourselves on the back and say we're doing an awesome job with reliability, but at the end of the day, if a single offer code is wrong or a single product image doesn't show up for a customer, then something is wrong. Reliability can only be measured in the eyes of our customers.

▶ **Effective.** This is a subjective term but centers around the customer experience. Are customers able to accomplish the task they came to the website for today? The task may be informational, like to find out when a warranty expires. It may be to download software, or maybe they want to buy something. That's where a satisfaction metric comes into play; we'll ask, "Were you able to accomplish your task?" We want to keep the measure of effectiveness customer-focused and not just look at whether they bought something, because they might not see that as an accomplishment.

Can you tell us a bit about your organization's optimization program?

We love optimization. Dell is a very analytics-focused company. We like to say, "If you can't measure it, you can't manage it." There's a core team of about 40 people focused on optimization and testing, and they are supplemental to the global teams who work on it part time.

Are segmentation, targeting, and personalization aspects of the program?

Segmentation is a big one. We've gone from a very complex segmentation model to a very simple segmentation model in line with our overall objectives. We're segmented by "for work" or "for home," so customers no longer need to choose a more granular entity like "small business," "medium business," "K–12 school districts," and so forth. I believe this is a huge win for our customers.

As we continue to simplify the way we segment customers, there's a risk of presenting more content to each visitor on the site. We're working on narrowing down the content to provide a personalized experience without the customer having to select into it. We use some automated targeting and have had a lot of success with that, but we're still working on how to best implement broad-based personalization. Personalization is the holy grail of marketing, and it will be the best of both worlds, but I have yet to see a company that does it really, really well.

How do you keep track of results?

We centrally store the test results and make them easily accessible, of course. However, tracking results still presents huge challenges for us. I don't think we're very good at it. The challenges are around capturing the environment around the test, because it's always changing. This is complicated by the breadth of products and customers we address, as well as the amount of globalization that we do.

For example, nobody thought adding security verification to the cart would be a big deal, but it significantly impacted conversions in a positive way. Let's say we apply the change to the cart, but over time we see cart conversion start to go down. We may ask: "What happened from between when we saw this huge lift and when we see it start to edge down?" "Has security verification stopped working?" "Are people just used to it?" or, "Did a change to payment types or financing options make it less impactful?" With test results you can only see a slice in time. Knowing what the site, and the environment around the site, looked like at the time of the test can help guide you.

Visual Examples

Cart Page A/B Test: Simplification and Coupons to Encourage Checkout

The objective of this test was to encourage users to complete checkout. The majority of the customer drop-off was occurring on the first step of the cart (**Figure 1**), also referred to as the "basket," which made it all the more important to try to improve the experience on this page. The tested recipes included:

▸ The default cart page as pictured in **Figure 2**.

▸ Recipe B (**Figure 3**) aimed to simplify the cart by removing the shipping information because it made the page very long. We made sure all the shipping information would appear in a subsequent step. The Checkout button is the primary call-to-action, so we removed CTAs that competed with it near the top of the page ("Save Cart for Future Access," etc.). We also added an extra Checkout button just above the 768 pixel fold line and above the Coupon Entry section of the page.

▸ Recipe C (**Figure 4**) included all of the simplifications of Recipe B and also removed the "Essential Add-On" element from the right side of the page.

▸ Recipe D (**Figure 5**) was just like Recipe A except the coupon codes were automatically included in the "Coupon Entry" section of the page.

Recipe C was the winning recipe because it provided the highest lift in a range of metrics. It provided about a 10 percent lift in RPV, over a 5 percent lift in AOV, and over a 15 percent lift in the conversion rate for orders over $1,000. If Recipe C were to maintain its lift in RPV throughout a year, it could provide an additional $115 million to the business.

Our recommendation was to push the winning recipe to all visitors, to continue to test designs that further simplify the cart and the overall buyflow, and until tested further, not to highlight coupons in the cart, because this might create a hesitancy to continue with the purchase.

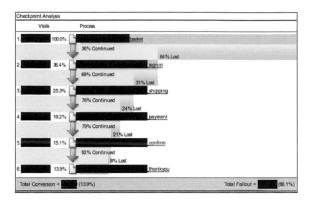

Figure 1 A cart fall-out report where confidential information has been redacted.

RECIPE A (DEFAULT)

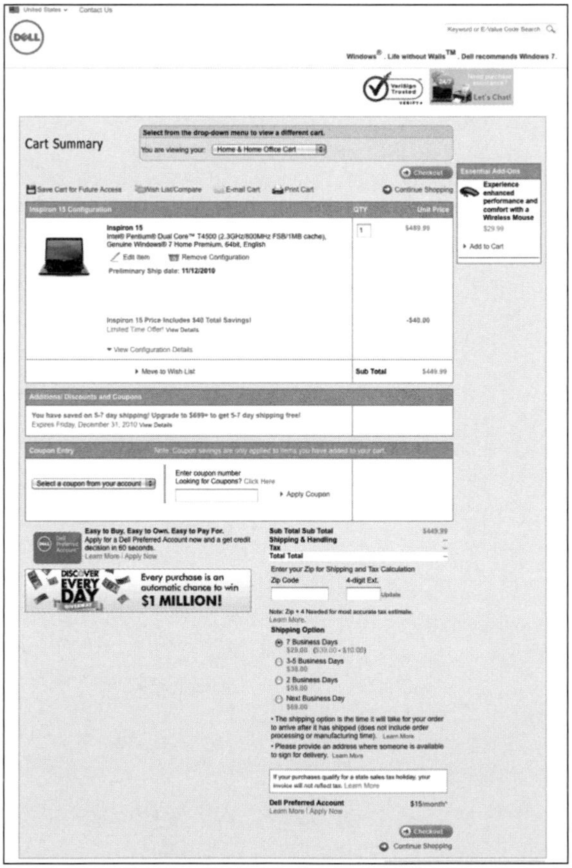

Figure 2 Recipe A: The default cart page.

RECIPE B: +10% RPV, +5% conversion rate for orders >$1,000

RECIPE C: +10% RPV, +15% conversion rate for orders >$1,000

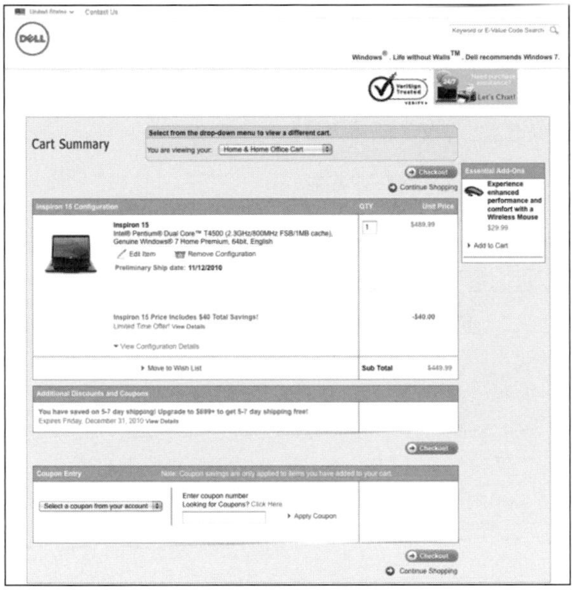

Figure 3 Recipe B: A simplified version of the cart.

Figure 4 Recipe C: A further simplified version of the cart without add-ons.

RECIPE D: -5% RPV, FLAT for conversion rate for orders >$1,000

Figure 5 Recipe D: Coupon codes automatically added.

Homepage A/B Test: Hero Personalization

We ran this test several years ago, and the objective was to determine whether providing a more personalized homepage experience would increase engagement and RPV.

Some analysis that influenced this test included:

► Customers return to the site several times before making a substantial purchase. We can therefore try to provide a more personalized customer experience based on what we think visitors are looking for.

► Homepage data showed that the majority of revenue and clicks came from users interacting with the subnavigation links. However, in order to see these links, a visitor first had to hover over the top navigation and self-segment by customer type

("For Home," "For Small Office," etc.). We wanted to test exposing the subnavigational links in the main body of the page.

► The default homepage (**Figure 6**) serves a lot of different types of visitors through a rotating hero banner with content ranging from PC promotions, to support, enterprise servers and services, and so on. Gaining consensus around what to display on the homepage at any given moment is not easy. That's the beauty of personalization.

We tested a simpler version of the layout with prominent subcategory navigation, shown as Recipe B in Figure 6. Rather than enter all visitors in the test, only visitors who had previously viewed the homepage and clicked on navigational links contained within "For Home," "For Small Office," or "For Small & Medium Business" were allowed to enter the test. If a

RECIPE A (DEFAULT)   RECIPE B: +5% RPV

Figure 6 The default and alternate versions of the homepage.

visitor didn't qualify for the test, they would continue to see the default homepage and their data would not be included in the control data.

Results showed that alternate experience provided over a 5 percent lift in RPV, and the majority of homepage clicks shifted to the newly designed area of the page. Because the homepage is the most visited page across all of Dell.com, this test represented a potentially enormous lift in revenue for the overall business. Our recommendations included pushing the winning recipe to all applicable visitors, testing simplifying the top navigation to reduce the number of categories, and testing organizing top navigation by the product categories rather than by customer segments.

Product and Cart A/B Test: Remove Chat Pop-ups

This test is a good example of how to quickly improve the business and the customer experience based on visitor feedback. We surveyed a sample of customers who had configured a system but not completed their purchase to ask why they hadn't completed their purchases. One of the top answers was that the chat box popping up during checkout annoyed them.

We tested removing the chat pop-up from the product and cart pages in Brazil (**Figure 7**). The results showed about a 5 percent lift in conversions and about a 5 percent lift in RPV. The recommendations from this test were to remove automatic chat pop-ups from Brazil; to conduct phased testing to remove them across geographies; to run a series of tests around making it easier for a customer to initiate a chat session by improving the CTAs and messaging; and to test improvements to rules for when automatic chat pops up to see if we could use it to help customers who may be struggling.

RECIPE A (DEFAULT)

RECIPE B: +5% RPV, +5% checkout conversions

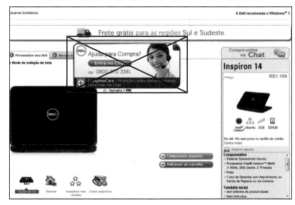

Figure 7 The default and alternate versions of the product and cart page.

Sandy Martin, Director of eMarketing & Administration

As the Director of eMarketing & Administration, Sandy oversees all of the online marketing strategies and vendor relationships for Dollar Thrifty. This involves optimizing spend for all marketing campaigns, including those that span the online and offline channels based on customer profiles from the rich Dollar Thrifty data mart.

Dollar Thrifty Automotive Group

Dollar Thrifty Automotive Group, Inc. is focused on being the low-cost provider in the car rental industry, and Dollar Rent A Car and Thrifty Car Rental serve value-conscious travelers in over 80 countries. In November 2012, Hertz Global Holdings, Inc. acquired Dollar Thrifty Automotive Group, Inc.

What are your business's goals?

We're in the car rental business, which is a commoditized market. Our overall business goal is to get butts in seats, and those seats are in our cars. We try to get people to the website and then drive reservations for the whole company. This mostly involves trying to acquire new customers. We're always in the acquisition game.

What are your customers' goals?

To get a car rental at the cheapest price possible.

Can you tell us a bit about your organization's optimization program?

We are all about passing any savings back to our customers, and optimization helps us keep our spending inline. We are always focused on how to get more out of every dollar that we spend. We pilot a lot and test the waters, because when we jump in full force, we want to make sure we're getting the most return out of our spend so we can offer our customers great deals.

We look for efficiencies and aim for a ten times return on investment for each marketing dollar spent. A lot of times we're able to way exceed that. We measure the success of our overall program by the fact that we've maintained the same media spend since 2008, and we've gotten more and more revenue out of that spend. And it's a modest budget.

Are segmentation, targeting, and personalization aspects of the program?

Segmentation, targeting, and personalization are very much in our wheelhouse. They help us drive more revenue from email than any other tactic we're using. Not everybody rents a car every week, so there's no reason for us to email our entire list every week. There are a lot of brands out there in similar situations.

Using segmentation, based on behavioral data, we try to determine when a customer is in-market for a rental car. We don't want to alienate our customers by sending them too many messages, so this keeps our email unsubscribe rate low and reduces costs for the emails we send.

A customer can make a reservation as "Mickey Mouse," and we would accept it, because we don't require a credit card or authentication to reserve a car. So, we don't know a lot about people who just make a reservation, but once they transact at a rental location, we can start matching up all of their historical and future data, and build a rich profile for someone. We build a profile for each customer, including data such as whether they opened an email, clicked on an email, clicked on a paid search link, visited the site directly, belong to certain loyalty programs, or made a reservation but didn't show up to rent the car. We also know their historical spend levels from rentals with us, which locations they rent from, which brands they rent from, which targeted ads or emails they've responded to in the past, and so on.

We assign a weight to each of those events, not just the first or last events. We look at all components across our channels that lead people to make reservations. For example, we know that within 45 days of clicking on an email a customer is more likely to make a reservation with us. Or, if someone starts to make a reservation but doesn't complete it, they'll likely receive an email the next Sunday asking if they would like to reserve the car they left in their cart. We can even target online advertising based on offline data. Most people are shoppers looking for the best deal possible, so sometimes a little extra communication, including clear messaging with a little urgency behind it, will help get them down the purchase path.

What advice would you give to someone in your position at another company about starting and scaling an optimization program?

I would advise someone that it's not all going to happen in one day, and you can't do this all on your own. You need partners who know how to do this to help you. You have to get the IT, web development, data management, revenue management, finance,

operations, marketing, and the fleet teams together. It's not an us versus them conversation; it's a let's do this together and share in the success conversation. If everyone is invested, it will work.

We optimized out of necessity. In 2008, our company was about to go under, and we didn't really have any alternatives. We had nothing to lose. A lot of people aren't in that situation, and taking on optimization can be daunting when you have so many items drawing your attention all of the time. When the economy was going down in 2008, our stock was tanking. In early 2009, we were trading at below $1 a share, and it seemed like we might go bankrupt at any minute.

We started spending less offline and more online, and narrowed down the online spend to just the essentials—and optimization was one of them. We also got funding for an analytics data mart that tied together our online and offline data for testing and behavioral targeting.

In 2013, Hertz ended up buying us at $87.50. We took a company that was about to go under and transformed it into the most profitable company in the industry. Without everybody working together, I don't think that would have ever happened.

Visual Examples

Reservation Page A/B Test: Email Opt-out

When a customer makes a reservation, the check box stating "I want to receive email updates and special offers" is always pre-checked. In Recipe A, a customer can easily deselect the box to opt-out of receiving promotional emails (**Figure 1**). Email acquisition is tough, and most customers see this page; it's our best way of getting email addresses.

We created a new design, Recipe B, so that if a customer deselected the box, we would alert them with a pop-up to confirm they had wanted to deselect the box (Figure 1). The main concern I had with this design is the impact it might have on our reservation conversion rate. This alert would pop up on the very last step of converting, where our bounce rate has traditionally been pretty low. If this new design was going to annoy people so much that they wouldn't make a reservation, I didn't want to use it. Therefore, we decided to put it to the test.

Recipe B increased email acquisitions by 9 percent, but it dropped our reservation rate by 7 percent. Based on the average value of an email versus a reservation, pushing Recipe B could lead to an over $20-million loss in one year. To me, this test was successful because it gave us an answer to our question before we hardcoded in a change and six months down the line asked, "Why did we lose so much revenue?" Our goals to get more reservations and more email addresses can lead to internal competition between teams, and this test allowed us to look at the whole business and customer experience we were creating as one team. Even though this test doesn't generate incremental revenue, it saved us from making a big mistake.

Email A/B Test: Hero Offers

We do a lot of testing in the actual emails. For example, we know that if we give 10 percent off a Mercury Grand Marquis or Ford Crown Victoria, it's really going to perform great. We also know the "wildcard special," where a customer pays the compact car rate but can receive anything from a compact to any type of car, is our best-performing offer.

One challenge our marketing department has is that we don't control price. We're told what we have to promote, and we have revenue goals for our email program, which can sometimes be challenging based on the available offers. Marketing teams will regularly change email offers from week to week and measure results, but there are too many variables changing each week to know what impact the offers are really having, especially when you factor in seasonality. Optimization fixes this by using A/B testing to send

RECIPE A (DEFAULT)

RECIPE B: +9% email opt-ins, -7% reservation conversions

Figure 1 The default and alternate versions of the confirmation page after the customer deselected the box to receive email updates.

different emails to different people and control for the other variables. We can even dynamically change the emails after they've been sent, so if customers are responding better to a specific offer, we can change the other emails we've already sent to show that offer.

An example of email testing appears in **Figure 2** for Dollar and in **Figure 3** for Thrifty. The same internal team works on both brands, even though we only

have about a 4 percent customer crossover between brands. People are generally either a Dollar customer or a Thrifty customer. In these examples, we tested multiple versions of the hero spot, varying elements such as the headline, car imagery, offer, and descriptive text. Based on the results from these tests we're able to adjust the emails our customers receive and view in real time.

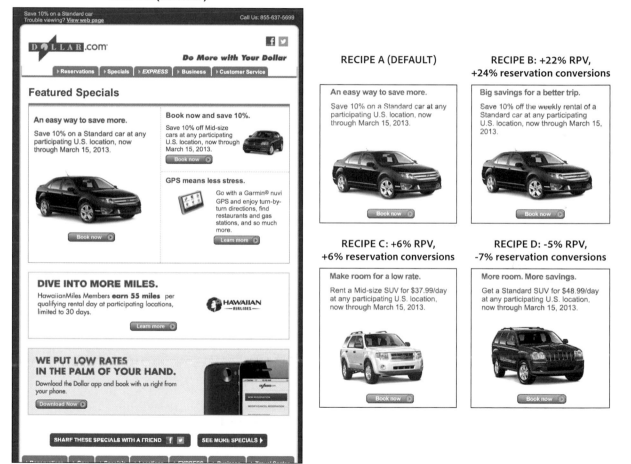

Figure 2 Test results from a Dollar email test.

RECIPE A (DEFAULT)

RECIPE A (DEFAULT)

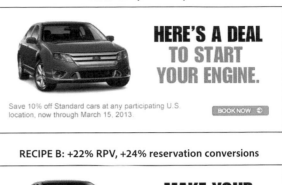

RECIPE B: +22% RPV, +24% reservation conversions

RECIPE C: +6% RPV, +6% reservation conversions

RECIPE D: -5% RPV, -7% reservation conversions

Figure 3 Test results from a Thrifty email test.

Zimran Ahmed, Director of Product Management and Strategic Planning

Zimran manages the Product Management and Strategic Planning teams for Pogo at Electronic Arts. Zimran has redesigned several of the business's core experiences to significantly increase revenue, feature adoption, play rate, and social graph density. These enhancements have led to customer experience improvements that have increased gameplay by two to four times.

Electronic Arts

Electronic Arts is a leading global interactive entertainment software company whose mission is to unite the world through play. Electronic Arts delivers games, content, and online services for Internet-connected, consoles, personal computers, mobile phones, and tablets.

What are your business's goals?

To make great games, and some profit, of course. You can play almost all of our over 140 games for free. We make money through advertising and premium gaming memberships, which provide special features.

If you play the games for free without registering, you are a guest user. If you register, you can continue to play the games for free, and you get some additional features. For example, free registered users can play against other people, chat, and save their progress in the game.

If they want, registered users can subscribe to Club Pogo, which is a premium version of the service that doesn't show advertisements and provides access to additional games. In addition, Club Pogo members get access to more social features, like earning badges, which show they completed certain challenges within the game. The folks that join Club Pogo love playing the games. We, as gamers, all do.

We have customers who have been subscribers now for ten years. It's amazing, and we couldn't ask for better or more fun customers.

What kind of games do you have?

Primarily evergreen games, which people like to play again and again because the core gameplay is so inherently fun and can withstand repeated playing. Evergreen games are easy to learn but can be difficult to master. They include classics like dominos, solitaire, and chess. In some cases, people have been playing these games for over 1,000 years, and the game hasn't substantially changed because they're so engaging. Newer evergreen games include *Scrabble*, *Bejeweled*, and *Minesweeper*.

Pogo took these core evergreen games that were very simple and wrapped service components around them to help customers play them in different ways. For example, we've added a chat feature so people can play the game and chat with other people at the same time. We've added a ranking system so people can determine their level of expertise for the game. We also created these things called challenges, which ask a player to play the game to a nonstandard win condition. For example, a challenge for Scrabble might be to use the letter Q 30 times in a week.

The player doesn't actually have to win Scrabble to win that challenge. Challenges extended the games' playability and add a twist to the games to help players connect with the games over time.

What are your customers' goals?

People play games when they're looking to be entertained. We have three different kinds of customers, with three different goals. I think of them as three different usage patterns:

▶ **Group 1.** They have a lot of time that they look to fill with structure and meaning, and play games to engage with other people in a safe environment.

▶ **Group 2.** They play these games primarily with family members, for short periods of time, to stay in touch with people they care about in their lives.

▶ **Group 3.** They play games because they really love the games, and they want to continue playing them at deeper and deeper levels.

Usually, customers in Group 3, and sometimes in Group 1, are interested in long play sessions, which are what we do best. A great experience for those customers is finding a game they love, spending a lot of time on the site, and then making friends within our online community.

Would you tell us about the product you were hired to build?

I was initially hired to create a "meta-game" that would help connect the different games. At one point, I think it involved building a virtual island. It sounded cool, but what we found from our research is that it wasn't helping solve a customer need. Our customers were struggling to understand all of the meta-experiences already on the site, such as ranking, tokens, avatars, challenges, and badges. We assumed that customers knew as much about

these features as we did and, in fact, they did not. So instead of adding additional new features, we focused on making all of our existing features easier to discover and understand.

We tried to focus on answering: What are the key experiences someone needs to have, starting from being a total novice to being a happy Club Pogo member? Better understanding the adoption path involved a lot of quantitative and qualitative research. For example, we conducted ethnographic studies, during which we went to people's homes and watched how they played. We also conducted diary studies, where we asked customers to record their actions related to gaming in a diary. Every so often we would call them to better understand what they had written about in the diary. We also upgraded some of those customers' memberships on the site to see how their gameplay would change. We used our analytics to try to quantitatively match up what we were hearing from the qualitative data.

High-level findings included:

▶ Our customers, especially our new customers, had trouble understanding the individual games and how to play them. They needed feedback on how they were playing so they could determine whether or not they liked the game.

▶ People understood the difference between paying to join Club Pogo and playing for free. However, we hadn't done a good job of explaining the difference between playing for free as a guest or playing for free as a logged-in user.

▶ Playing challenges and making friends drive loyalty, which we saw both qualitatively and quantitatively. Finding and understanding challenges, and making friends, were hard, so we needed to try to make it easier.

We needed to get really clear about the basic stuff before we got more advanced.

Visual Examples

To take visitors from being newbies to happy micro-transacting subscribers, we needed to contextually reveal the service as the visitors were ready to learn more about it. What I'm going to show you are redesigns for the pre-game page, which is the page the customer sees before playing the game, and the post-game page, which is the page the customer sees when the game ends.

These examples feature *Word Whomp*, which is a fun word game with gophers. When you play this game, you get tiles with letters on them. Each time you make a word out of the tiles, a gopher makes progress digging toward a vegetable. To win the game, all you need to do is make enough words so that the gopher reaches the vegetable.

Word Whomp A/B Test: Pre-game and Post-game Pages for Guest Players

The default *Word Whomp* pre-game page for guest players is shown in **Figure 1**. The pre-game page needed to be SEO optimized, let players start playing the game, and make it easy for them to sign in. The "Play as a Guest!" button was placed on top of the game art. The art for *Word Whomp* has a green background, and this made for poor contrast with the yellow CTA. Each game has different art, so placing the CTA on top of the game art in this way meant there was no single button we could use for every game that would provide high contrast. Therefore, a big part of this project became standardizing the 140 game templates so we could make changes to all games at once.

The new template, Recipe B, created a shaded area on the left side of the game art. We added this shading so we could use the same buttons for every game regardless of the colors in the game art. Other changes to the template include adding a clear CTA to "Register Free," because this is the next step guests

should take. We also explained the benefits of registration below the CTA. Just below the game art we added a blank avatar for the user with a link to "Sign In" and also added blank avatars for their soon-to-be friends with links to "Add a friend."

The default version of the post-game page is shown as Recipe A in **Figure 2**. The post-game experience is very important because that's when the player gets a lot of feedback on how he or she did. In the default example, the user lost the game, because he or she didn't make enough words for the gopher to reach the vegetable, which in this case was a carrot. Feedback from users was that they didn't understand why they had lost, because they thought the point of the game was to make as many words as possible to earn points. The default screen also focuses on points and includes other confusing metrics as well, like the number of tokens earned, the word score, a gold word bonus, a time remaining bonus, and the player's high score. There were even tabs for "Tokens" and "Tips" with more information, and several additional calls to action. There was too much confusing information on this page for a novice player. Ironically, the one thing this page didn't have was a very clear CTA to become a free registered user.

In the alternate design, Recipe B, we wanted to make it very clear whether or not the user had won. Because research revealed that players were interested in how many of the possible words they had made, we added this data to the page just below the win status. In this example, it reads, "You found 14 out of 23 words this round." We also included the score and number of tokens earned but didn't make them the most prominent elements on the page. There is only one very clear CTA on this page, and it reads, "Register FREE to save your progress," because that's the next step we want the user to take. Just below that yellow button is a blue underlined link that reads, "No thanks, keep playing." All the other information from the default experience has been removed. All a user has to do on

Figure 1 The default and alternate designs for the *Word Whomp* pre-game page for guest players.

RECIPE A (DEFAULT)

RECIPE B: +30% registration rate, +15% logins
(results from simultaneously testing pre- and post-game pages)

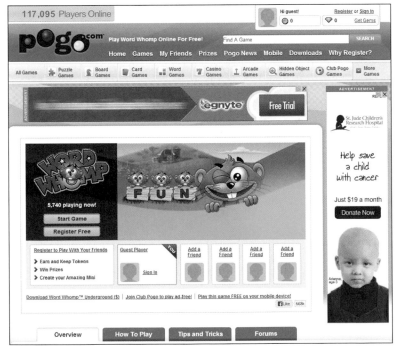

RECIPE A (DEFAULT)

Figure 2 The default and alternate designs for the *Word Whomp* post-game page for guest players.

RECIPE B: +30% registration rate, +15% logins
(results from simultaneously testing pre- and post-game pages)

this page is understand whether they won, and then decide between clicking on two CTAs: one to register and one to keep playing. This was a huge change to the template.

Results from A/B testing these changes were fantastic. They showed that the registration rate, which was our primary conversion metric, increased by 30 percent. Because it also became clearer to registered users whether they were logged in or not, the percentage of logins on these pages increased by 15 percent.

Word Whomp A/B Test: Pre-game and Post-game Pages for Free Logged-in Players

The default *Word Whomp* pre-game page for registered players who have logged in is shown in **Figure 3**. Even though the Play Now button is the most prominent CTA on the page, it is saddled by several competing CTAs on both sides. A CTA to join Club Pogo, with several value proposition bullets, takes up the left side of the screen. "How to Play," "Screenshots," and other links take up the right side of the screen. Logged-in users most likely already know how to play the game, and there are instructions within the game teaching them how to play, so these links seemed unnecessary. We wanted the primary logged-in user experience to be playing the game itself, not receiving ads pushing them to pay for Club Pogo.

The alternate version of the page, Recipe B, removes both of these sidebars and uses a simple variation on the winning template for the guest experience. Because the Register Free button no longer appears, the "4,376 playing now!" message is more prominent, and there was also room to add a "choose a chat room" secondary CTA just below the button. Now that the user has logged in, the screen shows avatars for any of the user's friends who have played the game recently and includes an "Add a friend" link.

The overall goal of this page is to allow our registered users to easily play the game and add friends, because those are the primary drivers that will lead to happy customers.

The post-game experience is shown in **Figure 4**. The default experience is very much like the default guest experience. The alternate experience uses the same framework as the alternate guest experience, making it clear whether the player won and letting them know how many words they found. It also adds more details about their game performance, because registered users are usually more advanced players. The primary CTA on the page is still "Play Again," because this is the primary customer goal. There is also a relatively small but contextually relevant advertisement for Club Pogo below the Play Now button, which lets users know they can find out their rank (their level of expertise with the game) by joining Club Pogo.

Results from A/B testing were dramatic. Due to these designs driving so much increased gameplay, we doubled our ad revenue. Our bounce rates fell, our registration rates increased, and our logged-in play rates increased. The site design is now standardized, so there is a lot more we can do.

RECIPE A (DEFAULT)

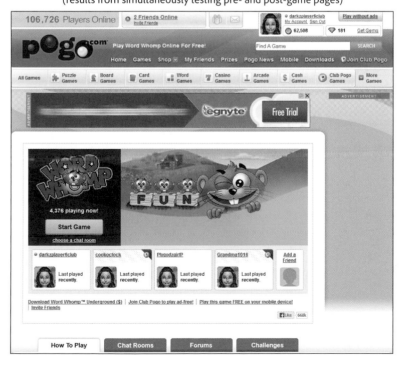

RECIPE B: +100% advertising revenue from increased gameplay
(results from simultaneously testing pre- and post-game pages)

Figure 3 The default and alternate designs for the *Word Whomp* pre-game page for registered players who have logged in.

Figure 4 The default and alternate designs for the *Word Whomp* post-game page for registered players who have logged in.

RECIPE A (DEFAULT)

RECIPE B: +100% advertising revenue from increased gameplay
(results from simultaneously testing pre- and post-game pages)

Nate Bolt, Design Research Manager

From 2002 until 2012, Nate was the CEO of Bolt|Peters, a user-centered design firm specializing in remote usability testing and ethnographic research. Nate is the co-author of the book *Remote Research: Real Users, Real Time, Real Research.* In 2012, Bolt|Peters was acquired by Facebook. In the year since the acquisition, Nate has worked on a range of Facebook products, including News Feed, Advertising, Photos, Messages, Graph Search, and Instagram.

Facebook

Facebook's mission is to give people the power to share and make the world more open and connected. As of August 2013, Facebook was ranked as the #2 visited website in the world (source: Alexa.com).

Can you tell us a bit about Facebook's customers and your role?

We think of them as three key categories: users, advertisers, and developers. The bulk of our users aren't necessarily considered customers. Users just want to connect with people they care about. Advertisers want to reach people who their products and services could help. Developers want to build things they think could be useful to the world and use Facebook as a platform to do that. As a Design Research Manager at Facebook, I help make sure that our users, advertisers, and developers have a seat at the table in the design process. The fourth seat at the table is the business, because Facebook has goals, too.

When designing, is there a line between data and creativity?

Design gut instincts sometimes turn out to be right, and sometimes they turn out to be wrong. It's important to balance between data-driven and creative-driven decision making.

I'm interested in the history of this topic, even outside of Facebook. Creative industries have been struggling for years to figure out if there's any sort of formula that they can use to build something that gives people joy. It's like when record labels in the '70s and '80s tried to predict how people would relate to different pop songs. Now, we're creating experiences through interfaces, and it's vastly more complicated. For example, Flickr applied user feedback and data to evolve from an online multiplayer game site, with real-time instant messaging, to a photo-sharing site.

Nobody who designs for a living is going to say, "Multivariate testing is going to solve the world's problems." Companies are now swimming in all this data, and it's awfully sexy in that it offers up the promise of how to make great interface decisions—to what extent that it is true has yet to be determined.

It's an incredibly nuanced issue. People on both sides of the fence have a lot of misconceptions about how people on the other side of the fence apply their respective expertise. In the mid-twentieth century, Edwin Land, the founder of Polaroid, said, "Market research is what you do when your product isn't any good." In some ways, that's still the case, because even in a sea of data and metrics, a creative gut instinct, or vision, or an idea is required to build something really awesome. At the same time, the data informs us and helps us optimize our existing products way faster and better than ever before. I don't see it as a conflict so much as two things—gut design instinct and access to experimental data—that are happening at the exact same time.

Which types of research methodologies do you incorporate into the design process?

At Facebook, we try to do as much research as possible. Our audiences of users, advertisers, and developers don't come to Menlo Park every day, so the challenge, especially for audiences we may not be as familiar with is to figure out how we incorporate them into the design process.

The core issue I face every day at Facebook is making sure that we still have a creative design process that incorporates real human beings that use the products. On the quantitative side, experimental design testing is a big part of that. On the qualitative side, observational research, card sorting, interviewing, and live remote research, during which we watch people use our tools, are all techniques we incorporate. We need to decide which research method is right for each scenario. When it comes to making big decisions, we'll incorporate a mix of techniques and often include redundant research methodologies. As we design, there are a ton of iterations, as well as sprint releases of our products to subsets of our users. We gather a lot of data to get a pretty good picture of how people are using a product before it launches to everyone.

How does innovation happen at Facebook?

I can speak to the research side of it. We're always looking for insights or understanding about our key audiences. The researcher helps frame the conversation, and then a product manager, engineer, designer, or anybody else will hopefully get inspired to build something really amazing.

One of the cool things at Facebook is, there isn't a super-corporate hierarchy, where product strategy is delivered in a memo that everybody has to carry out. There's a lot of organic collaboration between teams. Depending on the product release, many small teams may work together very closely. Teams are empowered to create what they think are the best experiences, using the best strategies, and present them accordingly. Everybody gets a chance to craft, review, and make changes. There's a huge focus on customer experience, and if we're seeing patterns and trends from one research method, like qualitative interviews or test data, everybody is willing to have a discussion around what that means.

Visual Examples

We're currently iteratively redesigning the News Feed. The News Feed is essentially the homepage for Facebook and one of the primary ways in which our users interact with each other. We've done more research on the News Feed redesign than any other product before. This is also the most tested product we have ever put out: There have been hundreds and hundreds of design experiments. As a result, we have made substantial changes both to the algorithm and the layout of the News Feed. About 1 percent of the world is currently seeing the redesigned News Feed. It is very slowly being rolled out to all users as we continue to run design experiments. In terms of results, all of the charts are up and to the right.

One of the main reasons we started this large redesign is our users want to feel like they're getting access to their whole network. They also want to understand the way in which Facebook structures their access to information. We conduct research to make sure that we're representing the interests of our users as we develop the new product. We have used eight, sometimes redundant, data gathering methods; six of which are qualitative and two of which are quantitative:

▸ The first data point we started out with was a ranking from the support team of the top feature requests for the News Feed.

▸ We then conducted an online survey of people who frequently switch how they sort their News Feeds. The default sort is by "Top Stories," and we reached out to people who switched to sort by "Most Recent." This survey collected a ton of open-ended responses.

▸ We then started getting into more data analysis, sometimes referred to as looking at our "system data" or "big data." Specifically, we looked to understand engagement between different types of stories in the News Feed, especially when sorted by "Top Stories" versus "Most Recent." This is a big question at Facebook.

▸ We then did a number of qualitative interviews. Jane Leibrock was the lead researcher on this project. Jane interviewed people who were in some way dissatisfied with their News Feed. We spent a lot of time with those people.

▸ We then did card sorting (detailed in Chapter 4).

▸ We then conducted six weeks of one-on-one behavioral qualitative tests with a new prototype that we were developing. We did this to test out the "NUXes," which I'm not sure is a term outside of Facebook. NUX stands for *New User Experience*.

▸ We then ran two rounds of online, remote user testing for the mobile version of the prototype. The News Feed has been redesigned across desktop, tablet, and mobile devices.

▸ During this whole process there were almost endless multivariate tests happening on the site to move and redesign parts of the interface. We use standard experimental multivariate test setups, and we run them through a system at Facebook called Gatekeeper. We did so many tests I wouldn't even know where to begin summarizing them. Every possible element that you could imagine was tested.

It was our job in the research team, in partnership with the product team, to merge findings from all these data gathering techniques. We collaborated with the engineers, project managers, and the designers to ask ourselves, "Well, here are the issues we're seeing crop up from all these different research methods. How can we address them?"

News Feed Redesign: Algorithm

There is an algorithm that decides which stories are displayed and in which order they're sorted. Lars Backstrom has been overseeing the optimization of the algorithm and provided the following information related to it.

"Every time someone visits the News Feed, there are on average 1,500 potential stories from friends, people they follow, and Pages for them to see, and most people don't have enough time to see them all. With so many stories, there is a good chance people would miss something they wanted to see if we displayed a continuous, unranked stream of information.

"The prime directive of the News Feed is to show users the stories that they will find most interesting. If our ranking system thinks that a user will find a post very interesting, we'll publish it near the top. If a story seems less likely to be interesting to the user, we publish it further down, below other things that seem more important. Our ranking certainly isn't perfect, and we are continually refining it, but we've run many tests showing that any time we stop ranking and show posts in chronological order, the number of stories people read decreases and the amount of likes and comments people produce decreases. That's not good for our users or for Facebook.

"The News Feed algorithm responds to signals from users, including how often they interact with a friend, Page, or public figure; the number of likes, shares, and comments a post receives from the world at large and from the user's friends in particular; how much a user has interacted with a type of post in the past; and whether or not the user, and other people across Facebook, are hiding or reporting a given post. This allows us to prioritize an average of 300 stories out of these 1,500 stories to show each day.

"The update to the News Feed ranking algorithm allows for the following: Organic stories that people did not scroll down far enough to see can reappear near the top of the News Feed if the stories are still getting lots of likes and comments.

"Early test data, with a small number of users, shows this improves the experience of the News Feed (**Figure 1**):

▶ A 5 percent increase in the number of likes, comments, and shares on the organic stories users saw from friends.

▶ An 8 percent increase in likes, comments, and shares on the organic stories users saw from Pages.

▶ Previously, users read 57 percent of the stories in their News Feeds on average. They did not scroll far enough to see the other 43 percent. When the unread stories were resurfaced, the fraction of stories read increased to 70 percent, which is over a 20 percent lift.

UPDATED NEWS FEED ALGORITHM:
+5% likes, comments, and shares from friends' stories
+8% likes, comments, and shares from Pages
+22.8% number of News Feed stories read

Figure 1 Results from the updated News Feed algorithm.

"The data suggests that this update does a better job of showing people the stories they want to see, even if they missed them the first time."

News Feed Redesign: Layout

One of the pieces of feedback that Facebook has gotten forever and came up in every kind of research method is, "the New Feed feels cluttered." If you think about that feedback, it's really hard to turn it into actionable design. Part of the challenge was decoding what that feedback meant and then turning it into a design. The teams felt like they needed more on what people meant by "cluttered," which is when card sorting came into play. Card sorting, and people slicing up their feeds with scissors, led to a lot of the inspiration for the new News Feed. The whole team then decided that what people really meant when they said "cluttered" was that they weren't getting access to the content that was important to them. Because if the News Feed is cluttered with awesome stuff, people don't really care. But if it has information or navigation that's distracting, then people say it's "cluttered."

The work then moved onto teams sketching, iterating, and prototyping. We used design in conjunction with analytics data. Everybody had the system data, but it takes a lot more effort to pair it with a mirrored data gathering technique that's more qualitative and lends a more human feel. Jane Leibrock, the researchers, and the experimental data analysts sat with the product, engineering, design, and project management teams, and information was shared with everybody. Decisions were made in as close to real time as possible. Conversations would go like this: "Here's what we just learned. What are we going to change *right now*?"

Content was the number one focus. The default News Feed is shown in **Figure 2**. Changes to the News Feed layout as viewed from both a desktop and mobile browser, because we designed for both at the same time, appear in **Figure 3**. These designs include making the layout cleaner and prettier, and the content bigger, and reducing the size of the left-hand navigation to create more room for content. Every single type of story that a user could see in their News Feed has been redesigned; that was the biggest part of the redesign.

We also added new types of navigation in the upper right, so users can now view stories within the following groups: photos, music, friends, or Pages, and people they're following. This gives people easier access to grouping stories. This change was secondary to redesigning all the content.

There is a constant focus on how much content interaction we are seeing. There are a lot of metrics we look at; some we can share, and some are double top secret. We see increases in metrics for people engaging with the News Feed more, including engaging with photos, comments, or clicks to stories, as well as people coming back to engage with the News Feed more regularly. Each of these is taken into consideration because they each represent different uses of the News Feed. There's no one metric that we look at to make every decision.

The rollout process started in March 2013, and we're using Facebook's Gatekeeper system to incrementally release it to all of our users. We are slowly rolling it out to make sure it's working as expected, and we continue iterating on it along the way. Most of our launches are like that now, to make sure we don't change experiences for the whole population at once without getting a lot of feedback. The data from the rollout is obviously the best data, because it's as real as real can get.

DEFAULT NEWS FEED LAYOUT

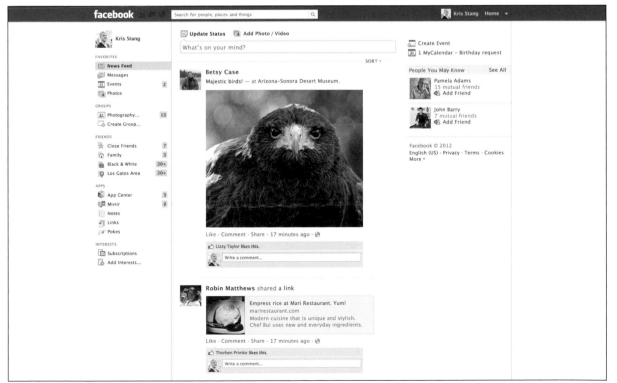

Figure 2 The default version of the News Feed that the majority of Facebook users still see.

UPDATED NEWS FEED LAYOUT

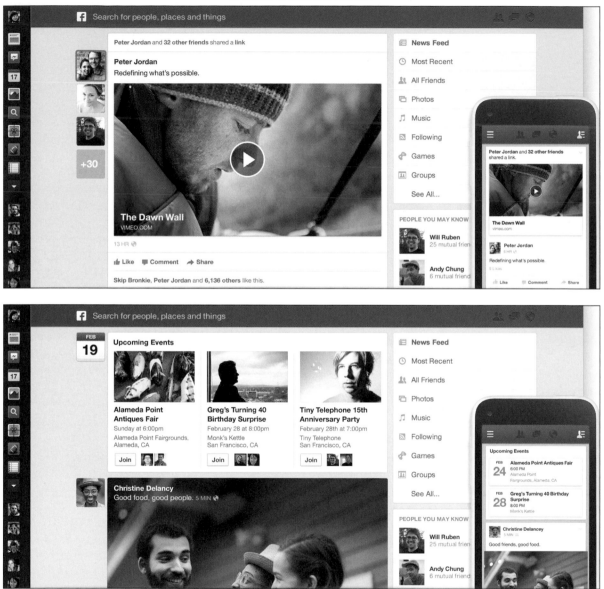

Figure 3 Two examples of the updated News Feed layout, including new left and right side navigational elements as viewed from a desktop. This design also includes the new treatment of a video story as viewed on desktop and mobile browsers. This redesign has led to a lift in engagement with photos, comments, clicks to stories, and users coming back to interact with the News Feed.

Simon Favreau-Lessard, Software Engineer

Simon Favreau-Lessard is a software engineer currently at Foursquare in San Francisco where he works on its advertising platform and search engine. After graduating from Polytechnique Montréal in 2007, he spent four years at Google working on its A/B testing platform and on the analysis of A/B tests across the company, including search, advertising, and the company's other products.

Foursquare

Foursquare is a free app that helps users and their friends make the most of where they are. When they're out and about, Foursquare helps users share and save the places they visit. And, when they're looking for inspiration for what to do next, Foursquare gives them personalized recommendations and deals based on where they, their friends, and people with their tastes have been.

Would you please tell us a bit about your role?

At Foursquare I am focused on monetization and advertising. On the side I built and now maintain our A/B testing framework, and help a lot of teams in the company on anything that's related to A/B testing. It wasn't part of my job. I really wanted to run A/B tests, and we didn't have a standard way of doing it, so I just decided to build it.

Wow. What are your business's goals?

At Foursquare we try to help you discover the real world. We recommend really great places, help you share them with your friends, share your location, and also see where your friends are. Through Foursquare you can get a lot of information about anyplace; as soon as you walk in, you'll immediately get great tips.

We have a great local search engine. If you're looking for a restaurant, coffee shop—anything—we're able to give you really good recommendations. We have over 40 million users, 4.5 billion check-ins, and many millions of location-specific tips. We also use that same data to target ads on search results. It's sort of like Google AdWords for the real world, where local businesses can pay to show up as an ad in our search results.

What are your users' goals?

People use Foursquare for a variety of reasons—from finding new places to visit, finding where their friends are, and finding out what their friends are doing to keeping track of where they've been in the past so that they can look it up and remember. For example, we can let someone know, "it's been nine months since you've been to this restaurant."

How does your business innovate?

It's a small company, with about 150 people, so innovation comes from basically everyone. If you have an idea, just say it. There are not a lot of layers. Everyone knows each other. Ideas can come from engineering, product management, marketing, design, business development, and so on.

Once we have an idea, we'll normally have design and product management try to scope it out, and make a lot of prototypes. Then we conduct user testing. We have a user experience researcher who will bring in users to look at early mock-ups. We try to get a lot of information from them and to make sure the designs are things that users actually want to use. After that, we'll implement them and test them. We A/B test almost all major features. If someone has an idea for a tiny feature they can just go implement it.

How do you measure the success, or value, of a design?

The ultimate metric for us is user retention. We always ask ourselves: Do people keep using the app when we make a change? That's a really hard metric to measure, and doing so requires a long-term view, so we may sometimes run tests for several weeks. For example, we may seek to understand whether visitors who used the product in one week came back during the next week. We try to understand how the test may have changed user behavior based on any metrics associated with them and whether the changes made them like our product more. However, if retention is the only metric we look at, we can't move fast, so we also use a lot of other metrics.

The other metrics depend on which part of the product we're changing. For example, if we're working on the sign-up flow, we'll look at funnel conversion metrics, like the percentage of people who started the sign-up process and also finished it. We'll then also look at retention to understand how many of those users are still using the app a week later.

How do you measure the effectiveness of the search and advertising products?

Testing on search results is nuanced and requires a certain amount of subjectivity when analyzing metrics. We need to distinguish whether or not a click-through on a search result is good. For example, if someone had to click on seven different search results, they may not have received good recommendations. We don't want our users to have to go through that. Ideally, they should only need to click on one or two results.

As another example, if we add more information to the search results, that can reduce the need for a user to click, even though we're improving the overall experience. So, if we make a change to improve search results, the number of clicks may sometimes drop. It's important to understand what we're changing in order to know whether the experience is good or bad for the user. We can't just have an absolute metric that tells us whether or not to launch a change; that's definitely not how it goes.

All of our search results are places, and people who use our app end up checking into places, so we're able to calculate a metric around whether we gave a good enough recommendation that the person ended up going there. For example, did they search for food and an hour later walk into a restaurant that was in the search results? If so, how high up was it in the results? When someone visits a place without clicking on a search result, we call that an "explore conversion" versus a click-through. It's also important to realize that sometimes people will visit a place, like a coffee shop or bar, a day or two after they searched for it. We know which places people have told us they've been to before, so we factor into our metrics whether someone is visiting a place for the first time, based on our recommendation.

For the advertising product we primarily want to increase revenue per thousand impressions (RPM), but we also look at other metrics to ensure we're not negatively affecting the user experience. So, in addition to revenue, we'll look at metrics like click-through rate (CTR) on the advertisements and natural results. Let's say we make a change that ends up showing more ads. That will probably increase revenue, but it may decrease the user experience. For example, we can show ads everywhere in the app and it will increase revenue, but that doesn't mean it's a good idea. If we can manage to show more ads and have the same overall CTR for ads, then generally speaking, that means the quality of the new ads that we're showing is likely similar to the old ones.

We repeatedly ask ourselves: Is this a good enough advertisement to show to the user? We try to show the most relevant ad to each user by matching our inventory of places being promoted to interested users based on all the data we have about them. If we make a change to the ad placement or algorithm, we want to make sure it's providing a positive user experience and that we're not shoving poor advertisements down everyone's throats.

For both search results and advertisements we take in several signals to determine relevance, and use machine learning to generate models based on those signals. Part of the challenge is figuring out the right weight to give each signal. An example of a signal in the model is "timeliness," where we try to determine what users are looking for based on the time of day. Different locations will have different timeliness scores. For example, we'll recommend more coffee shops in the morning, because we know that people go to coffee shops in the morning. Some restaurants are better for lunch, and some are better for dinner; so if it's noon, we'll give the user a different recommendation than if it's 7 p.m.

Using A/B testing, we then experiment with new search and advertising models, testing the old model versus the new one. Some models might apply very small tweaks to the order of the search results, and A/B testing helps us to understand changes to the CTR rates, as well as whether users are coming back more to use the search engine. Retention is always the best metric.

How do you communicate design successes?

We have demo days every other week, which last for an hour, or however long it takes. We try to get everyone to showcase what they've been working on, and demos can range anywhere from 30 seconds to several minutes. Additionally, after each A/B test, someone will write up the analysis and share it around the company along with links to past results. On our corporate wiki we store a list of all the experiments we've conducted, a link to the results dashboard, and a document with written analysis. It's useful to refer back to results to help inform future decisions and test ideas.

Have any themes or "best practices" emerged from your testing program?

If you can create a simple experience by removing information without having a negative effect on metrics, that's great. One example is when we ran a test to try to remove information from search results so we could fit more results on a mobile screen without causing users to have to click into more results or negatively impacting retention.

Also, for our business, we tend to look at test results segmented by new and existing users. New users are like a blank slate, and we can sometimes see larger changes in their behavior during A/B tests. For example, a test that changes conversions 1–2 percent for existing users may change it by 25 percent for new users. That data can hopefully help inform what the long-term effect of the change will be once existing users come to slowly adopt and appreciate it.

Finally, with A/B tests you only get data; you don't get reasons behind the data. You never know why people did anything; you just know how many people took specific actions. You should use A/B tests to guide your decisions, not let A/B tests make your decisions for you.

Visual Examples

Search Results A/B Test: Autocomplete

Analytics showed that a lot of people would click on the search bar and either not enter anything or start to type but not complete their search. We didn't know why. Perhaps they weren't sure what they were looking for.

We already had an autocomplete feature, but for this test we worked to make the feature much more robust. The default version and tested versions for the same search term in the same city are shown in **Figure 1**.

The default version of autocomplete only included basic categories like, "French Restaurant." For the

alternate version of the autocomplete feature we built a model based on the entire set of search terms people were using, not just categories that already existed. We also had the model incorporate the location of the person, because search terms vary by city. In the alternate version, "French Restaurant" still appears, but there are now additional options like "free wifi" or "gluten free." We hoped that the new version would not only make it easier for users to type on their mobile device, but also that it would educate users around the kinds of queries they could make. For example, maybe users didn't realize they could search for "free wifi," which could sometimes be useful.

Figure 1 The default and tested versions of the autocomplete search results algorithm when viewed from the mobile app for the search "fre."

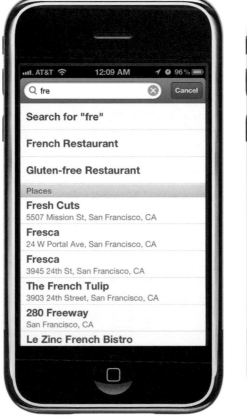

The two versions of the autocomplete feature were A/B tested on the mobile site as well as within the mobile app. We ran the A/B test for a few weeks, and the results were so strong that it was a no-brainer to push the new feature live to all users.

This had a huge impact, with a 10 percent increase in the number of completed searches. It's hard to come up with a good feature that really moves the needle as this one did.

Search Results A/B Test: Query Refinement

Another great feature we tested to educate users about conducting successful searches was query refinement. Based on a user's query, we tested showing them additional search terms they might find helpful. For example, if users search for "breakfast sandwich," they could be looking for many things:

Perhaps they're looking for a specific sandwich, breakfast in general, a bagel, or a café. Depending on where the user is, a search for "breakfast sandwich" may not return a lot of results, but a search for "breakfast" may return a lot. We used all the data from searches users conduct to generate a list of good recommendations for each search term, city, and time of day. This test was run on the mobile site and within the mobile app.

The default and alternate versions of a search results page appear in **Figure 2**. In the alternate version the query refinements appear at the bottom of the screen. The alternate version of the site and app led to a 13–14 percent increase in the number of completed searches. This feature was especially helpful to people when their search didn't return a lot of results, because the suggested terms could return much better results.

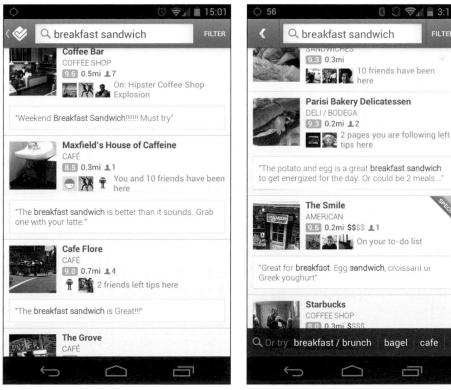

RECIPE A (DEFAULT)   **RECIPE B: +13 to 14% completed searches**

Figure 2 The default search results for "breakfast sandwich" and the tested version with query refinement suggestions at the bottom of the page, as viewed from the mobile app.

Jon Wiley, Lead Designer, Google Search

Jon Wiley leads the User Experience team for Google Search, working each day to make the search experience more usable, useful, and beautiful. Since 2006, Jon has had the opportunity to design for nearly every Google product. Prior to Google, Jon designed for Hoover's, managed web communications for Texas Governor Rick Perry, owned a theater, and performed improv and sketch comedy. Jon has starred in viral videos seen by millions, most recently as *The Autocompleter* on YouTube.

Google

Google's mission is to organize the world's information and make it universally accessible and useful. As of August 2013, Google was ranked as the #1 visited website in the world (source: Alexa.com).

How does Google innovate?

Innovation is a very exciting topic for me. At Google we have a relentless focus on our customers in terms of the problems they have and the perception of whether or not we're solving those problems. We have a fairly good process and methodology around innovation. We don't spend a lot of time dwelling on what was there before.

Innovation, and thinking about what we can do next at a high level, really involves going out into the world and listening. It's about being very open to seeing how people are going about their day-to-day activities, seeing the challenges they have, and identifying the opportunities we may have to address those challenges through our technology. We have a number of methods that we employ to listen to our users, and they're central to our development process.

As an example, we've been running a study for over a year now called Daily Information Needs (DIN). It's a fascinating study. We recruit people to participate,

and we have them install a mobile application called PACO, or Personal Analytics Companion, on their phone. It is a tool that we developed here at Google and have made available to the academic community for free. PACO uses a technique called "experiential sampling," which was developed by psychology researchers to collect data for social science experiments.

Throughout the day, PACO prompts participants and asks them, "What is the last bit of information you needed to know?" That information doesn't need to be tied to Google or the last thing they looked up on a computer. The study doesn't make any assumptions on how they might answer that question, because we're trying to address really basic information needs.

It turns out that people want to know about the weather and the time a lot. Of course they do; they're age-old things—time and temperature. The environment is tied to your day. There are also other questions like, "Why was my daughter mad at me?" which is very personal information that someone needed to know. The weather is on one end of the spectrum, and potentially, family psychology issues are on the other end. Within that spectrum, there is a range of information needs such as, "When do I need to check out of my hotel?" "Has my package arrived from Amazon?" and, "I need to learn about string theory for a paper I need to write."

We look at that spectrum of information and ask ourselves: "What are the things that Google is good at?" Questions like, "What is the weather?" or "What time is it in Shanghai?" we can do pretty well (**Figure 1** and **Figure 2**). But what about the other queries? From that point on it's a gap analysis. We look for ways to apply our technology and ability to organize information to help them find that answer or to connect them with someone who can help them, because there are plenty of resources on the web with which to connect them.

For example, in the DIN study, a question someone asked was, "What color should I paint my bedroom?" If you ask Google that, I think you'll get some okay responses. Google at this point is intelligent enough to know you're asking about bedrooms and colors,

and you'll probably get some good web results for that. But if you're listening to a conversation between two people, and one of them has a fair amount of knowledge about interior design and the other asks that question, the first response would not be "red" or "green." The first response would be a question like, "What colors do you like?" "How many windows do you have?," or "What are the materials you have in your furniture?" They would start asking questions that open up possibilities and avenues for answers. We think about a simple question like that and the natural track that would follow from someone trying to answer that question, and then we look at Google and say, "What can we do here?" "How can Google start asking questions in return?" or "How can we help people refine their query so they can get to a better answer faster?" These open-ended questions generate a ton of additional questions about how we could try solving that problem. We might

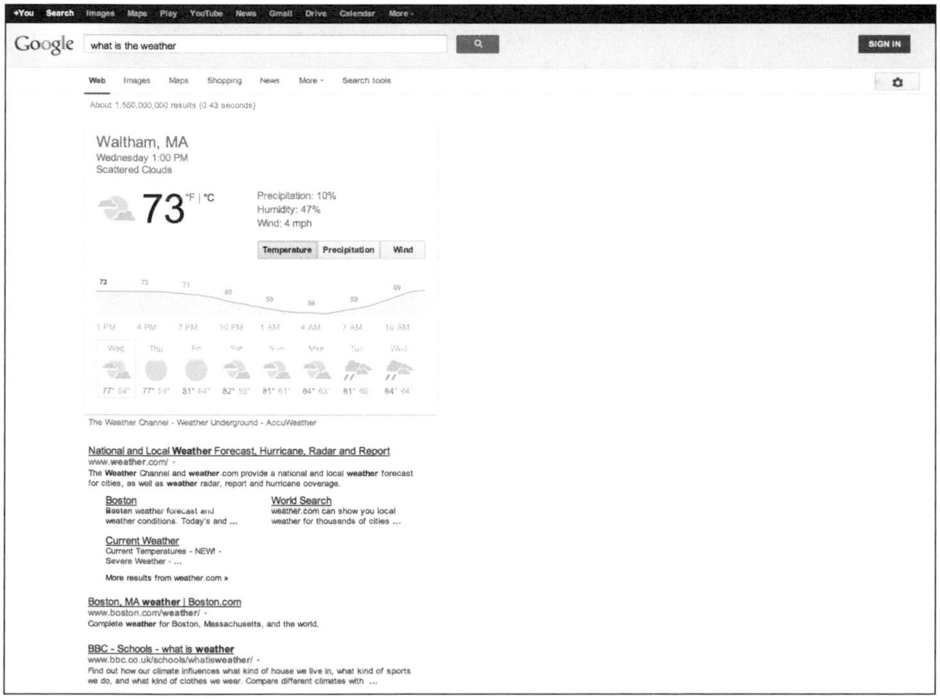

Figure 1 A Google search result for "what is the weather."

Figure 2 A Google search result for "time in shanghai."

find we need to invent some new technology or do a better job of indexing websites that have information about interior design. We try to innovate by always asking ourselves really hard questions about the gaps between people's needs, what Google can do to help, the technological limitations, and how can we try to get around them.

Another example of how we listen to customers are field studies. In these we'll conduct very open-ended interviews. Field studies are about going out and having a conversation with people to see what kinds of problems people are facing.

We also have technology innovations. For example, a jump in technology might come from the engineering team. Then my team, the UX team, will ask ourselves, "Now that we have this technology, how do we apply it to a need people may have?"

How does an innovative idea start to become a Google product or service?

Once we've got a problem we want to solve for, and a path set to solve it for our users, we start developing a product or a series of product solutions. At this point, it's primarily an evaluation phase based on practical measurements, including aspects that are both qualitative and quantitative.

Qualitative aspects include observing users. We have research labs on campus, and we recruit users to come in and use our products. For example, they might use prototypes or go through card-sort experiences. It's your typical user-research lab environment. Our labs are equipped to measure a multitude of devices, including mobile, desktop, laptop, and tablet. How people use multiple devices throughout their day is a big part of our research, because we want to make sure we create a great experience across devices.

There are also high-level quantitative aspects of what we do. Maybe what Google Search is most famous for is running hundreds and hundreds of experiments. We have the luxury to run a lot of experiments. We have a fantastic infrastructure for it. We can run a lot of experiments and gather a lot of statistically significant results in terms of how our solution is performing based on user behavior.

At the same time, experiments don't measure everything. They're not perfect. They can tell us what users do, but very rarely can they tell us why. So we pair our quantitative analysis with our qualitative analysis. From the data, if it looks like users are having a problem with a particular part of the solution, we'll go into the lab to see if we can learn what's really happening at that point.

We also combine the quantitative and qualitative measurements when we run surveys on search results. Asking is a great way to get information, though you have to factor in the biases, because there's a self-selection component to the fact that someone decided to answer a survey. You also have to be very careful when asking users what they want and what they perceive, because people aren't always able to accurately articulate the reason for their behaviors. You may end up getting swayed in the wrong direction if you only rely on self-reported information. For these reasons, it's very important to observe people firsthand and to look for patterns and trends in the data.

There's also an internal process we call "dog fooding," as in "we eat our own dog food." As Googlers, we use our products every day. Googlers use almost all of the same products as our users to run our business. Gmail, Google Calendar, Google+ Hangouts, and Google Search are all examples of products we use internally. Googlers tend to be some of our hardest critics on the quality of the service we're providing. We're never quite satisfied. It does mean that Googlers can be perpetually grumpy, because a lot of times we live on the cutting edge of these products

and see that "Oh, this is a bug," or "This doesn't work." The products get a lot of stress testing just right here inside of Google. We try to suffer the pain so our customers don't have to. We also have to recognize that Googlers represent only a small fraction of use cases and points of views of the problems to be solved.

All of these aspects—qualitative, quantitative, dog fooding, surveys, and also user-submitted feedback—play a role. One aspect doesn't dominate the evaluation. We take each as one grain of sand in a lot of grains of sand in terms of evaluating the success of our products. Throughout this process we're continually iterating and refining our solutions as much as we can.

How do you balance optimizing existing products and services with creating entirely new experiences?

That is very hard to solve—even at Google. How do you take optimization, or the daily keeping the lights on—making things faster and better, launching and iterating—and balance that with taking a longer view, really trying to get out of the box and try some truly disruptive things? To answer that, we go back to how we innovate: really listening to users, being open-minded about the problems they have, and not tying potential solutions to any particular ideas about existing technology.

For example, a few years ago we launched Google Instant, which is a search feature that shows results as you type. We first developed that product by asking, "How can we make Google faster?" Google was already the fastest search engine in the world. We wanted to make it faster because we knew that speed, and being able to get to an answer quickly, were critical to how people think Google is helping them solve their problems. We came up with some solutions where we said, "For us to do this, we would have to change the speed of light." And we thought, "That one's tough." But asking those questions pushed us to ask, "What are some optimization solutions, short of changing the speed of light, in our technology and algorithms to make this possible?" We try to find a big problem that users have and start exploring ways in which we can help solve it.

People sometimes say not to ask customers what they want. I don't believe in that. There's the possibly apocryphal Henry Ford quote, "If I'd asked people what they wanted, they would have asked for faster horses." That quote gets at the heart of what I was saying earlier about listening and observing users. People then take that quote and say, "You shouldn't ask people what they want, because all you'll get is 'faster horses,' not innovation." I think that's a misguided view. It's certainly dangerous to ask users what they want, because it could be hard for users to conceive of the solution. But when you ask, "What do you want?" and they say, "Faster horses," you need to listen to them. What they actually said was, "I need a faster way of getting from point A to point B." We can then ask ourselves, "Using all of our technical expertise, what could we do that would make that possible?"

The approach we take at Google about innovation is we just try to listen to people. The answers are there. People are telling you—maybe not directly, maybe not verbally—but people are telling you what the problems are in their lives. Listening is the hard part. This is why innovation is hard. This is why everybody is not an entrepreneur building a start-up. Listening, and turning what you learn from listening into an innovative solution, is really hard to do. It's hard even for Google to do. Certainly, we try to get better at it, and we have pretty well-refined processes for it. The great thing about working in technology, and on the forefront of this problem-solving space, is we never know when a disruption—that brand-new innovation we never saw coming—is going to come along. It's fun and exciting.

The most recent disruption is the development of touchscreen mobile devices. I think practically everything is going to have a touchscreen pretty soon. Interacting with a keyboard and a mouse versus

physically interacting with software makes a big difference to the experience. That's a big disruption. It changes how we think about things. For example, mobile devices are driving voice interaction through Google's Voice Search. This leads to the ability for Google to ask questions and for a user to have a conversation with something like Google. This transforms what kinds of things people think they can do with their lives, and those changes cascade throughout people's lives. So, when I think about innovation, it's about innovating within the company's current products and services, but also innovating in the space where lots of people are trying to solve all sorts of problems. And those solutions feed off one another. It's a really exciting space.

Design experiments aren't always well received by designers. What is your point of view?

This is a really interesting and complicated issue. When talking about the analysis of design, there's a story that's frequently brought up about Google. The story is about a gentleman named Doug Bowman, who is a very talented designer. When Doug left Google, he wrote a blog post about Google overanalyzing design, which was picked up in the press. His examples involved an overreliance on quantitative data to make subtle design decisions, such as whether a border should be three, four, or five pixels wide or testing 41 different shades of blue. Doug was highlighting something that is always a danger in terms of any analytical approach to thinking about design, which is an overreliance on one particular method of analysis. We have several methods; they each have their weakness and their strengths. We need to apply judgment around when each approach should come into play.

I very much use data with design because that's the way in which I can measure whether my solution is working. Data is a very important aspect of design.

We need to be able to answer, "Are we solving the problem we want to solve?" "Are people using it?" and "Are people happy with the product?" Measurement involves listening, feedback mechanisms like the ratings you get in an app store, and quantitative design experiments. When you start getting to the scale of companies like Google, where we have people who are using our products all over the world, in multiple languages, multiple times a day, you have sophisticated methods of measuring whether or not your design is really solving the problem. Those methods make a real difference in terms of the actual satisfaction that people have with the solution.

I think a lot of the debate is driven because in the press it's a good story. Right now, the latest story is flat versus skeuomorphic design, as if those are two sides of a coin. The whole debate around these things is just silly. There's a spectrum there, and more important, there are different solutions to different problems. Some solutions are more appropriate to the set of constraints of one problem, and another problem may have a different set of constraints, requiring a different set of solutions—those are all fine.

It matters whether or not a user is getting the right and relevant answer from a search as quickly as possible. Even a handful of milliseconds are things we want to shave off. So, if a particular horizontal rule, with a particular color of gray gets people to their answer 100 milliseconds faster than another particular shade of gray, all things being equal, I'm going to pick the one that gets them there faster. This is one of the things that sets Google apart from other companies and may be why it's sometimes a little harder for designers in other companies to see their way through this debate. The sophistication of the measurement technology and analysis we have, in terms of listening to our users beyond just what they say, enables us to measure subtle changes in the experience, good and bad, and that optimization is important. Those optimizations add up. Each one might be very small, but if you add them all up, in

terms of the full set of the different types of problems people come to Google Search with, those optimizations make a difference.

What success metrics do you track?

When we think about the search experience, there are a lot of things we look at measuring. We try to always match up quantitative data with the qualitative observations in the lab. If people are having trouble in the lab, we observe whether why they are having trouble matches what we see in our live experiments.

There are tons of metrics that we look at as we try to make a judgment of whether people are having a good experience. I can't go into a whole lot of detail about all the particulars. As a designer who works on Google Search, my goal is to reduce the amount of friction between a user having a question and getting an answer to it. In terms of the actual metrics, most simply, we measure this: Are we helping people answer their information needs more often? The three most important aspects of that are the speed of serving the answer, the quality of the answer, and the ability for the user to ask the right question:

▸ The speed of Google Search is very important. We know if we increase latency too much for the search experience, people start having a bad experience. We know this from talking to people and them expressing, "It's slow and not a good experience." We also know this quantitatively by measuring engagement with search. The slower the search product is, the less engaged users become. They may not ask as many questions and may stop their research early. As an example, for some search results, we load a lot of images, and images add latency. We have to balance these features with images against the speed of the page. We have run A/B tests that simulate additional server processing time of a few hundred milliseconds when returning search results. The tests found that the average daily searches per user decreases over time but begins to increase back to normal once the delay has been removed (**Figure 3**).

▸ Answer quality can be difficult to measure through purely quantitative means. We have a whole other program in which human raters evaluate search results. For any algorithm change, or any ranking change, we have a very large program in which we're evaluating results against a set of metrics, including relevance and quality. Results should be of good quality with relevant information and devoid of spam.

▸ "Query formulation" is what we call people being able to know what to ask and how to ask it to get the answer they want. Users might have an information need, but turning that into a question Google can answer may be difficult. "What should I ask?" is sometimes the hardest thing to figure out. A lot of what we do is help users to quickly get to the question they want to ask. We can look at a pattern of searches and say, "This person probably didn't find what they were looking for." For example, within a particular session we look for people doing a lot of refinements and asking the same types of questions over and over again but not clicking on results; or, people clicking on a lot of search results links but not seeming to land on an answer. When we perceive people having trouble or struggling, we know they're probably having a bad experience. Sometimes, query formulation can be helped with an aspect of the design users don't see or aren't making use of, so we need to make it more visible. Conversely, something in the design might be too visible, getting in their way and slowing them down.

Another important aspect is access to search. Now, we have mobile devices and tablets, and they reduce the friction to get to Google to ask a question. Voice Search is another aspect of reducing that friction, because typing into mobile devices, especially long

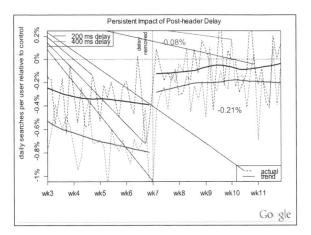

Figure 3 The average daily searches per user decreases if an artificial delay of 200 or 400 milliseconds is added to returning results. Average daily searches increase once the delay has been removed (in week seven in the graph) and trend toward the control value.

questions, is hard to do. As we'll discuss, the Knowledge Graph and Google Instant help users ask deeper questions and more quickly find relevant answers. All these play a role in lowering the barriers people have to asking a question and getting an answer for their information needs.

Since Larry Page became CEO again in 2011, Google has been even more focused on the user experience across products. Can you tell us more about the role design plays at Google?

That's been a big and exciting journey for Google, and for me, too, for the last few years. We're shoring up our design chops while maintaining all the stuff that's cool to Google. In some organizations, design might happen mostly upfront, like as part of the standard waterfall process where things get handed off. Google's designers tend to work from the very beginning through the very end of projects.

We start with the problem that our users are having that we're trying to solve. Designers are involved in brainstorming lots of solutions. We want to try to figure out amazing experiences for solving the problem. A team is then tasked with winnowing down the solution space to some promising sets of potential solutions that optimizes any number of variables, including how many people could be impacted, the degree to which the problem is being solved, and the speed with which we could deliver a solution compared to the speed of our other solutions, such as search. Designers participate all the way up through launch, when "we've got to tweak that pixel," and "we've got to change that piece." Designers also help to optimize solutions post-launch, because engineering will sometimes approach us to help polish something they have that needs an improved experience.

How is Google organized for design?

We have a number of design roles at Google. Within the design discipline members of my team include interaction designers, visual designers, and motion designers. My team also includes user experience researchers and specialists in qualitative and quantitative research. We also have an interface copywriter who spends a lot of time thinking about the text in our interfaces to create the best possible experience. All these roles are fairly common throughout the industry. As companies and teams scale they tend to have more specialization. A long time ago, when I worked at smaller companies, I was the only person who was a designer and I wore a lot of different hats. At Google, because the teams are large and the problems we're trying to solve are large, we end up specializing.

Teams at Google are organized around solving particular problems. For example, for Image Search, some people are focused on interaction design and some are focused on visual design. All team members are focused on multiple form factors. I don't have a mobile team or a tablet team; everyone is focused on solving a task across devices.

There's also a large support organization in terms of the products we're creating. Scaling up a product, through engineering, for an actual launch, is a very different beast than running through some fail-fast prototypes. The standard team makeup consists of a partnership between product managers, engineers, and designers.

How do product managers, engineers, and designers interact?

It depends. Teams tend to self-organize around skill sets. Organizing is about finding the right mix of skills to come up with ideas, build them, try them, and ship them to users. I've worn all those hats at Google. On some teams I've been the person fixing bugs and triaging; sometimes I'm the person really defining the vision for the product, and sometimes I'm organizing the team and getting people to execute on a solution. Although it's probably a fairly rare scenario, you might have a very thoughtful and visionary designer who is pushing a product vision through design work; the product manager might have a role that's more execution-driven and focused on making it all fit together with the engineers. It varies quite a bit across Google.

There are a whole lot of engineers at Google. There are fewer product managers by title, but they're abundant compared to the number of people with "design" in their titles. It's like that at many companies. Creating highly scalable, well-developed, and fast solutions requires a lot of engineers. Engineers build the solutions and make them work by fitting all the pieces together. How many people we have working on product is a strict function of that, because we need to have a very healthy product team in order for the business to make things. On the design side I can create a whole lot of products just by moving things around in Photoshop. Photoshop, and similar tools, are force multipliers for ideas. Actually going out and building them is another thing. It's kind of like the difference between an architect with the blueprints they create and the engineers and construction workers who have to go make those ideas real; that can be a much more challenging job.

We have a very engineering-driven company here at Google. Engineers are not just asking, "Is the code accurate?" "Is it tested?" and "Is this a great algorithm for solving this problem?" A lot of times our engineers are very involved in thinking about the user experience. Our engineers get involved in helping to define the solution space, and the same is true of our product managers.

I think the ideas of measurement and data analysis are part of the computer science DNA of the company. Larry Page, Sergey Brin, and Eric Schmidt are all computer scientists. Science is about trying to arrive at truth through analysis and experimentation. Scientists can be skeptical and are always asking, "Is it working?" "Could it work better?" and "Is what we think is true, actually true?" Questions like those are instinctual in the way a lot of people at Google think, especially if they have backgrounds in computer science. It's built into how they operate.

Carrying that through to design is a very natural thing for Google to do. I wanted to be an astronaut, and although I figured politics was against it, I still have a scientific mind. This isn't something that's unique to Google, but science is very, very strong in Google's culture, and it's also very strong in our design culture. We wouldn't be able to design at Google if we didn't have great relationships with our engineering and product partners. In order to have great relationships, designers need to be able to talk the talk and walk the walk. Science is inherent in the makeup of the people who started Google; it's part of our DNA and runs throughout the company.

Visual Examples

When we talk about big foundational changes, they tend to be less in the actual pixels and tend to be more in the capabilities of Google Search. Big changes come with big new capabilities. It's rare that we see a complete transformation, with an orders-of-magnitude difference in metrics, based on the design changes we make. The impact of the two changes we'll discuss, on the search results page and on the search box, were large by the measure of the day-to-day use of Google Search.

Search Results Page: Querying Sets

At Google we always run little experiments; one was called Google Sets. If you entered "Titan" and "Mimas," which are two of the moons of Saturn, it would fill in the blank with the other moons of Saturn, such as "Rhea," "Pandora," and so on. By the way, amateur astronomy is one of my hobbies, although I get to do less of it now than when I lived in Texas.

Fast-forward a decade, and Google has gotten to the point where we can start to really understand some of the people, places, and things that users are searching for. We call this the Knowledge Graph, and it contains hundreds of millions of objects with billions of facts and connections between objects. Google has a great amount of information and is starting to have knowledge about the world.

As we were developing the Knowledge Graph, I kept pulling up queries where users were looking for sets of things (**Figure 4**). So, we started developing this particular carousel feature to give rich information about these types of sets. Now, when a user searches for "moons of Saturn," they get a very nice set of the Knowledge Graph's names and images of the major moons, the Knowledge Graph card for Saturn, and links to all of the great web content (**Figure 5**).

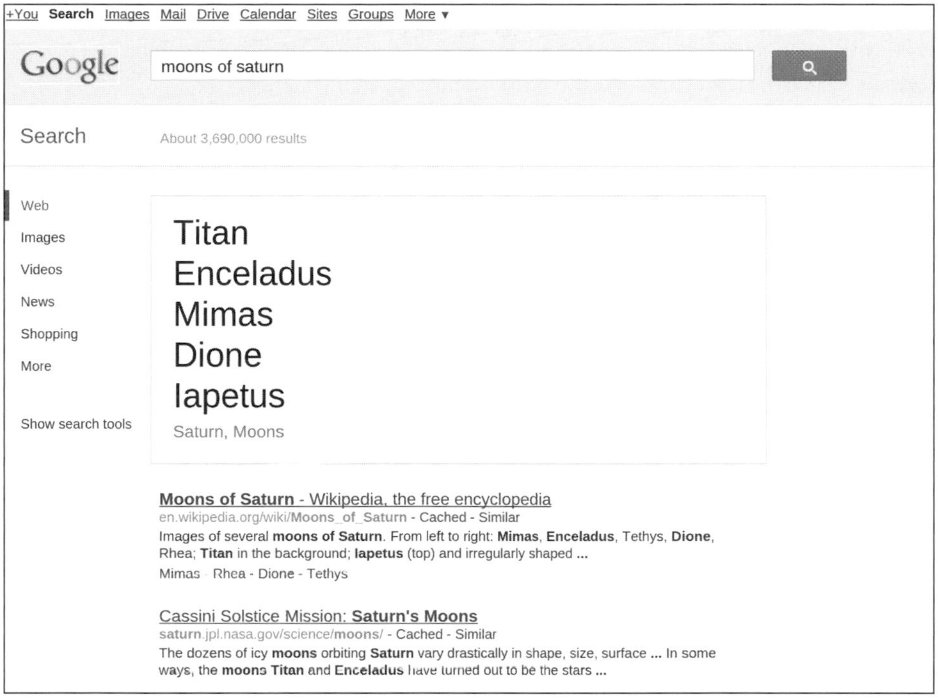

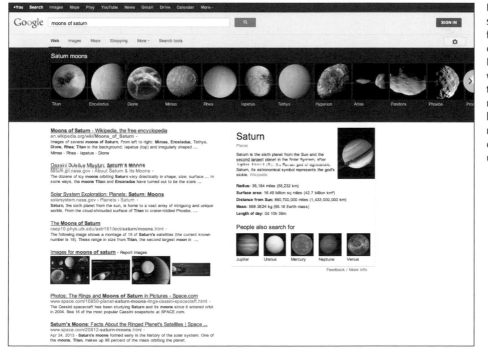

Figure 4 An example of a search for a set of items, in this case the "moons of saturn."

Figure 5 The tested search results redesign for a set of items. This design uses Google's Knowledge Graph, which contains information about hundreds of millions of objects and billions of facts and connections between those objects, such as the moons of Saturn.

This works on desktops, tablets, mobile phones, and more. This is a very rich and beautiful feature for these sets. You really get the sense that Google knows what you're asking about.

This is a fairly large change to the search results page. When brainstorming designs, we asked ourselves, "How do we go about representing these sets of information so we're doing good by the set and showing a good representation of the set's entities?" and also "How do we design across all the sets so the interface is something people can start to become familiar with, understand, and make use of on the search results page?"

If I was just shown the design in Figure 5, I probably would have been a little scared. I might have thought it could be disruptive in a bad way. We sometimes have concerns about whether adding features to Google may be more disruptive than helpful. We did a whole lot of research for this design, both qualitative and quantitative.

In qualitative lab studies we watched people use the feature and had conversations with them about their experiences. Users reacted in the lab very well to this. We found people were using the cards and carousel to get a nice quick summary when searching for people, places, and things. Users remarked that the card and carousel helped them understand that Google "gets what I'm talking about."

There's also a lot that went into our quantitative analysis and experiments. Through running experiments we were able to see whether or not people were successful on the search results page. Quantitatively, the carousel and card designs encouraged people to research the topic, and related topics, in much more depth than they were previously. It led them to ask more questions and learn more information about all of the knowledge in the set of those entities.

Before, a query for "moons of Saturn" may have gotten some great web documents, but then the user's research may have ended. Now, it gives them more of a platform to really dive into and say, "Yes, I want to learn more about Titan. I've heard about it in the news," or to click on Rhea and really see these are beautiful different worlds. Users are clicking more on web results and learning about all this great information available from NASA or Wikipedia. The card and carousel are about complementing the web results, and are part of the entire experience on the search results page. That's something we worked really hard on in terms of the design. The experiments quantitatively show that people are diving deeper into these sets, whereas before they may have stopped earlier.

We went through a series of design iterations based on research and worked hand in hand with engineering to iterate on this multiple times. We continue to add more ways of looking at sets that might require a carousel, like local information. I'm from Austin, so I'm always interested in Mexican restaurants in Austin, Texas. If a user types that into Google, they'll get a similar feature that allows them to have a deep exploration of this topic (**Figure 6**).

As we expand the ways to display structured information, there will be a continual evolution to make sure we stay true to our goals of giving users a way of exploring content and getting them help where and when they need it. The exploration tools help them to do this much faster. Our Knowledge Graph, and all of the features associated with it, are helping people enter a whole new class of queries that they really couldn't get to before. This is a good example of what has been a fairly complicated problem. It's been a tough needle to thread in terms of landing on a solution.

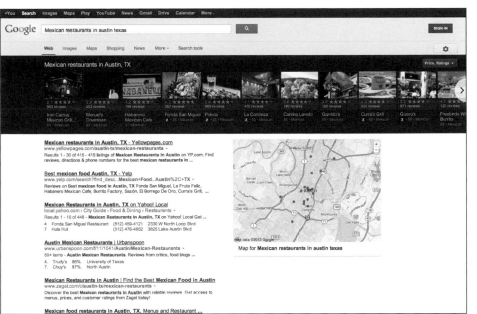

Figure 6 The tested search results redesign for a set of restaurants in a specific location.

Search Box: Search Box Size, Text Size, and Google Instant

The search box is a key part of the search experience. It's the window through which users have a dialogue with Google. If you look at the Google search box through the years, it's historically been pretty small. The reason is that the way it was originally implemented used the default size of a web form input box. Not a lot of effort was made to display it in any particular way, to change the size, or anything like that. Compare the design of the search box with the Knowledge Graph carousel and cards; the Knowledge Graph has a strong visual impact, whereas the search box doesn't. The search box is probably doing its job best if you don't think too much about what it looks like.

From December of 1998 (**Figure 7**) to a full decade later in December of 2008 (**Figure 8**), the search input box stayed roughly the same size. Then, in September of that year, it suddenly got bigger, as displayed in **Figure 9** in a screen shot from December of 2009. It's remained at the new, larger size through today, as shown in **Figure 10** in a screen shot from August of 2013. This very tiny change, which people may not have consciously noticed, actually had a pretty big effect on people's search happiness. When we say, "search happiness," we mean their overall happiness with their experience.

A couple of things happened in this change. By making the input box larger, we made the font inside of the box larger, too. People can see what they're typing more clearly because the font is bigger. Users can confirm they're typing what they meant to ask. The size more easily helps people catch things like spelling mistakes, although Google's already pretty good at that. Because query formulation can be pretty hard, the really big impact came with Google Instant, which adds autocomplete predictions as the

Figure 7 The Google homepage in December 1998.

Figure 8 The Google homepage in December 2008, which had changed very little since 1998.

Figure 9 The tested and redesigned Google homepage in December 2009 with a larger search box, which showed a large positive impact during testing.

Figure 10 The current Google homepage, in August of 2013.

user types (**Figure 11**). We had this feature prior to increasing the size of the search box, but the size of the autocompletions were commensurately small with the size of the input box. When we made the search box larger and all those autocompletions larger, people noticed them a lot more. This had the instant effect of people clicking on the autocomplete queries and getting to the results they wanted faster than when the search box was smaller.

Google Instant helps users to ask the questions that they meant to ask. When a suggestion appears via autocomplete, which is closer to what a user meant and they click on it, it's very likely they will get to the result they wanted more quickly than had they typed in their original query. Hopefully, they'll spend some time with the results and that will be indicative of a good experience.

This change didn't come up in the qualitative user testing in the labs; it was too subtle. But when we shipped it and ran experiments, we quantitatively saw that it made a large change. For any individual person, it may have made a difference in one or five out of ten searches. But globally, and over time, it makes a huge difference if users don't have to type in their questions two to three times, because they get what they want the first time. Google Instant can save each user two to five seconds per search, and based on global search volumes, that could be a savings of 11 hours every second. Google Instant has connected people with easier and faster ways to get their information, and the design substantially contributed to its success.

Figure 11 An example of autocomplete for Google search, which based on the number of people searching on Google can save up to 11 hours of typing every second.

Linda Tai, Director of Analytics

Linda Tai heads analytics and testing at Hightail. Prior to Hightail, Linda led marketing analytics and datamart teams at Intuit, Yahoo!, and Genealogy.com. In her previous career as an advisory engineer at IBM, Linda focused on disk drive manufacturing failure analysis to optimize the manufacturing test process. Linda holds BS and MS degrees in mechanical engineering from the University of Michigan and the University of California, Berkeley.

Hightail

Founded in 2004, Hightail, then called YouSendIt, started as a simple way to send the large attachments that email couldn't process but has since grown to offer robust online file storage, and sharing and management capabilities. Today, Hightail serves more than 43 million registered users across 193 countries, including professionals at 98 percent of the Fortune 500.

What are your business's goals?

We have a "freemium" business model, meaning we offer both free and paid products. Our free service allows people to save and share documents in the Hightail cloud, with no file expiration. We also have a premium subscription-based account that allows customers to send even larger files, gives them unlimited storage, and offers advanced control features.

What are your customers' goals?

Our customers are professionals who want to share their content, like graphics, legal documents, music videos, and architectural blueprints instantly and seamlessly across devices. They also want to be able to control permissions to view, edit, and share their content.

How do you measure the success of a test?

As a software as a service business (SaaS), we have a recurring revenue model through subscriptions rather than product sales. Because of the nature of our business, we optimize for monthly recurring revenue (MRR). We have also used lifetime revenue (LTV) as a success metric, based on retention curves of what percentage of customers we retain since they first subscribed (**Figure 1**). We update these curves on a quarterly basis for each product in order to model test results.

We also take care to evaluate important auxiliary metrics, because we want to be careful that we aren't optimizing for one metric at the detriment of another. For example, if a test results in a healthy

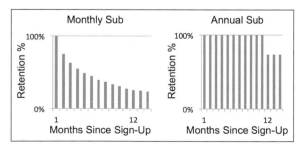

Figure 1 Retention of monthly and annual subscriptions.

MRR lift of 8 percent but registrations decline drastically, we figure out how to resolve the registration loss before rolling out the new design to all visitors.

Visual Examples

The following visual examples are from before YouSendIt changed its name to Hightail.

Homepage A/B Test: Remove "Buy It Now" CTA

Our homepage gets a very large amount of traffic, and it is the primary landing page for new visitors from organic search. The default version of the homepage, Recipe A in **Figure 2**, included two competing CTAs: "Free Trial" and "Buy It Now." For both of these CTAs, the credit card information is taken at the time of registration. For "Buy It Now" the credit card is charged immediately, whereas for "Free Trial" the credit card is charged 14 days later, assuming the customer hasn't canceled.

The Free Trial button historically receives more clicks and generates more subscriptions than the Buy It Now button. The alternate design, Recipe B in

Figure 2, shows only the "Free Trial" CTA. We thought that removing the Buy It Now button might increase subscriptions because customers would no longer need to choose between the two primary CTAs.

The results of this test were surprising because the default version of the page won, and Recipe B led to a 6 percent decrease in overall revenue. Our takeaway from this test was that the Free Trial button is more enticing and may seem more legitimate when paired with the Buy It Now button.

Plans Page A/B Test: Increase Product Storage Limits

Our Pro product included 5 GB of total storage, and because our market is competitive, we decided to test how sensitive our users are to storage limits by offering four different versions of the Pro plan (**Figure 3**):

▸ **Default.** 5 GB storage

▸ **Recipe B.** 10 GB storage

▸ **Recipe C.** 50 GB storage

▸ **Recipe D.** 100 GB storage

RECIPE A (DEFAULT)

RECIPE B: -2% revenue

Figure 2 The default and tested designs for the homepage.

Each version was the same price, so for Recipe D users would get a 20 times better deal on storage than for the default. We thought that Recipe D would certainly win.

The results were surprising, with the Default and Recipe B winning in a statistical tie. Recipe C led to an 11.6 percent decline in revenue, and Recipe D led to an 8.3 percent decline in revenue. In Recipes C and D, people were opting not to purchase at all even though we were offering them a better value. There could have been many explanations for this. Customers may have thought it was far more storage than they thought they needed; they may not have known how much space they needed; or the large numbers may have intimidated them.

This test taught us that we couldn't assume to know what our customers want. Just because we, as Silicon Valley professionals, value high volumes of storage doesn't mean our customers will. At the same time, it's important not to draw too many conclusions from just one test. For example, the results of this test may have differed had we messaged the larger storage capacity differently, and we will use testing to find out.

RECIPE A (DEFAULT)

Figure 3 Four different storage limits for the Pro plan were tested.

RECIPE A (DEFAULT): 5 GB

RECIPE B: 10 GB: +0.1% revenue

RECIPE C: 50 GB: -11.6% revenue

RECIPE D: 100 GB: -8.3% revenue

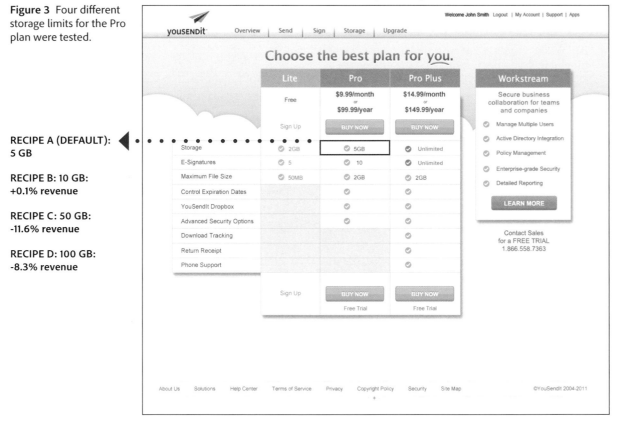

Phil Corbett, Product Owner for Digital Dashboard and Program Manager for A/B Testing

Phil is responsible for IBM's digital dashboard, which measures performance across IBM's business units in every geography. For the last seven years, Phil has also worked with a team of IBMers to support internal clients for A/B testing.

IBM

IBM is a global technology and innovation company headquartered in Armonk, New York. It is the largest technology and consulting employer in the world, with more than 400,000 employees serving clients in 170 countries.

What are your business's goals?

ibm.com's business goal is to provide our customers with the right expertise at the right time in the buying cycle. The products and services we drive revenue from are not necessarily something you can put in a shopping cart. The site includes services like downloading a white paper, watching an informational video, or reading an article. Relevant content drives customers to take actions that allow us to continue to communicate with them. We listen to our customers and are vigilant about measuring the effectiveness of our content for them.

What are your customers' goals?

That's a great question. We have a wide array of service, product, and content offerings. Our customers vary, and their roles can be technical or nontechnical. Examples include software customers coming to buy products or renew maintenance online, mainframe customers coming to upgrade service online, and C-Suite Executives coming to learn about our services.

One aspect that's shared across all our customers is that their time is valuable. We share in that like-minded view and try to make it as easy as possible for them to find the content they're looking for; hopefully, they'll then come back when they need something again or continue the conversation with us through other channels, like chat or a sales representative.

Can you tell us a bit about your organization's optimization program?

If they're digital leaders, everybody is trying to optimize their site regardless of where they're sitting. My team has internal clients, and the business goal for my team is to meet our client's expectations. Like other business-to-business companies our sites have a lot of stakeholders.

We've conducted a couple of hundred tests over the last several years, and it's growing faster and faster. So far, we've conducted 26 tests this year, and it's only May, so our speed is increasing. It used to take us a while; it used to just be me! Now we have more support from four to five people who are the core of the testing team. It's a band of people doing this because we love to do it. One of the things I'm working on is getting a larger formal team in place.

We're scientifically proving whether the designs are working or not. A lot of the times the tests will reveal data the teams are not expecting, and that's just the way that it is. We've gotten better, learned so much over the years, and streamlined the process to make it easier for tests to get set up and QA'd. We're educating all our internal clients, not just on why to test, but how you constantly have to iterate and keep the customer in mind all the time. One of our current challenges is making sure we actually implement the findings.

How do you measure the success of a test?

We have primary and secondary goals for each test. They can be anything from engagement or awareness to more traditional conversion-type goals like downloading code or trying a demo. On the ibm.com homepage, we're currently optimizing an algorithm to test showing different customers different content.

Our Smarter Planet site has some business tie-ins, but it exists more to share with our customers how IBM is making the world a better place through expertise and innovation. For example, it features how we leverage Watson's computational power, which is known for beating Ken Jennings at *Jeopardy!*, and apply it to the healthcare space. Watson can take in symptoms from patients and help determine a better treatment. There's no form completion around Watson; it's about engagement.

How do you keep track of results?

We have an internal blog that we use to keep track of results (**Figure 1**). The blog gives people some ideas to consider for testing. For example, we recently posted six themes we've found with our testing over the last six to eight months. The blog also explains to people how to get started with testing and has a form people can complete so we can help them test in their area of the business (**Figure 2**).

Figure 1 IBM's internal optimization website.

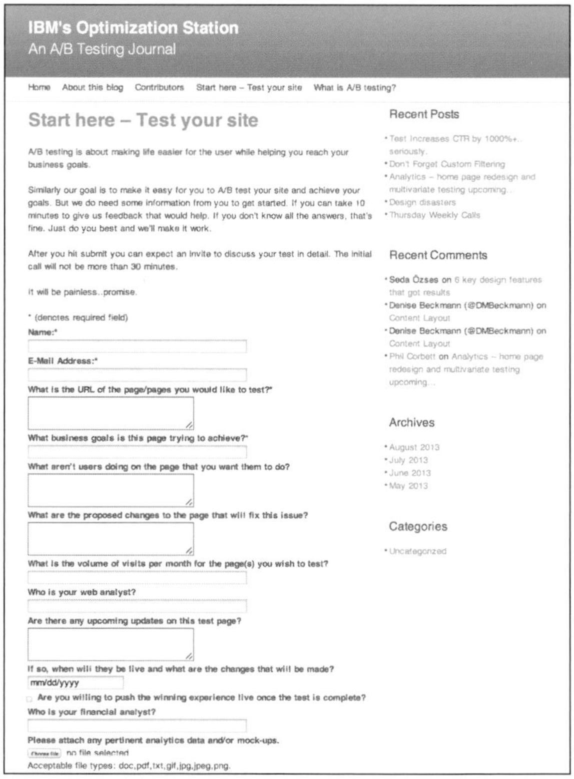

Figure 2 A form anyone in IBM can fill out to submit a test idea.

Visual Examples

The following two business cases are from when we started testing back in 2007. They follow the customer journey as they download intellectual capital.

Global Pre-login Page Element Discovery Partial Factorial Multivariate Test (3 elements x 2 alternatives): Messaging, Layout, and Link Style

Once a customer clicks to download intellectual capital such as software, a white paper, or a demo, and if they haven't already authenticated on the site, they will be taken to our global pre-login page. On this page they can click to sign in, proceed without an IBM ID, or register for an IBM ID. The primary conversion metric for this test was the sum of clicks to any of those three options. This page was run across the global template, so visitors from across the site who were interested in a range of products and services were entered into it.

The default version of the page appears in **Figure 3**. The three elements tested were:

- ▶ **Headline.** The default minimized the name of the product, demo, or white paper the customer was interested in by placing it beneath a headline in a small font; the alternate placed the product name in the headline.

- ▶ **Layout.** The vertical layout was tested against a horizontal layout that we hypothesized might be clearer, because it differentiated the two main actions by placing them in boxes labeled "Returning visitors" or "New visitors," shortened explanatory text, and also shortened the second link from "Proceed without an IBM ID" to simply "Guest login."

- ▶ **Link style.** The standard light blue underlined links with icons were tested against a larger font in a dark blue color without icons.

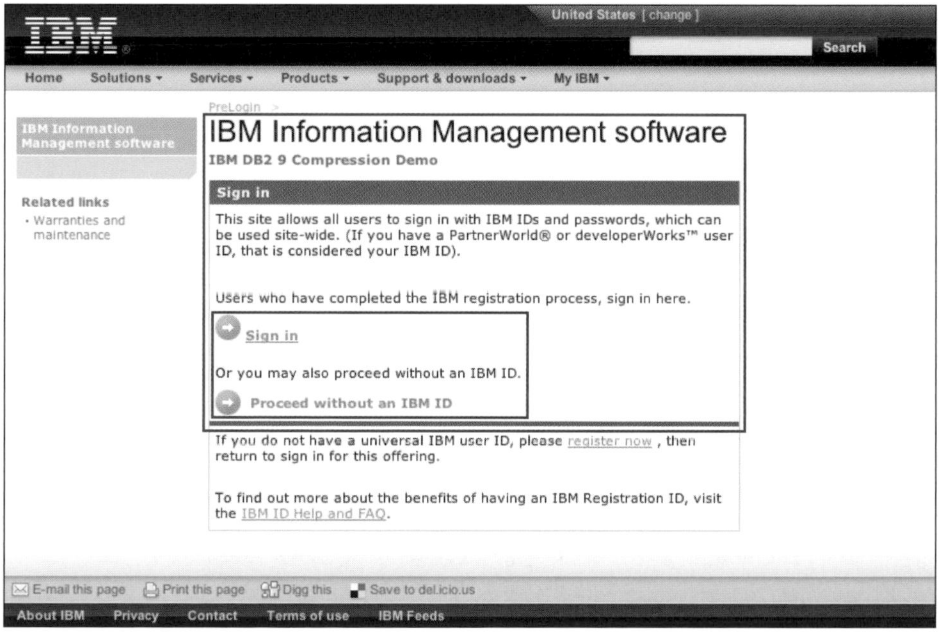

Figure 3 The default version of the page highlighting the three tested elements.

The winning version of each element is shown in **Figure 4**. The alternate versions of the headline and layout won, and the default version of the link style won. The most influential element was the layout. The winning version of the page led to a measured 5.67 percent lift in clicks to sign in, proceed without an IBM ID (or guest login), and register now (**Figure 5**).

Global Proceed Without an IBM ID Page Partial Factorial Multivariate Test (3 elements x 2 alternatives): Help Links, Address Form Fields, and CTA

The goal of this page is to have customers who don't have a login provide some personal information for us to better understand who is accessing our intellectual capital and to ask permission for our sales to contact the user at some point in the future. The primary conversion metric for this test was completed form submissions.

The default version of the page appears in **Figure 6**. The three elements tested were:

▶ **Need help box.** The default page contained three links to help customers who may be confused by the form. We hypothesized that these links may be a distraction, because they seemed redundant with one another, as well as with the explanatory text already on the main body of the page. The alternate version tested removing this element altogether.

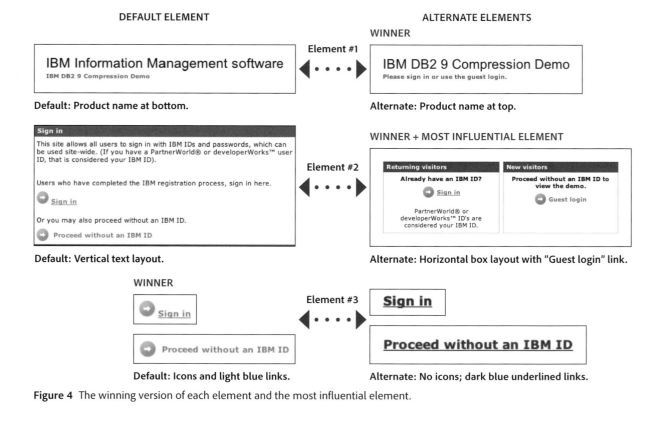

Figure 4 The winning version of each element and the most influential element.

RECIPE A (DEFAULT)

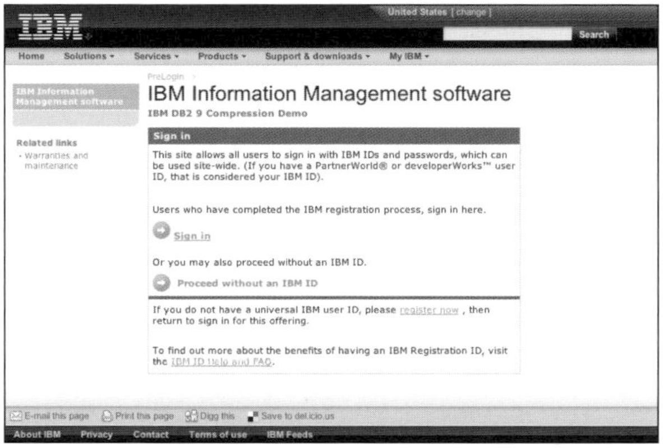

WINNER: + 5.67% clicks to: Sign in,
Proceed without an IBM ID (Guest Login), and Register Now

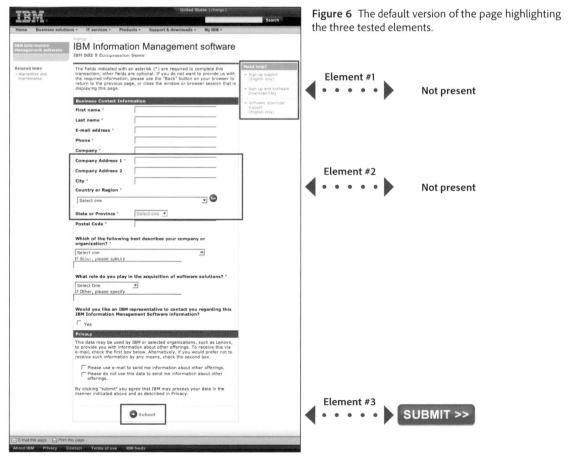

Figure 5 The default and winning versions of the page. The winning version of the page contains each winning element.

RECIPE A (DEFAULT)

Figure 6 The default version of the page highlighting the three tested elements.

Element #1 · · · · · Not present

Element #2 · · · · · Not present

Element #3 · · · · · SUBMIT >>

► **Address fields.** This section of the form asked for the customer's company address, city, country or region, and state or province. All of these were required fields on the default version of the page. Although the more information our salespeople had, the better, we also knew that users may not want to type in too much personal information. The best way to understand the trade-off was to put it to the test, so the alternate version tested removing these elements altogether.

► **Call-to-action.** The standard blue text link with an icon was tested against a large blue button to submit the form.

The winning version of each element is shown in **Figure 7**. The alternate versions, which removed the "Need help" box and the address fields won, and the default version of the CTA won. The most influential element was surprisingly the call-to-action button. The winning version of the page led to a 5.16 percent lift in completed form submissions globally across the site (**Figure 8**).

Figure 7 The winning version of each element and the most influential element.

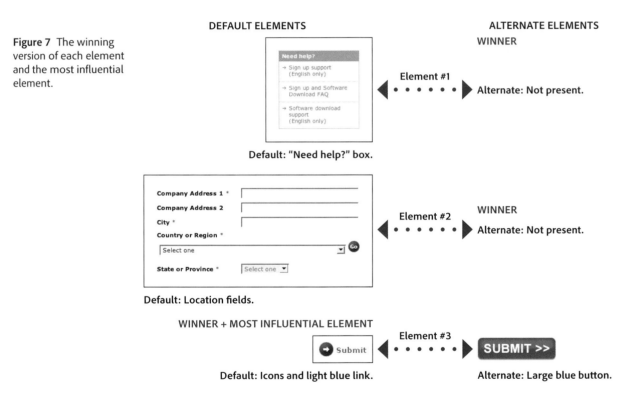

RECIPE A (DEFAULT)   WINNER: +5.16% completed form submissions

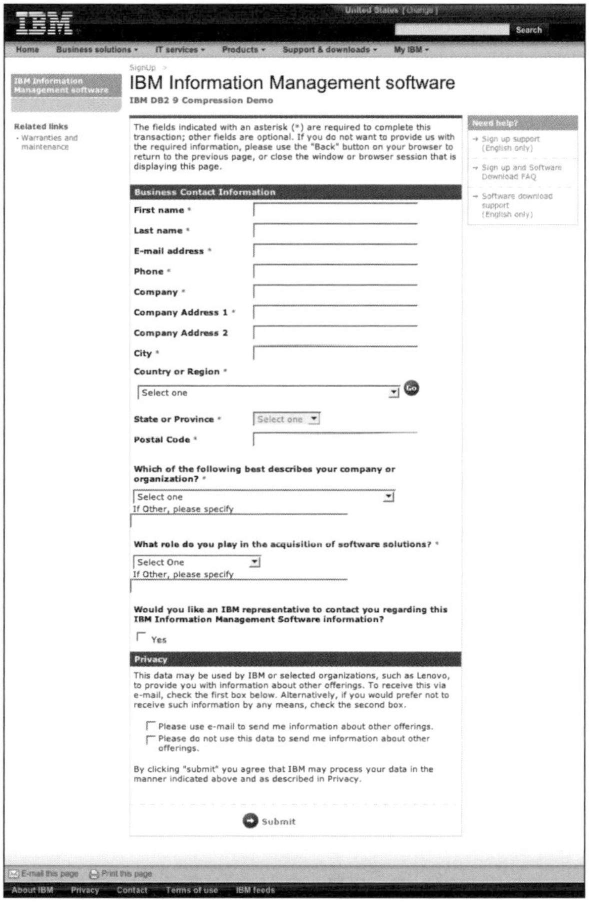

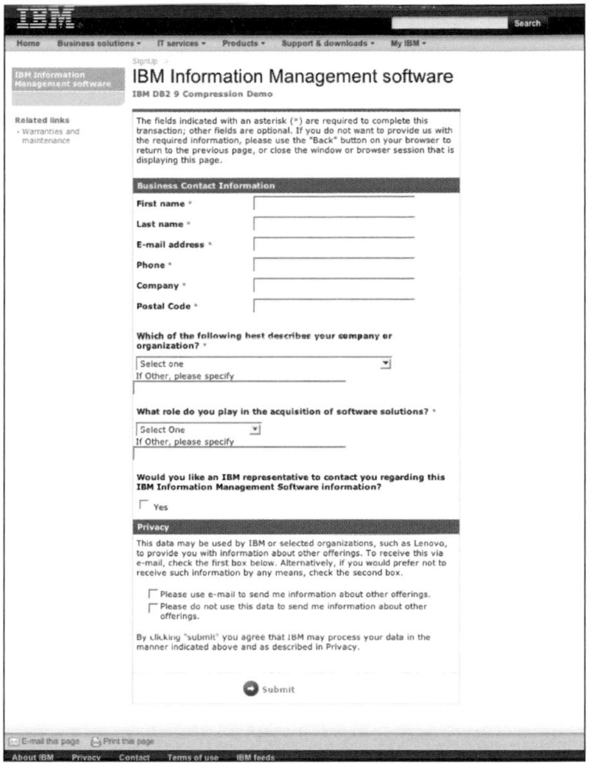

Figure 8 The default and winning versions of the page.

Amy Parnell, Principal Designer

Amy has worn a number of hats at LinkedIn, including lead designer, design manager, and principal designer. Throughout her various roles, Amy has always combined hands-on product design work with design mentorship, and direction and management of projects and people.

Amy recently led the redesign of the LinkedIn Homepage, Profile page, and Content and Community products including LinkedIn Today and the global navigation. Amy had to ensure the metamorphosis of these product designs met or exceeded key business metrics, rolled out within the same quarter, and above all was a smooth transition and created value for LinkedIn's members. Amy previously redesigned the Yahoo! Homepage, My Yahoo!, and Yahoo! Buzz. Amy holds one patent and has two patents pending for user interface inventions.

LinkedIn

LinkedIn is the world's largest professional network, with 225 million members in over 200 countries and territories around the globe. As of August 2013, LinkedIn was ranked as the #8 visited website in the world (source: Alexa.com).

What are your business's goals?

To connect talent with opportunity at massive scale.

What are your customers', or users', goals?

That depends on the audience segment and where they are on their career path. For example, our general users want to present a professional identity that helps them get found for new opportunities. Our recruiters and hiring managers want to find the right talent. Our outbound professionals want to network and find new business opportunities. Our

fastest-growing segment is students who are making decisions about their education based on the career outcomes of other students and alumni.

What is a good user experience with your business?

A good user experience is when we can simplify and hone an experience to help our members easily find the information they need, improve their professional identity, or get better at what they do. Our goal is to improve their productivity and increase their exposure to new opportunities. Examples of this include:

▸ Profile guided editing, which is when we can make helpful profile suggestions via a lightweight Q&A, which aids them in quickly and easily completing their profile. Having a completed profile helps them get found for new opportunities and maximizes their professional brand.

- Discovering new career opportunities through "jobs you may like," or having a recruiter send an InMail with a new opportunity. Many employed professionals are delighted to discover they are in demand or an even better position is available, helping them get closer to their career aspirations.

- Reading influencer posts about their industry, discovering great content via their network, or joining groups and discussing their skills and expertise—all ways that our members continually grow their knowledge base and expertise, making them better at their job and more marketable for the next position.

What are the largest challenges businesses in your industry are facing?

Fighting for people's time in a busy world. Presenting relevant information at the right time, which requires the ability to anticipate a person's needs before they may know them themselves. Keeping an experience simple and reducing the noise—presenting the single most valuable piece of information versus an endless menu of options.

How does your business innovate?

We have a number of ways we empower our employees to innovate. We have monthly hack days and quarterly incubator projects, and we frequently add these projects to our product roadmap. Every single employee is empowered and expected to come up with new business or design ideas. We are a ground-up product company.

Can you tell us about your organization's approach to design?

Often the project begins with an innovative concept from a designer on the team. The concept will first get circulated among designers and the specific product team, gaining momentum and the team's excitement. Then it may get included in presentations at product and company level all-hands, as a preview into where a product is headed, which gets the whole company rooting for the project. For completely new product ideas, another channel is our incubator program where new product ideas are pitched and selected by the executive team, and then an engineering and product team is commissioned and resourced to make it a reality.

During the development of a concept into a reality, the design will iterate and go through various review cycles with the design and product team. We'll frequently use our user research and data to inform the design idea and strategy, and then test the experience with our members when we have something tangible to demonstrate. If possible, we'll identify features or portions of the design we can build and A/B test along the way to test major hypotheses or high-risk changes that could impact key metrics. Once we have the go-ahead to move forward with the new product design, we'll roll it out to a small segment of our member base, and then gradually ramp up the experience to all members.

What role does user research play in design?

Research at LinkedIn happens at any point in the process. It can be conducted before design begins so we can learn about members during the design phase or after a product is launched to inform the next iteration. Each research project is conducted in collaboration with designers, product managers, and other product partners. They participate in user interviews to hear firsthand what members think and feel.

We believe in "insights by any means," blending different research techniques that we use according to what we're trying to learn. This includes both qualitative and quantitative methods, formal and informal, in-house and in the field. User research is essential to ensure our products are designed with consideration of our member's day-to-day realities, and how we can connect with them emotionally. We gain an understanding of the user's general experience, and then go deeper into specifics in order to identify opportunities we may not have considered.

How do you measure the success, or value, of a design?

We identify what our goals are and what success means at the outset of every design project. Success is frequently a combination of driving positive usage and engagement metrics as well as positive feedback from our members. We use industry standard measurements, such as pageviews and unique users, as well as flow analysis to understand which pages they came from and where they went to next.

If there's a linear flow we want them to get through, we'll look to see why they abandoned ship. Did they get confused? Was it taking too long? Did they just get fed up? Then we'll make iterative changes, like reducing a step, to see if that helps them complete it. We ask ourselves, what would make this easier? Are we asking too much? A lot of it is just trial and error through A/B testing. We also look at explicit feedback we get. We have a help center where users are able to file tickets, and we go through those on an ongoing basis. We do our best to try to help our users.

For example, one of the goals with the new profile design was to create a platform for professional identity that "makes our members look awesome." We value our member's experience above everything else and take any feedback we receive, whether it's signals from metrics or direct feedback, very seriously and constantly refine and improve our products based on this input. Our designs also strive for "global optimization," which means it's not just about moving one particular product-specific metric. It's about creating a cohesive experience across all of LinkedIn: Our previous version of the profile had a top section that repeated a ton of the information that was lower on the page.

Another example is the global navigation. Our previous version of the global navigation had 40+ links on it and we redesigned it down to about 15. From a business case standpoint, we'll hear, "Why would you remove that link? Even if it only gets 1 percent of the clicks, it's still some engagement to that product."

You have to balance that data with how much information is thrown at a user every day. We're fighting with other inputs in the world for their attention. We needed to sacrifice clutter and weight for longer-term engagement and organic repeat visitors to the site. There are trade-offs, and sometimes you have to go with your gut. The other option would have been to throw everything on the page and let the user have to figure out what to do. We found with previous incarnations of the page and navigation where we did that, users didn't know what to do. If you were just designing by the numbers, you would keep adding more and more.

How do segmentation, targeting, and personalization impact design?

Hugely. We constantly cater our designs to the specific audience segment and individual member. We consider their "persona" as well as their unique, personal characteristics. We are very focused on ensuring all member experiences on LinkedIn are as relevant and personal as possible. Personal relevance impacts the content we showcase, the recommendations we make, and the products we suggest. However, we do try to "design with one pen" so we adhere to a consistent design aesthetic, brand, and interaction pattern library.

For example, when you come to your homepage, you're going to see a personalized feed of updates from people you're connected to and people and companies you follow. The structure of the page stays the same, but the content is personalized.

There are also certain tools that some people may use more than others. For example, in our new mobile phone application, the navigation is personalized and responsive to user behavior. There are a few fixed navigational items, and there are shortcuts to things we see the user doing the most. We also let users add their own shortcuts. We want to make sure we give users the right information, at the right time, to help them do their jobs better. We also create specific tools for different segments. Our flagship product is LinkedIn Recruiter, and that's a completely targeted product that's designed for that one type of segment. All of the above also applies to designing for mobile.

How is your business organized for design and optimization?

User Experience Design (UED) is part of the product organization. Our SVP of Product includes "& User Experience Design" in his title, because he values the experience as a critical aspect of the product's success. Three key aspects make the UED team successful:

1. We are equal partners with our product managers, engineering leads, and other functional stakeholders. We contribute to product strategy and have the ability to detain a launch if we feel the experience is not up to par.

2. Our team includes web developers, which means we are both equally accountable for the quality of the experience and the fit and finish of the final implementation.

3. We frequently move people around. We don't let designers get stuck in one silo.

These three key aspects ensure that we execute an extremely high quality product experience. Our design team thinks about LinkedIn as a cohesive business, not just one product vertical. This practice also benefits the individual: They gain a wealth of experience across numerous products and audience segments.

Regarding optimization, our team continually tests and optimizes its products. There is no concept of "it's done." Instead, we rally behind "next play." Once we complete a milestone, we're immediately on to the next iteration.

How has the field of design changed in the last few years?

I believe our current industry trend is for digital product companies to build in-house product design teams. There is less dependency on external agencies to create digital products or experiences, as compared to around the year 2000 and the era of mega digital agencies like Organic, ModemMedia, Razorfish, and so on. Internal product design teams are able to have more ownership and leverage long-term product research to iterate and improve their business.

Any key pieces of advice about starting and scaling a design practice?

Get the culture, values, and trajectory started in the right direction. It's extremely hard to change later.

Visual Examples

Email Template A/B Test: CTA on Mobile

We will frequently A/B test CTA buttons on emails or other prompts. Often a simple language change will have a dramatic change in click-through rate (CTR). We will also frequently test order and placement. Often, moving things into a different position will have a big impact; for example, having a button in a banner, versus a right rail, versus embedded in the content. We recently updated our email templates to ensure the CTA button was above the fold on a mobile display. We saw a huge improvement in CTR, because mobile users could now see what to click without scrolling (**Figure 1**).

Figure 1 The default email template had CTAs below the fold; the redesigned template pictured here with above-the-fold CTAs, led to a huge increase in the click-through rate.

Profile Template A/B Test: Guided Editing

We frequently test steps in a flow, such as registration. We ask: "Where is the drop-off?" "Will it help if we reorder the steps?" "Consolidate them?" and, "Break them in to more steps with less information or fewer inputs and choices?"

For example, I worked on guided editing of a user profile. Previously, when a user went to edit their profile, we would put them on a page with all these blank form fields. It was a ton of form fields and it was a ton of work for the user. We wanted to make it easy, lightweight, and not overwhelming. We changed

it to a guided process in which we walked the user through editing their profile one field at a time.

It meant we had to prioritize. We may only ask three or so of those questions in a sequence, and then we're done. Someone may argue that we don't get that fourth, fifth, or sixth piece of information. Overall, it's okay because it's net positive, and we don't need to get it all at once. We can look at profile completion data and see that completion rates increased. We can also segment the data by basic completion versus rich profile completion and see that we moved more people from one segment to the next with guided editing.

When we designed the profile guided editing flow, we tested a few variations of the entry point, which is a prompt that sits on top of the user's profile. Most of the options we tested used different language in the messaging and call-to-action button (**Figure 2**). One version of the A/B test skipped the prompt altogether and simply asked the first question in the guided editing flow—a question you could confirm with a yes/no answer: "Hi [*name*], do you still work at [*company name*]? Yes / No" (**Figure 3**). That option outperformed any marketing messaging we could use. Whether the response is a yes or no, we've started a conversation with someone. If they say yes, we can ask the next question. If they say no, we can ask, "Where do you work now?" Once they answered that first question, we'd ask another, and they were hooked into the flow. This design helped clear the barrier to filling out a profile that felt like so much work by turning it into a lightweight human conversation.

These tests helped pave the way for the types of sweeping changes we've been able to make at LinkedIn. If we're able to simplify, we're able to increase new member growth and overall customer satisfaction—that's what drives the business forward.

Our design philosophy is if we keep it human, lightweight, simple, and conversational, it will pay off.

RECIPE A (DEFAULT)

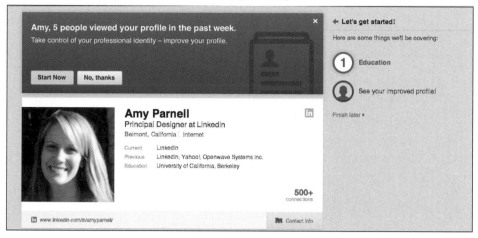

Figure 2 The default version of the guided editing experience, which asked a user whether or not they wanted to start editing their profile.

RECIPE B

Figure 3 The winning alternate version, which jumps right into the profile editing process.

Kenyon Rogers, Director of Digital Experiments

Kenyon Rogers built and continues to oversee the expansion of Marriott's centralized optimization program. Marriott's optimization team provides thought leadership, support, and enablement services to the global Marriott organization.

Marriott International

Marriott International is a leading lodging company with over 3,700 properties in 74 countries and territories worldwide.

What are your business's goals?

Marriott International's goals are to provide impeccable service to our customers by fulfilling all of their needs.

What are your customers' goals?

Our customers fall into three groups: owners, franchisees, and guests.

- ▶ Our owners are looking to increase shareholder value of the company through expanding the pipeline of available rooms and bringing in more franchisees and guests.

- ▶ The franchisees look after "heads and beds," meaning they're looking to make sure each guest has easy access to everything he or she could possibly need. They look to two metrics to indicate the demand and the health of the hotel: Revenue per Available Room (RevPAR) and Average Daily Rate (ADR).

- ▶ Our guests' goals are to find the right travel opportunity based on their travel needs. As these goals get more specific, they become dependent on the phase of the travel experience: pre-planning, planning, travel, on-property, and post-stay. As you can imagine, our guests' goals during each of these phases are starting to revolve more around digital (adjusting reservations from a mobile phone due to a delayed flight, etc.).

Our digital research team has goals for room bookings, the Marriott Rewards program, and Marriott credit card acquisitions. We're primarily focused on distribution of our inventory through our website, Marriott.com; our mobile platforms; and our partners, like Expedia.com, Travelocity.com, Taobao.com in China, and so on. If certain properties have deals, we want to make sure our partners have access to them, too. Marriott's digital platform is a great strength, because it affords us the ability to move rooms and evangelize hotel properties better than our competitors. Although it's easy to see results quickly from optimization, travel and lodging are usually not spontaneous purchases, so influencing long-term incremental growth is challenging.

How do you measure the success of a test?

Bookings, room nights, micro-conversions, and offline metrics are used in tandem to assess the long-term impact of our efforts. Directly measuring revenue during a test is nuanced for several reasons. Prices fluctuate in lodging, so we have guests booking hotel rooms ranging from the hundreds of dollars to the hundreds of thousands of dollars on their credit cards through Marriott.com. Similarly, because lodging is pseudo-perishable, the same room's price can vary depending on how far in advance the room is booked. It's also important to remember guests can cancel reservations without getting charged, so we need to make sure to understand whether the rooms that were booked led to completed stays.

This just means that we need to be very careful when calculating results. For example, we'll use segments based on a traveler's location, where they're going, their loyalty status, and whether we think they're traveling for personal or business reasons to determine whether we think their behavior is changing due to the tested experience. Marriott.com is currently responsible for about 23 percent of all room nights booked, so we also need to look at the business holistically to understand any channel shift when we run tests. For example, in many cases, we'll still get the business whether it is booked through Marriott.com, a partner like Expedia.com, or through our call center. Through testing, we need to illustrate whether we're driving an overall increase in bookings and room nights.

Incorporating all of the above, we are able to estimate an increase in revenue from testing. In 2011, we identified 9 campaigns out of 55, with a total average increase in revenue of around $168 million. In 2012, we identified 11–13 campaigns out of 57, whose average was $450 million.

In many cases we have tested winners several times to confirm results and have seen some consistent results year over year. We will also test combining winning designs to determine whether the net effect is additive or whether one winning design will overwhelm the rest.

Visual Examples

Homepage A/B Test: My Account Panel Appearance

Marriott.com sees over 400 million visits on an annual basis, and about 80 percent of our bookings are influenced by our Marriott Rewards members, who make up only about 20 percent of our online traffic. This is part of a series of tests that was intended to understand which variation would be a better landing page for Marriott Rewards members, understanding that they're the minimum of overall traffic but the majority of revenue.

We ran a test in which the homepage would load with the "My Account" panel open in the upper right of the page (**Figure 1**). This panel allows Marriott Rewards members to more quickly log in, and we saw about a 1 percent lift in room bookings with statistical significance. At first we didn't understand how that could possibly be true, because booking a room was far downstream from the homepage. So, we ran the test multiple times later in the year and saw the same results. In our analysis, a lightbulb went off: The new design increased logins by 2.5 percent, and when a member has logged in, our reservation process goes from a four-step process to a three-step process, because they can skip the step where they enter their personal information. That tiny result helped evolve how we've framed testing for our Rewards customers. There was initially some pushback around exposing the "My Account" panel due to it blocking content, but the test showed that whatever the panel was blocking must not be especially meaningful content.

Homepage A/B Test: My Account Panel Placement

Because the aesthetic of the homepage with the "My Account" panel open wasn't to our liking, we tried a few variations. One version tried having it open only on hover, but that didn't test as well as

RECIPE A (DEFAULT)   RECIPE B: +2.5% logins, +1% room bookings

Figure 1 The default and alternate versions of the homepage. Recipe B has the "My Account" module in the upper right open, whereas Recipe A does not. Even though the cards in the center of the page differ in the above designs, they were not part of the test and change regularly.

having it open. We then decided to test pulling the "My Account" panel into the cards (**Figure 2**). The primary card in Recipe A was to book a room, and we were confident that it was easy to find. The question we were asking with this test was whether we could prioritize at least one additional topic. We made the "My Account" card equally prominent in Recipe B, and there was no impact to bookings, which suggested that we could further engage our most valuable segment to log in without distracting our non-Rewards members. This test also helped to increase traffic to learning more about Marriott Rewards and our credit card, all without negatively impacting bookings.

Homepage Automated Targeting: Two Card Offers Based on Individual Visitor Models

The goal of this test was to increase traffic into our booking funnel by tailoring promotions based on information we knew about the visitor. All of the

visitor data used for this test was anonymous and not tied to any personally identifiable information: We take our customers' privacy very seriously. This test set aside the middle two cards in the homepage for targeting (**Figure 3**). Those two cards would change on a visitor-by-visitor basis based on anonymous data associated with their cookie, such as their location and their browsing behavior on Marriott.com. We created over 14 different sets of offers, and they were displayed based on where the automated model determined visitors might be looking to book a stay. There were offers for popular northeast destinations, such as New York, Boston, and Philadelphia; popular West Coast destinations, such as San Francisco, Honolulu, and Las Vegas; and so on. The results from testing this automated model against the control were wonderful. It generated a 21 percent lift in room bookings, just by showing people offers they were more likely to find helpful.

RECIPE A (DEFAULT)

**RECIPE B: +6.5% logins,
+57% clicks to learn about Marriott Rewards,
+26% clicks to learn about Marriott Rewards Credit Card,
FLAT in room bookings**

Figure 2 The default and alternate versions of the homepage. Recipe A has the "Book Right" in the front and the "My Account" module open in the upper right. Recipe B has the "Book Right" and "Marriott Rewards" modules both open in the front. The other cards in the recipes change regularly.

TARGETED CONTENT: +21% room bookings

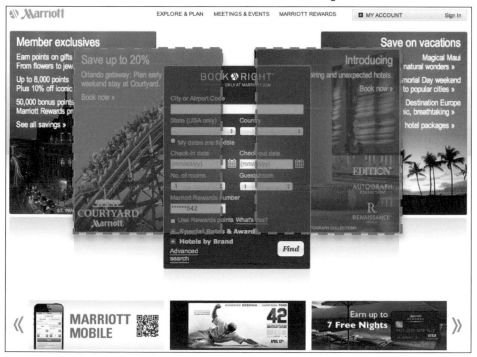

Figure 3 The two highlighted cards would be determined individually for each customer based on anonymous visitor data and the visitor's perceived preference. The homepage with cards generated using this type of modeling was tested against the default version of the site where cards were manually changed for all visitors at regular intervals.

Hotel Page A/B Test: Clickable Hero Image

This flight of tests came about in Q4, because performance for our non-Rewards members was low for the year, and we had extra budget allocated to improving it before the end of the year. The Marriott Marquee and Renaissance properties have their own sites, and they are the top of the funnel for our non-Rewards members.

Photo tours are popular with customers, but in order to access the photo tour, a customer would need to click on the "view photos" link on the bottom-left side of the hero image (**Figure 4**). For Recipe B we tested hyperlinking the main hotel image by making it clickable and having it lead to the property's photo tour. This led to an 18 percent lift in photo tour views and a 1.5 percent lift in nonmember bookings.

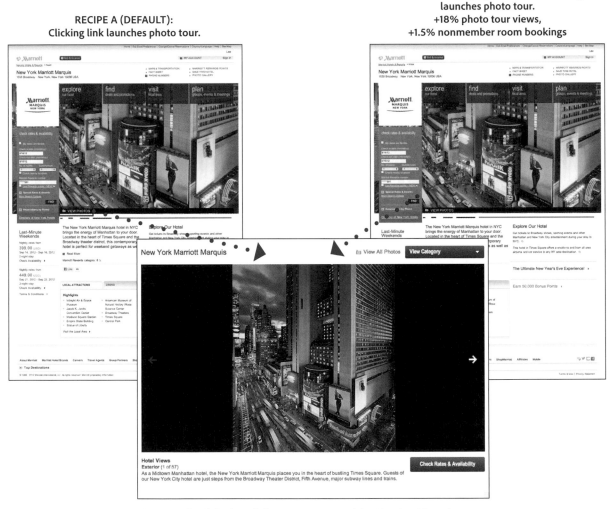

Figure 4 The default and alternate versions of the Marriott Marquis homepage. In Recipe A the large property photo is not clickable, but in Recipe B it is.

Kyle Rush, Deputy Director of Front-end Web Development

Kyle managed online fundraising that brought in $690 million during the course of the 2012 Presidential campaign. As part of his role, Kyle over-saw over 500 A/B tests that led to estimated improvements in the overall donation rate by 49 percent and the email acquisition rate by 161 percent.

Obama for America

Obama for America was the campaign to reelect the President of the United States, Barack Obama.

Would you please tell us a bit about your role?

I was the first engineer when I started in June 2011. I got to build out the whole front-end development team, which ended up growing to about 25 people by the end of the presidential campaign. That number fluctuated because we had interns helping here and there. Project management, quality assurance, and design were separate teams, although we took a few designers under our wing to try to teach them responsive web design. We worked very closely with the digital analytics team. They were great at statistical analysis; they were huge nerds and awesome about it. We had two dedicated people from that team who were amazing and helped the engineers and designers with A/B testing.

Earlier in the campaign my role was making sure pages were created and got out there into the world. We built and launched a new platform for online fundraising and optimization: contribute. barackobama.com. Once we had more engineers on my team, my role became more about product management and architecting fundraising. I oversaw all the online fundraising, from both the product and technical aspects, and that included a lot of optimization.

Thanks to our A/B testing program, the overall donation rate went up by 49 percent, and email subscriptions went up 161 percent: Those both account for a lot of money. Those are estimates based on all of the experiments that we ran. Obviously, we can't ever know for sure.

What were the site's goals?

We had four big goals:

1. Fundraising, which included email acquisition.

2. Get Out The Vote (GOTV). We could have all the money in the world, but if we're not getting people to vote on election day, that's a problem.

3. Help our users to organize support for the president. There were so many people in so many parts of the country who wanted to get involved in the election. This included efforts like getting people to knock on doors, make phone calls, and host neighborhood events. Whatever type of organizing people wanted to do, they could do it through the website.

4. Communicating information around the president's current and future policies. For example, we had a nice interactive page called "Life of Julia." It allowed you to follow a hypothetical woman name Julia and watch what would happen with or without the Affordable Care Act that was passed by the president.

Our primary goal was fundraising: It was always around dollars. Unfortunately, that's so important to win a political race. I don't think anybody at the campaign wanted it to be that way, but that's the state of things. One way in which the Obama campaigns, both in 2012 and 2008, differed from our competitors' campaigns is that we were a lot more grassroots. The Romney campaign's money mainly came from big corporations and high-value donors. Of course, we had some high-value donors, although the average contribution to the Obama campaign was much lower than to the Romney campaign. But we had more donors than they did—by a lot.

Part of fundraising was email acquisition. I didn't run the email program, but because I dealt with people once they landed on the site, I was responsible for helping to grow the email list. Our email list was probably the largest in the nonprofit world, with about 15 million email addresses. Although we always had advertisements running to get people to donate, and we also had outbound communication through Facebook and Twitter, our emails were, by far, the most effective way to get people to donate money. Upwards of 90 percent of our donations came in as a response to the emails we sent. We spent a decent amount of time optimizing email acquisition pages, but for the most part, we focused on optimizing fundraising pages.

What types of customer research did you conduct, and why?

We did a lot of one-on-one user testing as well as a lot of A/B testing. The overall goal of both was to make the experience easier for the user. User testing will teach you things you would never learn from A/B testing. It's such a critical thing to do. If you actually talk with your users and listen to what they're saying, you'll get great ideas on how to improve the user experience.

We would sit down our users on the donate page, and ask them to make a donation. We recorded the sessions, including the screen they were looking at, as well as their faces so we could track their eyesight. We conducted user testing with everyone ranging from students through retired people.

We also ran over 500 A/B tests. A lot of people think A/B testing is psychological tricking. It's not tricking, and psychology is involved, but it's about making the experience easier and faster. We had opinions, but we wanted to test our opinions. The changes to the page were iterative. We didn't make a single change—at all—to the site without testing. That even goes for a single new line of code, which is a change the user wouldn't see, because we wanted to make sure we weren't introducing bugs into the donate pages.

Did the qualitative user testing and quantitative A/B testing techniques build off of one another?

Absolutely. For example, by looking at our analytics we found that, aside from the "Credit Card Number" field, the "Employer" and "Occupation" fields on the donate form had the two highest error rates (**Figure 1**). We couldn't figure out why. To us, those seemed like simple questions. I would have filled out my employer as being "Obama for America," and my occupation as being "Web Developer."

Event Action	Total Events	Unique Events
	1,952,458 % of Total: 0.29% (674,461,714)	1,546,925 % of Total: 0.56% (277,776,643)
1. has errors	420,203	267,807
2. card number	136,421	103,935
3. employer	131,650	113,077
4. occupation	128,303	110,136
5. phone number	117,982	102,808
6. invalid or unsupported card type	116,735	90,320
7. expiration	103,876	87,316
8. you must specify an amount	88,635	77,983
9. required	59,343	20,942
10. state	53,102	48,569

Figure 1 The total number of errors, as well as unique errors, measured on the donation page using analytics during a set period of time.

As we looked more into the data, we saw people were submitting things like "none of your business." At first we thought it's a weird and personal question, and there's nothing we can do to improve the error rate, because there's a law requiring that those fields be collected with donations. Then we started doing user testing. When students and retired folks reached those fields, we found they didn't know what to enter, because they weren't employed. To see if that helped, we ran an A/B test that put a line of copy on the page reading, "If you are retired, enter 'retired' in both fields." We didn't add copy specifying what students should enter, because we thought the new copy explained how to use the fields and that students would figure it out. We tried to have the pages be as minimal and simple as possible by eliminating copy and design embellishments.

The control and new design are in **Figure 2**. The A/B test showed that adding that one line of copy dropped the error rate by 63 percent for the employer field and 58 percent for the occupation field. We think this is because people who didn't have a job had no idea what to put there. Nobody on our team was unemployed, so we never would have thought

of that if we didn't do user testing. That's an example of how we looked at site data, used what we saw to conduct user research, and then tried a change to the page through A/B testing to measure the impact.

How did you scale both user testing and A/B testing programs?

The A/B testing program was pretty robust. We would assign tests to engineers to set up, and as soon they were done, they would get put into a queue. The queue would range from having between 5 to 15 experiments. Because traffic to the site wasn't steady, the number of tests we could run at any given time varied. Testing got heavier toward the end of the campaign as we got more engineers. There was almost always a test happening every single day on the donate pages—no matter what day it was.

Our most important best practice was to always have a test running on every page. If you have a live site with traffic coming in and you're not gathering data from your users, then you're wasting potential to learn. You never know, maybe your site will get profiled on CNN or Reddit, and you will get a huge

DEFAULT

ALTERNATE: -63% errors on Employer field, -53% errors on Occupation field

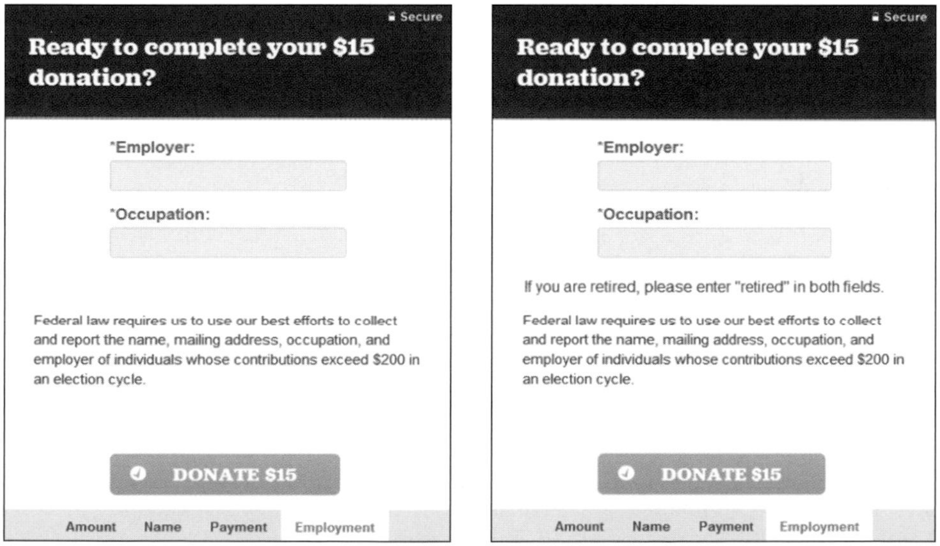

Figure 2 The default and alternate designs for the employer and occupation step.

amount of traffic. If you already had a test running, that's great; if not, it may be too late to try to think of one. You should also always be learning from the people who come to your site, even if it's just 50 people a day.

User testing is more difficult to scale because you need to get actual people to come into the office. We asked a Volunteer Coordinator for the campaign to send us as many volunteers as she had. We then trained the QA team on how to conduct user testing. It was a little slow as we were learning, but after a few days we were conducting about five user tests a day over a several-week period. We rarely asked participants to try using new variations of the site, because we could get results on variations quickly with A/B tests. Instead, we would ask them to use the existing version of the site, so we could try to figure out ways to improve the product. The good thing about qualitative user testing is you don't need much of a sample size to get good feedback.

It sounds like you were able to get A/B test results very quickly. For how long did tests typically run?

It all depended on how much traffic was coming into the site. It's a simple math equation to figure out when you'll reach statistical significance. We would aim to get 30,000 visits into each tested variation, including the control. We would test anything we could, even background colors, just so we could get experiments out and into production. We had a lot of traffic, and we tested in so many areas of the site that we had results to look at almost every day.

If we sent out an email that day, we would have a ton of traffic, and we could normally reach statistical significance for two to three experiments on the site within four hours. On landing pages from advertisements we could get a result for one experiment in about a day. Experiments using organic traffic depended on the news cycle. A splash page may take two days if there wasn't a lot of traffic, and even

lesser trafficked sections of the site could take up to a week to get a result. When the Democratic National Convention (DNC) happened, there was so much traffic that we got results in ten minutes.

We also got an incredible traffic surge the day the Supreme Court upheld the Affordable Care Act, also known as Obamacare. At the time, our queue was already down to about five tests, and we went through them in just a couple of hours, because we had never expected a traffic surge like that. We huddled behind Manik Rathee, who was the front-end engineer implementing experiments that day, and we thought up new tests on the fly. We had enough traffic to get results on each test within minutes. Soon our colleagues from other teams gathered around us to see what the excitement was about. It was a captivating day to say the least.

What was up for grabs for testing and what wasn't?

Political messaging and brand styles were not tested. Messaging is pretty tricky on a political campaign. For the most part, the messaging was delivered to us top-down: It's what we were selling. Messaging was run outside of the digital team by a totally separate team under David Axelrod. For example, his team came up with the "Forward" slogan, and used a lot of data from polling and focus groups.

Although we often tested different copy, we weren't testing different political messaging. Some of the best copy used real examples of why we needed money, like to help somebody else knock on doors, to help fund a commercial, or to communicate the grassroots nature of our campaign within the context of the current state of affairs. For example, the Citizens United ruling was really big for us in fundraising. Under that ruling, Political Action Committees (PACs) could raise as much money as they wanted; there was no limit. Explaining that was effective messaging to get people to donate. We also tested multiple versions of email subject lines.

We also inherited the 2008 campaign's brand styles from their Design Director, Scott Thomas. He was able to tailor a brand back in 2008 that was a big deal for us to inherit, because it was so clean and everything matched in print and in digital. The attention to detail was unseen at the time, even for a corporation. We didn't do a lot of testing branding-wise, although we ran some focus groups. For the most part, we knew we weren't going to switch the logo, because that was a huge part of the brand, and the colors obviously needed to be red, white, or blue.

What types of metrics did you track?

We had any metric you could measure or think about measuring. For testing email sends, we had standard metrics like the conversion rates of emails opened, clicks to the site, aggregate money raised per click and per user, segments by geography, and Facebook data when people connected through Facebook. On the site, revenue was our primary success metric. Other high-level goals were the conversion rate for donations and the conversion rate for email acquisitions. Secondary goals included conversions on subsequent pages and reducing the error rates in form fields.

We structured the site to daisy-chain conversions: We would first ask you to sign up for the email list; we would then ask you for a donation; and we would then ask you to save your payment information for next time or to join a group in your area. We measured conversion rates through each of these steps. For the most part, determining a winner was pretty cut and dried, because most tests had no large difference in revenue or conversions. If we had a statistical tie, we would keep the control. The reason was that most variations altered the user interface, and we wanted to keep the site as simple as possible to minimize chances for user confusion.

Sometimes, deciding the winner could be difficult due to conflicting results. For example, a test may have provided a bump in revenue, an increase in errors, and a decrease in the conversion rate on the next page. When we measured all those metrics, it wasn't always clear if a test had won or not, so we had to have a discussion afterwards. Quantifying the value of each goal in advance helped us to easily figure out which of the goals was more important.

We would also almost always run a test more than once. Sometimes the results between tests wouldn't match, which made picking a winner more difficult. Toward the end of the campaign, we would run a test three times, and if it won two out of three times, we would call it the winner; if not, we would move on to the next test.

The best success metric of all was when Barack Obama was reelected to be the President of the United States of America.

How did segmentation, targeting, and personalization impact design?

Some of the ways we segmented people included donors versus nondonors and whether or not they had an account, were logged in, or had saved payment information. For example, if someone had saved payment information and they landed on the donate page again, we would pre-populate it with all of their information.

Even though segments are fascinating, they really, really complicate the A/B testing environment. Treating segments differently, although it can sometimes be beneficial, requires you to execute so many more tests. For example, at one point in the presidential campaign we were building eight different versions of a page for eight different segments, and that was a huge drain on resources. That kind of segmentation became unmanageable, because we didn't have 80 developers working on fundraising pages; we only had six or seven. By the end of the presidential campaign we tried to streamline development as much as possible and were only producing pages for a maximum of two different segments.

Email is more scalable for segmentation. In the beginning of the presidential campaign we had four different versions of emails based on whether someone was a previous donor, a nonprevious donor, and their geography. By the end of the campaign we had upwards of ten different versions of an email for each send.

How did you keep track of results?

We had a shared online spreadsheet through Google Documents with information about every experiment we ran. It was very, very important for us to record every single experiment so that nothing got lost. The pages may be taken off of production, so we needed to record everything. After each experiment ended, we would store a screen shot of the control; screen shots of the variations; a screen shot of the results; the start and end dates of the experiment; the hypothesis; baseline conversion rates; the changes in conversion rates; the URL to view the experiment's results; whether it was an A/B or multivariate test; the page type: email sign up, donate page, splash page, and so on; and which element on the page varied: image, copy, UX, or page speed test.

Most tests resulted in a statistical tie, and about 20 percent of them won. Testing is very humbling, because you'll come up with variations that you think are just so obviously better than the control, and most of the time they're just not going to work. On some pages we could sometimes go a month without beating the control variation, but we never stopped optimizing. We would have engineers come in and leave every day—with a loss—for a month. That's a pretty hard situation to deal with, because you feel like you're losing all the time. It's hard work and gets especially tough after you pull out all the lower-hanging fruit. However, it makes it that much sweeter when you have a winning variation.

Did President Obama know about the optimization program?

Teddy Goff, our Digital Director, was very interested in online fundraising. Optimization results were in the reports sent up to the campaign manager and the president. I'm sure this stuff came across his desk—in what capacity, I'm not entirely certain.

Visual Examples

Platform A/B Test: Speed

Page speed was tightly linked to the conversion rate. Our fundraising platform worked well for us in the beginning, but there was a clear way to make it better. In order to do so, we had our vendor turn their platform into an API. That way we could build our own hosting platform but still use the vendor to process the donation, which also meant we wouldn't have to reengineer the reporting.

We then built the new fundraising platform with the whole goal of making it super fast. **Figure 3** gives a

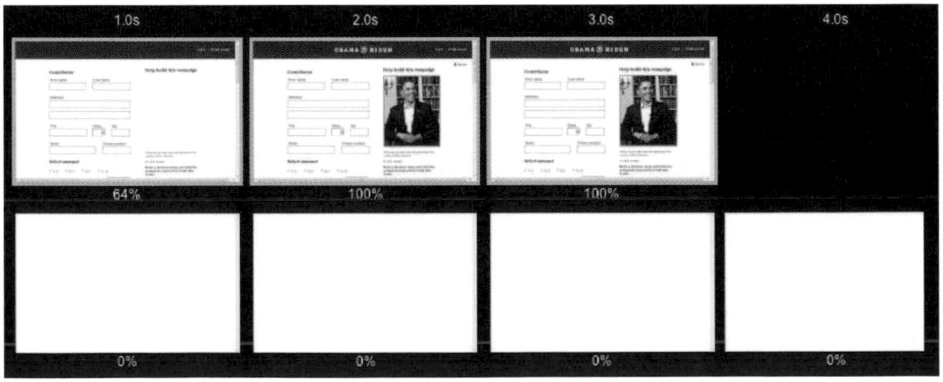

Figure 3 Results from a platform speed test: The default site is on the bottom, and the new much faster site is at the top.

visual comparison of the page load time of two URLs. The computer takes a screen shot of the donate page every tenth of a second. The same donate page is shown loading using the new platform at the top and using the old platform at the bottom. The new platform loaded the forms for the donate page in about a second, whereas the old platform took over four seconds for them to load. At one second, the new platform had "painted the page," which is a term meaning there's something on the page. Even though the logo and the image of the president hadn't yet loaded, the forms on the page were usable. These pages were totally identical, so it's crazy how much faster we made the new platform load. When we A/B tested the new platform versus the old one, that difference in speed gave us a 14 percent lift in the conversion rate, which alone was worth about $32 million in additional donations.

Reducing Errors A/B Test: Removing Credit Card Field Type

We started with the donate page from the 2008 campaign (**Figure 4**). We wanted to reduce any possible user frustration, so we used our analytics (Figure 1) to implement error tracking on each form field. During the timeframe pictured, you can see that there were 420,203 total errors, 136,421 errors on the card number field, 131,650 errors on the employer field, 128,303 errors on the occupation field, and 116,735 errors on the card type field. There shouldn't have been so many errors on those fields. One interesting thing here is by looking at the "Unique Events" column, you can see that a lot of people were getting an error more than once, which wasn't good. We used reports like this one to figure out where to spend our time.

Interestingly, most of the error reduction tests didn't impact conversions on the donate page but had an impact on the subsequent action we asked users to take. If a user didn't have errors on the donate page, they were 7 percent more likely to complete

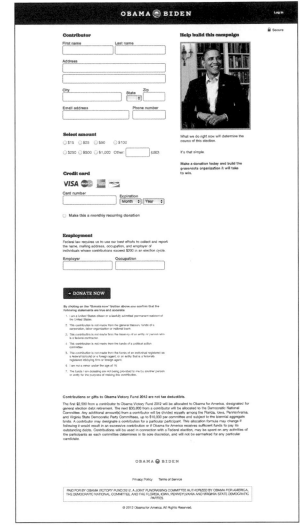

Figure 4 The default version of the donation page when the 2012 campaign started. This page was the final version after testing during the 2008 campaign.

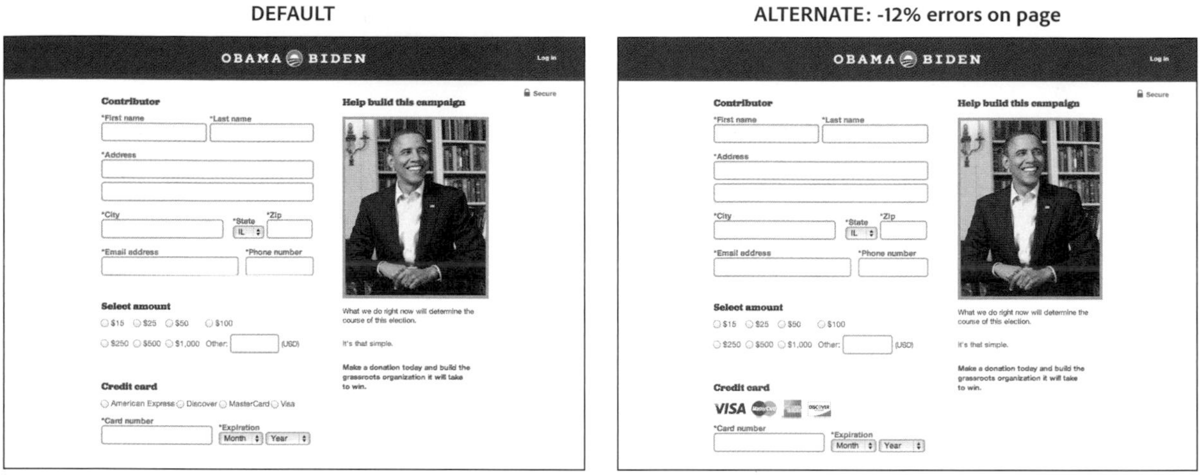

DEFAULT

ALTERNATE: -12% errors on page

Figure 5 The default and alternate versions of the donation page with a redesigned credit card selection element.

the follow-up action, which was to save their payment information. Learning that changed the way we measured things significantly. Before, we were just tracking the conversion rate on one page, and when we started tracking the whole chain we realized the isolated pages aren't microcosms; together they form the whole experience.

We attacked the "invalid or unsupported card type" error first. Those errors happened when someone selected the wrong type of credit card or missed that they should select their credit card type. We thought 116,735 errors seemed very high, especially because those errors didn't need to be occurring at all. We also thought they could easily be fixed by removing this field and auto-detecting the card type based on the card number. **Figure 5** shows the default and alternate design where we replaced the field with images of the four credit card types that we accepted. This small change reduced the overall errors on the page by over 12 percent. That's how we started chipping away at these errors.

Reducing Errors A/B Test: Noting Required Fields

When we looked at the form, there was no indication of which fields were required and which fields weren't. It seemed obvious to show which fields were required, but our mantra for the site was "If it's not needed on the page, don't add it." So before noting which fields were required, we wanted to test whether doing so made a difference. The control, and the variation with asterisks over the required fields, are in **Figure 6**. The new design got over a 9 percent reduction in the number of overall errors on the page, which was great.

Donation Page A/B Test: Splitting One Form into Four Steps

After 14 months of optimization, the page we started with in Figure 4 looked like the new default page in **Figure 7**. We had been trying to beat the page in Figure 7 for a month without any winning tests. The page still looked like a long form, so our hypothesis was that it might appear to be cumbersome and hard to complete. There were 15 fields in the form, and we thought that splitting them up into smaller forms might help the conversion rate.

DEFAULT   **ALTERNATE: -9% errors on page**

Figure 6 The default and alternate designs for the page. The alternate version includes asterisks to note required fields.

DEFAULT   **ALTERNATE: +5% donation conversion rate**

Figure 7 The default and redesigned versions of the donation flow, moving from a one-step to a four-step process.

We decided to test turning it into a four-step process, the first step of which is pictured as the alternate Figure 7, so that users wouldn't feel overwhelmed by the length of the form. The four steps were:

1. Donation amount

2. Personal information

3. Billing information

4. Occupation and employer

We considered many factors, but the primary factor we used to determine how to split up and order the fields were the error rates. We wanted to put the easiest actions first to lower the barrier to engagement and also produce a sense of investment in the user before they reached the more difficult parts of the form. We worried that asking for money upfront might seem off-putting, and that instead, starting by asking for their name would make it more personal. But we tried both and found it was best to start with the donation amount. All a user had to do was click on one of the squares to select their donation amount, and then step one would fade out into step two. Users didn't need to take the time to type in any information or risk incorrectly entering information and causing errors. We also thought the fading animation was a good use of positive reinforcement after completing a small action. It was like a reward, and we hoped users might think, "That was cool; how do I make that happen again?" The second step was personal information, which users needed to type in. Billing information generated a lot of errors on the default version of the page, but not as many as the occupation and employer fields, so we placed the easier-to-complete fields first.

We weren't sure whether this new version of the page would work. It was a gamble, because it took a decent amount of development time. The results showed that it increased the donation conversion rate by a little over 5 percent. That may not seem impressive, but we thought it was a fantastic result, especially because it came after over a month of testing with no winning results for this page.

The other benefit was that the new design was a dream for metrics. With the smaller pages it was easier to figure out exactly on which steps people were dropping off. We measured the drop-off rate for each screen and used that data to organize our time. For example, if the step had a 40 percent drop-off rate, then 40 percent of our time would go to improving that step.

Reducing Errors A/B Test: Credit Card Number Formatting

On the new form, the analytics showed that entering the credit card number properly was the number one cause of errors and also the step in the flow with the largest user drop-off, so we spent a lot of time executing experiments on that screen.

For this experiment our hypothesis was that it's difficult to enter 16 digits from your credit card. We tried thinking of ways to make it easier. Credit card companies have already thought of this, because when you look at your card, the digits are grouped. For example, VISA card numbers are split into groups of four digits. It's easy to remember four digits, but it's hard to remember 16. American Express® has a slightly different grouping schema. So, we wrote some JavaScript that would recognize the card type, group the numbers the way they appeared on the card, and even adjust the font's size and kerning to look more like the specific credit card, which also ended up making the font a little larger. The default and the variation are in **Figure 8**. The variation showed a 15 percent reduction in errors on the page.

DEFAULT   ALTERNATE: -15% errors on page

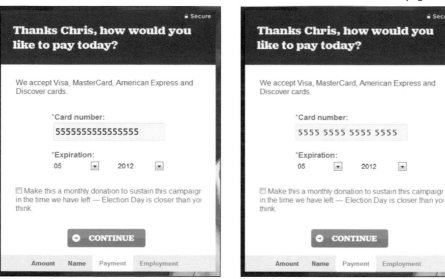

Figure 8 The default and redesigned credit card fields. The text field in the redesign mimics number fonts and group-ings based on the credit card type of the user.

Save Payment Information Page
A/B Test: Headline Copy

Users who saved their payment information after making a donation, or by simply creating an account on the site to save it, were extremely valuable to the presidential campaign. Once a user had saved their payment information, they could donate in the future using a product we created called Quick Donate. Quick Donate allowed users to donate with a single click on the web, a single click in an email, or through a single text message.

We would send these users an email with several links in it for different donation amounts and also a phone number to which they could send SMS messages. If a user clicked on the link to donate $10 in the email, then $10 would be donated to the campaign using their saved payment information in one click. If they text messaged "10" to the phone number, they would also immediately donate $10 to the campaign.

This program was cutting edge, because nobody had engineered donations through email before, and at the time the Federal Election Commission (FEC) did not allow political campaigns to use cell phone carrier short codes to raise money through text messages (the FEC later reversed this decision after Quick Donate launched). The program was so successful that by the end of the campaign, more than 1.5 million Quick Donate users had donated $115 million. Quick Donate users donated four times as often and gave three times as much money. This program received a lot of optimization because of its success.

The default and alternate pages to save payment information are pictured in **Figure 9**. This experiment focuses on copy and is sort of mind blowing because the header is all we varied. The header on the control said, "Save your payment information for next time." We changed only a couple of words, so the variation read, "Now, save your payment information." We tested a lot of variations of the headline, but that was the winner. We thought the

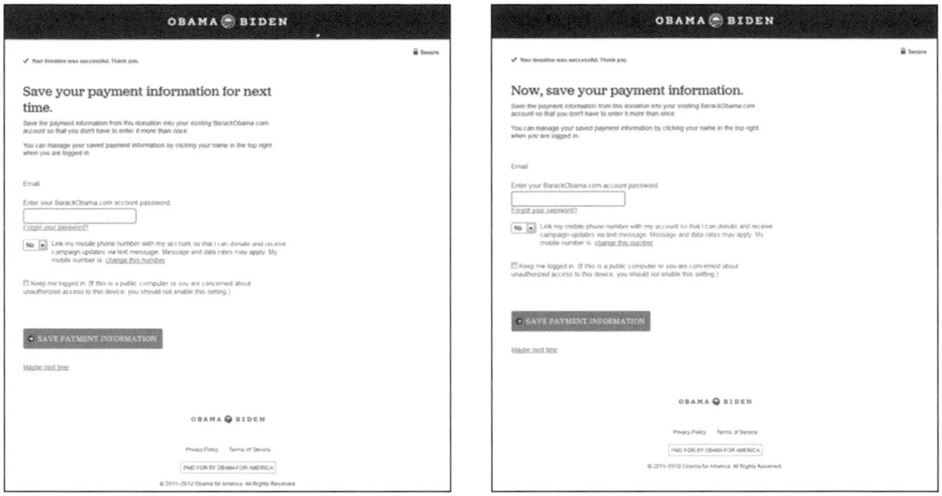

Figure 9 The default and alternate versions of the Save Payment information page. The alternate version of the page has a redesigned headline.

DEFAULT

ALTERNATE: +21% saved payment conversion rate

default headline made the request to save payment information seem disconnected from the donation, whereas the alternate version did the exact opposite. That single headline change increased the conversion rate on this page by 21 percent. The ROI on that is through the roof!

Contrast this with the earlier test that redesigned the donate page into a four-step process, took several weeks of development and design, and yielded a 5 percent lift in donations. Whereas changing a few words in a headline, which took a developer two minutes to set up, led to a 21 percent increase in saved payment information. Complex functionality isn't something you should test in the beginning stages of an optimization program; you should pick the low-hanging fruit first.

Two Term Fund A/B Test: Adding Video

This was a page collecting donations for what we called the Two Term Fund. We did a lot of testing on video. Most of the time we saw that videos reduced conversion rates, so we kept videos off pages. However, an A/B test that added video to this page showed over a 49 percent increase in revenue (**Figure 10**). Note that's not just an increase in the

donation conversion rate but over a 49 percent increase in the dollar value of donations. That is huge!

Unfortunately, this was an isolated test, and we could not reproduce the results in future video tests. I think what this says about video tests is that the audience who views the page and the content of the video are both very important. There is no hard-and-fast rule that a page with video will always win against a page without video. The performance during this test had to do with very unique video content about Romney that got people fired up and wanting to donate.

Targeting A/B Test: Login Indicator vs. None

We wondered whether people who had saved their payment information were coming to the site at a later time, forgetting they had already saved their payment information and having to enter it all over again to make another donation. If so, this may reduce their likelihood to complete the donation process a second time. We worked with our digital analytics team to look into this, and it turned out that a ton of people were making donations without using their already saved payment information.

DEFAULT   ALTERNATE: +49% revenue

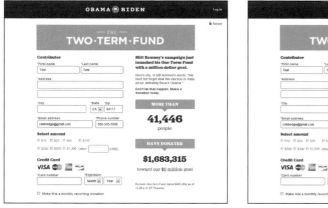

Figure 10 The default and alternate version of a landing page testing the appearance of a video.

So we ran a targeted A/B test, just to the segment of people who had already saved their payment information (**Figure 11**). Users entered this test through an email, so even if their browser session had expired or they had cleared their cookies, we were able to create a link that read, "Log in to use your saved payment information" on the page. The alternate version of the page with this link increased the donation conversion rate by over 9 percent for this segment of users.

Dinner with Barack Page A/B Test: George Clooney

Photography was a huge part of the Obama brand. We had several photographers who took lots of amazing photos of the president, the first lady, and everyone else. We took advantage of this by testing photos anywhere you could imagine. We found that there are many variables in photos that can affect conversions, but possibly the biggest impact had to do with the context in which the photo was used.

Our hypothesis for this test was, "George Clooney will increase donations." We tested two versions of the Dinner with Barack page: one offering dinner with the president and one offering dinner with the

DEFAULT

ALTERNATE: +9% donation conversion rate

Figure 11 A test targeting the appearance of a login link only to visitors who have saved payment information.

president and George Clooney (**Figure 12**). Unfortunately, the page with George Clooney didn't win and led to a 14 percent drop in the donation conversion rate over the regular Dinner with Barack page. Why wouldn't you want dinner with both of them?

Donation Page A/B Test: Reinforce Email Content on Landing Page

We sent users from all the different emails to the same donation page, and it didn't really make sense. We had a hypothesis that if we changed the donation page to match the context that was set in the email, the conversion rate would increase (**Figure 13**). This email was sent on the day the Supreme Court upheld the Affordable Care Act, which as I mentioned was a crazy day, because we got a ton of traffic. We tested putting a stamp reading "UPHELD," on the donation page, because it was relevant to the email and the news. This new page increased the conversion rate by 3 percent, which might not sound like a lot, but it was an easy change to make and we took that result with us everywhere.

This test was a big winner for us, because it changed the way we did things a lot. After this test, whenever we sent out emails, we would try to have the landing page be like the email the user had just read. Before this win, we would just assume that the same picture of the president would increase conversions, but the winning design didn't have the picture of the president on it at all.

Donate Page A/B Test: Removing Suggested Donation Buttons

We came out with crazy ideas. We asked, "What happens if we take away all the predefined amounts and just ask the user to enter the amount of their donation?" During this test (**Figure 14**) the variation increased revenue by 50 percent at a very high-confidence level. We thought, "We are geniuses!"

DEFAULT

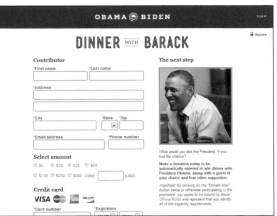

ALTERNATE: -14% donation conversion rate

Figure 12 The default and alternate versions of the Dinner with Barack page.

Unfortunately, this is another test we were never able to reproduce. It worked once, and I don't know why. We tested it several times, and because it didn't win again, we went back to the control. These sorts of situations can be so humbling. A 50 percent increase in revenue was amazing. Imagine if we could have kept that up through the whole campaign? After this experiment, we started testing winning ideas more than once.

DEFAULT **ALTERNATE: +3% donation conversion rate**

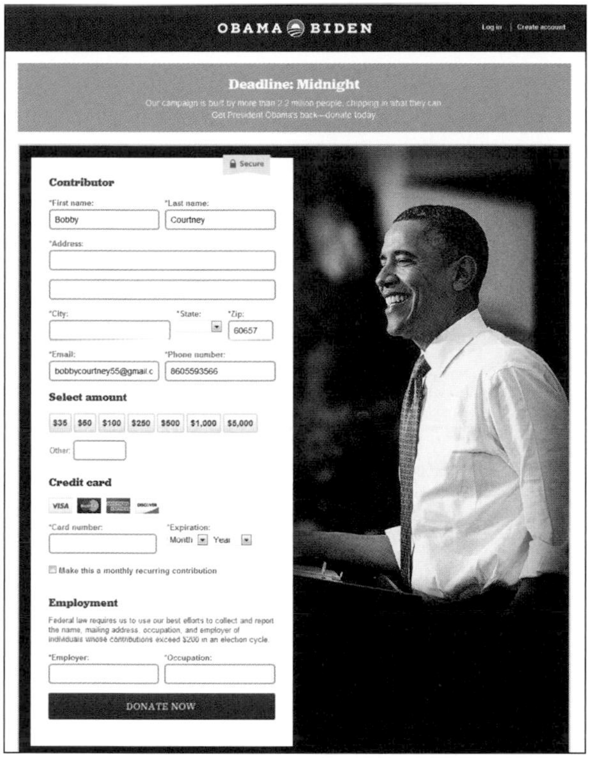

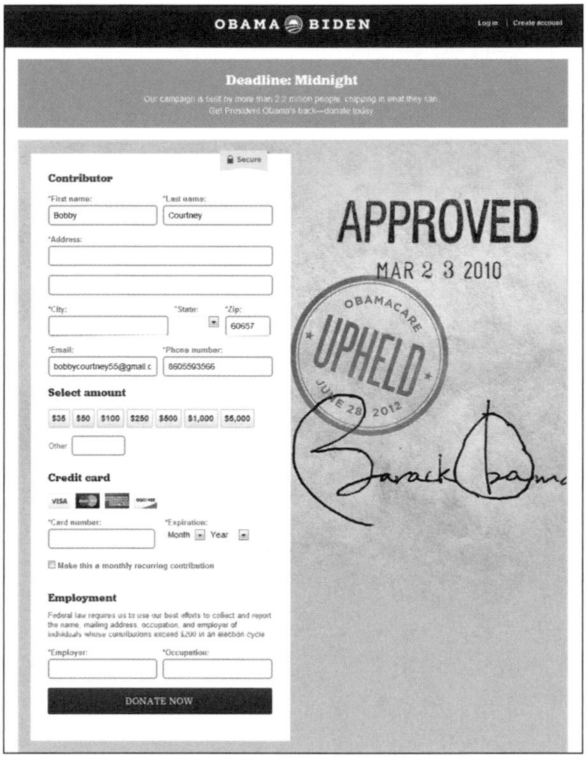

Figure 13 The tested redesign of the donation page after the Affordable Care Act had been upheld by the Supreme Court.

DEFAULT **ALTERNATE: +50% revenue**

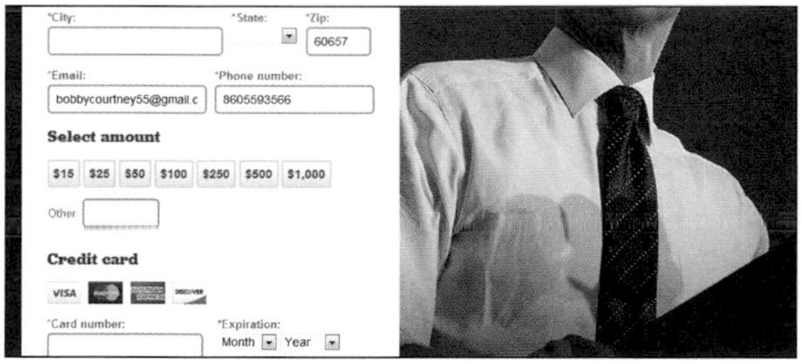

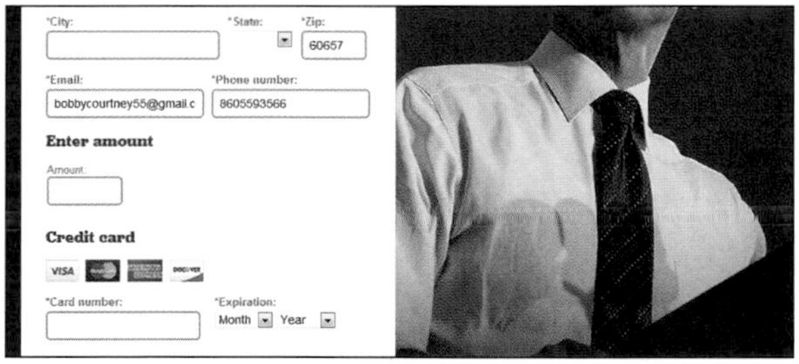

Figure 14 A redesign that worked once to dramatically raise revenue, but not in subsequent tests, by removing suggested donation amounts.

Donate Page A/B Test: Removing Dollar Signs

Someone suggested this idea from what they had learned about the psychology of restaurant menus. Upscale restaurants remove the dollar signs because that supposedly gets their customers to spend more. So, we tried removing the dollar signs from the buttons on the donate page (**Figure 15**). The variation showed a measured 36 percent increase in revenue. This is another test where we thought, "We're crazy geniuses!" Unfortunately, we tested it another five times, and in future experiments it didn't make a statistically significant difference, so we left the dollar signs on the page.

Donate Page A/B Test: Auto-focus on the First Name Field in Step 2

Google blogged that when users landed on its search page, they would auto-focus on the search field, and that increased the conversion rate of the page. We tested auto-focusing on the "First Name" field, and it led to over a 6 percent increase in donation conversions (there is no image, because the designs looked the same but the functionality was different). I've reproduced this result across different websites.

Donate Page A/B Test: Gray Background Color for Form Fields

The default form fields had white backgrounds. When we changed their background colors to gray, we thought they stood out more and also looked emptier (**Figure 16**). Hopefully, this would make users more likely to want to fill them in. Even though users probably know they're on a page with form fields, there might be some subtle psychological cues that occur when the contrast ratio of the background colors between the page and the forms is increased. Just by turning the background color from white to gray we increased the donation conversion rate by 11 percent.

Donate Page A/B Test: Adding Presidential Quote

Late in the campaign someone joined the team who said something along the lines of "We have so many great quotes from the president. Why don't we put one on the page? They're so inspirational." We tested putting a long quote and a shorter quote on the page. The shorter quote, which read, "Stand with me, work with me, let's finish what we've started," led to over a 10 percent increase in revenue (**Figure 17**). That was a great win.

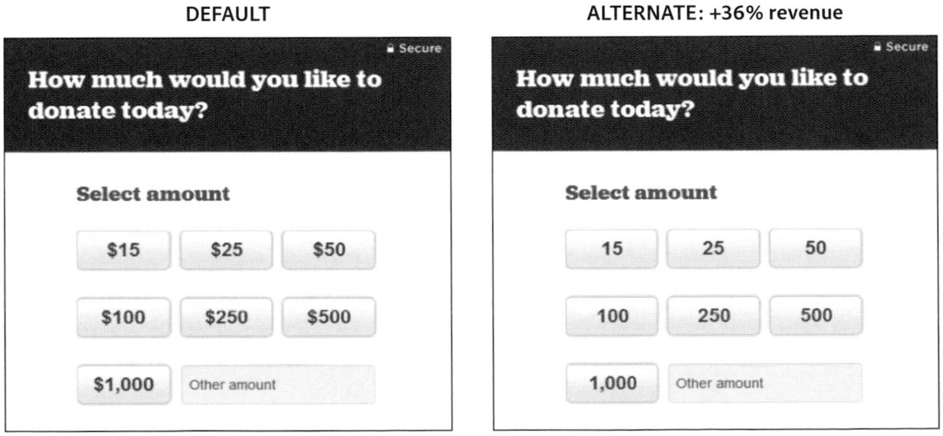

Figure 15 Another redesign that worked once to dramatically raise revenue, but not in subsequent tests, by removing dollar signs from suggested donation amounts.

DEFAULT

ALTERNATE: +36% revenue

DEFAULT

ALTERNATE: +11% donation conversion rate

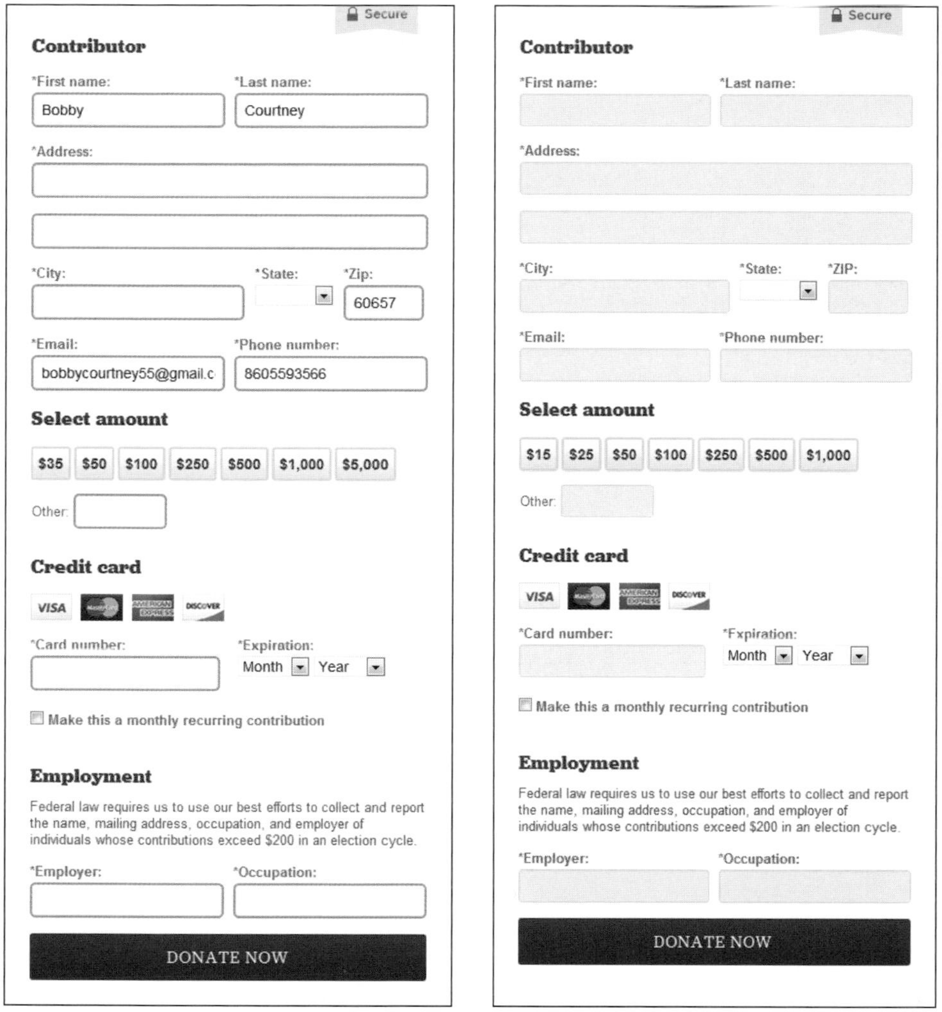

Figure 16 The default and alternate designs of the form fields. The redesign tested changing the form field background color to gray.

Figure 17 Testing adding an inspirational quote to the donation page.

DEFAULT

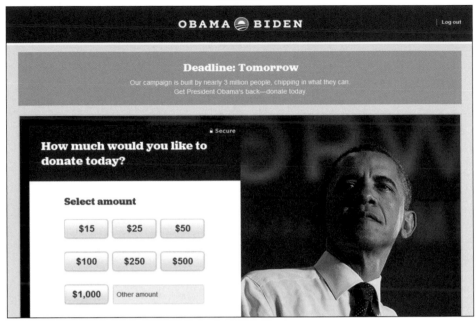

SHORT QUOTE: +10% revenue

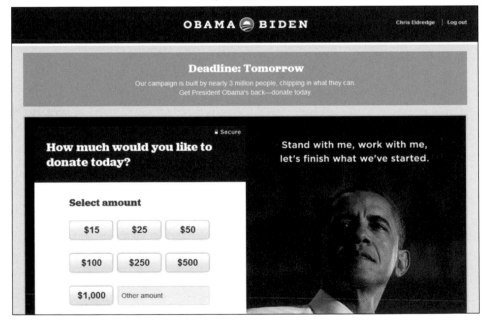

Summary

We started the presidential campaign with the page in Figure 4, which was the exact page the campaign had ended with in 2008. It was a highly optimized page by 2008 standards; the team then had done a great job with it. When it was handed down to us, we obviously knew that A/B testing was going to be very crucial to improving the site's goals, because a lot had changed between 2008 and when we started working on the new presidential campaign in 2011.

We ended the 2012 campaign with the page in **Figure 18**. It had been iteratively changed a lot over the course of 2011–2012 through hundreds of A/B tests. There's a reason behind everything on this page. The donation box is white, and the rest of the page is dark. The reason is that we knew the image of the president was important, but when it came to users landing on the donation page, we didn't want them focusing on the image; we wanted them making a donation. The white stands out. It's hard to not look at the white on the donate form. Your eyes can stray, but they will come back. It's the brightest part of the page, and it has the highest contrast ratio of everything on the page. Your eyes will naturally go to where there's the highest contrast ratio. If the whole page was white, it would be boundless.

The buttons used to be light gray, but we ran a test and ended up changing them to blue (**Figure 19**), which led to an over 2 percent increase in revenue. In light gray, we think they didn't have a high enough contrast ratio with the white behind them. We had to find a way to make them stand out. We didn't want users to have to scan the page to understand what was being asked of them. We wanted the user to focus on the buttons and not be able to avoid them. They really stand out when viewed within the entire page (Figure 18).

Figure 18 The final design for the donation page. This design was reached after running hundreds of A/B tests throughout the course of the 2012 campaign.

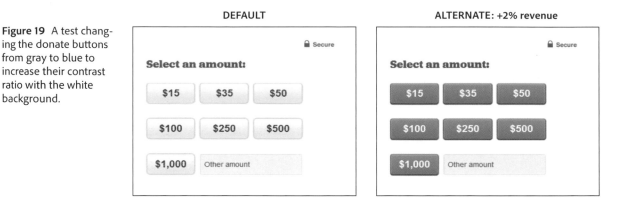

Figure 19 A test changing the donate buttons from gray to blue to increase their contrast ratio with the white background.

The progress bar steps are in green, because green is good. We purposefully removed all the red from this page, except for in the logo, because red is associated with error states. On an earlier version of the page, the donate button was red. For some reason, in 2008, people loved the color red. Now, users on the site see red only when there are errors. There used to be a Next button under the donation amounts. The page with the Next button was asking the user for two micro-conversions: to click on the amount to donate and then to click Next. Only the first click was necessary. On the final version of the page, the Next button would appear only if the users chose "Other amount."

I had never worked on something that was so calculated before. Something else that was new for me is that I've never had anybody copy my work before. When you're working for the president, your work is a little bit more in the spotlight. The Romney campaign copied our donation page with similar imagery and the same form steps. The press even wrote about how their campaign copied some sections of our site word for word. It was so funny how their campaign copied us. Also, several times co-workers would shoot me an IM pointing to a start-up that was using our same form setup, with the same animations and all. It was really cool to see that people were noticing our work and implementing it on their sites. It was a wonderful experience.

Blake Brossman, Founder and COO

Blake founded PetCareRx in 1998 with the passion to find ways to provide medications at reasonable prices for pets that might otherwise go untreated. Blake has significant business development experience and is a noted speaker in the areas of direct marketing and pet retailing. He is also a member of the national board of the Cystic Fibrosis Foundation. He's the proud parent of Humphrey, his Abyssinian cat, and his American Bulldog Samantha, who likes to drool all over Blake and his family.

PetCareRx

PetCareRx's philosophy is that every pet deserves lots of love, proper nutrition, complete protection, and personalized care. In this spirit they provide treats and toys; foods and vitamins; flea, tick, and heartworm protection; and a vast range of prescription and nonprescription medications, all at a great value and with the convenience of home delivery.

What are your business's goals?

Our goal is to get the customer to buy a product and then want it again. We don't need one-off customers. The one-off customer business is a sloppy business. We want lifetime customers, and people won't re-order something they still have. For example, if people run out of milk every five days, they go to the store every five days. Pet medication is on a timeline, too. Continuity is sometimes mistaken for loyalty, but it's not. Loyalty is about having a great customer experience; continuity is based on buying something on a regular basis.

We also look to bring in qualified consumers and convert them at a high rate so our advertising dollars go further. For example, if I said to a stadium full of people, "Everybody, I would like to sell you this dog

bone right now," maybe 10 percent would say "yes" and make it all the way through the funnel. But if I went to a dog convention and said the same thing, the conversion rate might be 75 percent. Prequalifying visitors is about finding the pet convention people in the stadium.

What are your customers' goals?

Total health and wellness for their pets, including health maintenance and new and better ways to help treat chronic conditions. If a pet is unhappy, you know about it because the pet owner is unhappy. Pets can't talk, but owners can read their pet's signals. When I first started in the pet industry, somebody told me, "If a dog won't eat it, it won't sell, even if it's good for them."

Not every customer is equal. A customer who comes in and buys a dog bone may be less valuable than a customer who buys prescription medication. We try to identify which customers will be better customers. For example, if we know the breed or age of their dog, we know what they should prepare for in the dog's future. Another example is demographic location. If it's snowing outside, the dog probably isn't running in the park. But if it's warm out, the dog could be outside and affected by fleas and ticks. Being able to personalize messaging to consumers improves the conversion rate because people don't want a stadium pitch.

What prompted you to start PetCareRx?

My dog, Lou, got cancer. It was very expensive to try to treat the disease. It cost $700 for a week's supply of seven pills. I had a necessity: I had to have the drug every week, so a continuity relationship was formed. I had no other choice, because without the drug, my dog was going to die, and I would do anything for a pet.

In my research I found out that the wholesale cost was $0.07 per pill. I learned how many other people were in the same position I was. People like me wanted to keep their pets alive. The loyalty of going to a specific doctor to buy expensive drugs was less important than the continuity of being able to afford keeping my pet alive.

How do you find customers needing pet medication without a stadium pitch?

In order to better find customers needing medications we started by selling supplies. When a customer buys a supply, like a certain size dog bed, we know that they have a dog, they're taking care of their dog, and the approximate size of their dog. That qualifies them for the next part of our experience, which is offering them medications based on their dog's size.

Because we went out with a more general qualification—for supplies—we were able to attract and convert a more general type of customer. We also know that a dog bed has a lifetime of four months before it's ruined and smells, so that product also has continuity. We are currently working on incorporating other general products into our business. Next up is dog food. If there's one thing we know, it's that every dog has to eat.

That's an inspiring entrepreneurial story. Did you try expanding your business into areas that didn't work?

Yes, we expanded into fish. Using common sense, we mistakenly thought pet owners were all equal: If we understood dog and cat owners, we would understand fish owners. We tried to sell them tanks, supplies, and food—everything they would need except the fish.

What we learned is that fish owners are more like hobbyists than pet owners, and the funnel would need to completely change for them. Fish owners wanted to know a lot about breeds: where they're from and how to maintain them; that information wasn't relevant to dog and cat owners. As we tried to become experts in the subject we came across a lot of failure.

Visual Examples

Homepage A/B Test: Trust Messaging

The default version of our homepage appears in Figure 3.3, and Chapter 3 includes insights from our analytics data for this page. In summary, because over 70 percent of the homepage visitors were new, and many of them abandoned the site from the homepage, we wanted to test emphasizing the PetCareRx brand promise. We thought that if we could explain how we're a licensed pharmacy with vets on staff, new visitors would be more likely to make a purchase. We tested alternate versions of the light blue box in the upper-right corner of the page. Creative comps of the alternate recipes are displayed in **Figure 1**:

▶ **Recipe B.** Mixes warm imagery with clear value proposition bullets. All of the alternate recipes bold keywords in the value proposition and include the same pharmacist and dog imagery.

▶ **Recipe C.** The value proposition is in a sentence instead of bullets.

▶ **Recipe D.** A bulleted warning about the dangers of offshore pharmacies.

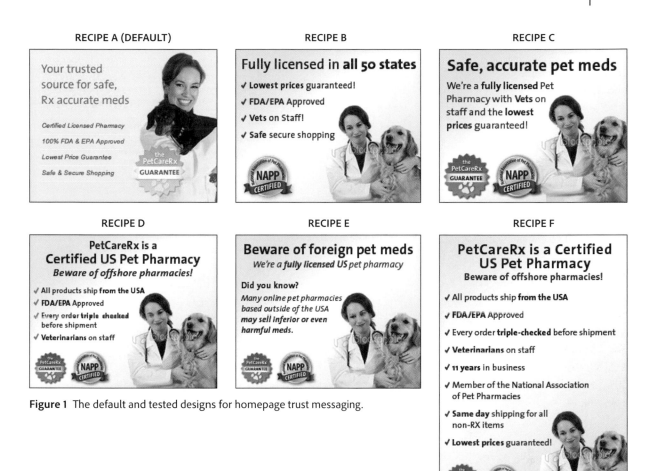

Figure 1 The default and tested designs for homepage trust messaging.

▶ **Recipe E.** A more explicit warning about the dangers of offshore pharmacies.

▶ **Recipe F.** The trust messaging area was expanded to twice the size to include a lot of value proposition bullets and a warning about offshore pharmacies.

Every single recipe was flat for RPV, which was the primary success metric. Even though the new designs didn't win, it's important not to give up. The next homepage test in our roadmap was a layout redesign, detailed in Chapter 3.

Dogs Category Page A/B Test: Banner Size, Messaging, and Imagery

The default "Flea & Tick" page is shown in **Figure 2**. Insights from our analytics included:

▶ Most clicks were to the subcategories in the middle of the page, not to the top blue banner.

▶ Conversion rates were higher when a customer clicked directly into products on our homepage rather than into subcategories on this page.

▶ In the past we have seen customers respond well to cute dog imagery.

RECIPE A (DEFAULT)

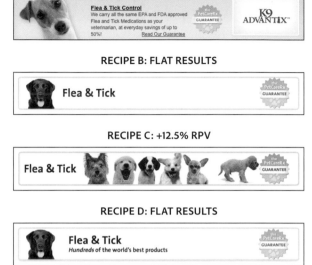

RECIPE A (DEFAULT)

RECIPE B: FLAT RESULTS

RECIPE C: +12.5% RPV

RECIPE D: FLAT RESULTS

Flea & Tick
Hundreds of the world's best products

RECIPE E: +14.9% RPV

All Flea & Tick
All non-Rx products ship today! If your order is placed by 2pm ET.

RECIPE F: FLAT RESULTS

Flea & Tick

RECIPE G: -13% RPV

All Flea & Tick
Lowest prices guaranteed!

RECIPE H: FLAT RESULTS

All Flea & Tick
All the same FDA approved Flea and Tick medications as your Vet!

Figure 2 Tested banners and their results for the Flea & Tick page.

The impact of this data was to test decreasing the size of the banner to pull up subcategory navigation to be higher on the page. We hoped that this would help visitors to more quickly end up on the page for the product they were most interested in, and convert. We tested several different banners that were at least 50 percent shorter than the default, and their wireframes are shown in Figure 2:

▶ **Recipe B.** Simple and easy to read without small text like the default.

▶ **Recipe C.** Multiple images of cute puppies and our guarantee icon.

▶ **Recipe D.** Emphasizing the breadth of the product selection.

▶ **Recipe E.** Emphasizing same-day shipping.

▶ **Recipe F.** Minimizing the size of the banner to pull subcategories higher.

▶ **Recipe G.** Emphasizing lowest price guarantee.

▶ **Recipe H.** Emphasizing that we carry the same medications as a vet.

Some banners were flat; the low price guarantee banner led to a large decrease in RPV; and two banners led to substantial lifts in RPV. The banner with the cute puppies provided a 12.5 percent lift in RPV, and the banner with the black Labrador retriever emphasizing same-day shipping won with 14.9 percent lift in RPV. For this test, cute puppies were good, but same-day shipping was better.

Cart Template A/B Test: Discount and Promotional Messaging

This was one in a series of fascinating tests around discount and promotional messaging. This test was run against the default shopping cart template for all customers, shown in **Figure 3**. Insights from our analytics included:

▶ The majority of visitors who view the cart eventually continue to checkout, which was great data.

▶ However, some visitors browse around the site after adding a product to their cart, and some of them end up abandoning.

The impact of this data was to test whether reinforcing the price savings we provide for customers on the cart page would increase their likelihood to checkout:

▶ **Recipe B (Figure 4).** The price discount is explicitly noted for each product line-item in the cart, as well as at the bottom of the cart.

▶ **Recipe C (Figure 4).** The same as Recipe B, with additional messaging at the top of the cart stating the total savings and Pet Points the customer will earn. For example, "Checkout now and save $51.52, and earn 160 Pet Points." Pet Points is a rewards program we developed. Customers earn Pet Points with each purchase, based on the size and type of their purchase, and they can use Pet Points in future purchases to increase their savings.

Even though the designs were applying standard best practices for messaging discounts, all recipes provided flat results. This shows the power of testing when used to confirm so called "best practices." However, we didn't give up. We tried testing similar messaging on the next stage in the flow: the checkout page.

RECIPE A (DEFAULT)

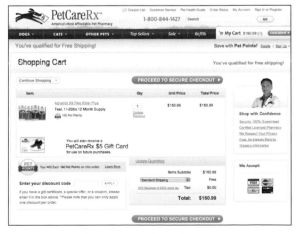

Figure 3 The default version of the shopping cart.

RECIPE B

RECIPE C

Figure 4 Tested redesigns for the shopping cart. Results for both recipes were flat.

Checkout Template A/B Test: Cart A/B Test: Discount and Promotional Messaging

This test was run on our default checkout page, shown in **Figure 5**. Insights from analytics revealed:

▶ Many customers use the back button to leave this page and return to other pages on the site.

▶ Customer research indicated that customers might be looking for any number of assurances before feeling confident checking out.

The impact of this data was to start by testing a variety of messaging, much of which appeared elsewhere on the site, to determine if showing it on the checkout page would increase the likelihood of customers to complete a purchase. All alternate recipes included new messaging at the top of the page in a yellow box, as shown in Figure 5:

▶ **Recipe B.** Offered customers free shipping if they place their order within the next ten minutes. The yellow box included a timer that would count down from ten minutes.

▶ **Recipe C.** Free shipping messaging without a countdown timer.

▶ **Recipe D.** Messaging of $5 off their next order if they check out now.

▶ **Recipe E.** Reinforcing the savings over standard vet prices.

▶ **Recipe F.** Reinforcing how many Pet Points the customer will earn.

The results of this test were surprising. Only Recipes E and F provided lift, of 9.18 percent and 11.24 percent, respectfully, and Recipe F was the clear winner. It was great to see that customers responded so well to the Pet Points messaging in Recipe F, because Pet Points help to encourage customer loyalty while giving us an opportunity to reward our top customers.

RECIPE A (DEFAULT)

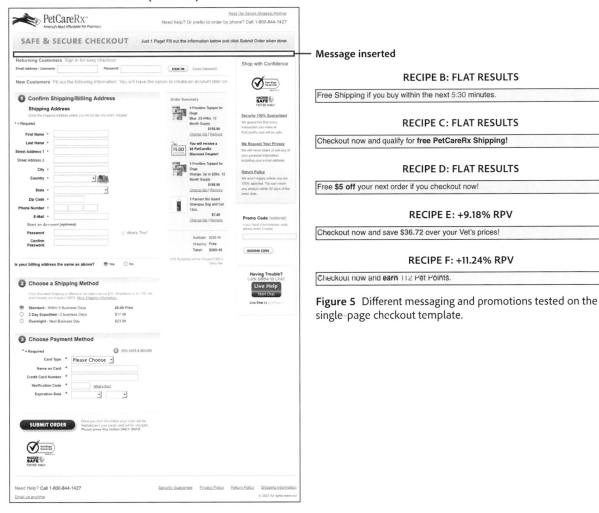

— Message inserted

RECIPE B: FLAT RESULTS

Free Shipping if you buy within the next 5:30 minutes.

RECIPE C: FLAT RESULTS

Checkout now and qualify for **free PetCareRx Shipping!**

RECIPE D: FLAT RESULTS

Free **$5 off** your next order if you checkout now!

RECIPE E: +9.18% RPV

Checkout now and save **$36.72** over your Vet's prices!

RECIPE F: +11.24% RPV

Checkout now and **earn** 112 Pet Points.

Figure 5 Different messaging and promotions tested on the single-page checkout template.

Roger Scholl, Vice President of Operations for Saks Direct

Roger oversees the user experience, product management, merchandise operations, and quality assurance teams; these teams work closely with the marketing analytics team to scope, design, implement, analyze, and respond to test results and other customer feedback.

Matt Curtis, Senior Manager of Marketing Analytics

Matt is a member of the digital marketing team and business owner of web analytics, personalization, and A/B testing.

Saks Fifth Avenue

In the summer of 2000, Saks Fifth Avenue launched saks.com, offering an enhanced, personalized, online shopping experience. You may shop at saks.com in many ways: by a distinct look, a specific designer, or an individual item. saks.com is committed to providing the same legendary service and style found in all Saks Fifth Avenue stores.

What are your business's goals?

To improve the customer experience, increase RPV, drive customers to brick-and-mortar stores, and to expose any product at any time on any device.

What are your customers' goals?

To achieve the best style with best-in-class customer service.

How do you measure the success of a test?

We look for statistically significant results and define success metrics before the test is run. Usually, the primary success metric will be RPV, conversion, or average order value (AOV). We'll sometimes use other key performance indicators based on the individual test, such as the number of email sign-ups.

Have any themes or "best practices" emerged across your testing results?

We initially focused on a lot of edge cases and questions around functionality on lower trafficked areas of the site. We now are more careful about only prioritizing tests that can "move the needle" and also try to avoid tests where we don't anticipate statistically significant results.

Visual Examples

Since 2009, we have taken a cross-functional approach to answering business questions by optimizing the customer experience and new development strategies, and reworking existing features and functionalities. Here are two examples of early tests.

Section Pages A/B Tests: Left-hand Navigation Link Order

We ran a series of tests across several section pages to understand how best to organize the links in the left-hand navigation. We were primarily interested in whether to place the links in alphabetical order or to order them by traffic volumes, as well as where to place the very popular "Premier Designers" and "Lifestyle" links. This test was run across the following section pages: Jewelry & Accessories, Men's Store, Women's Apparel, and Beauty & Fragrance.

The results differed by section page, and the Women's Apparel results are featured here. **Figure 1** shows the default version of the page, and **Figure 2** shows wireframes for the variations in the left-hand navigation:

▶ **Default.** "All Women's Apparel" categories in alphabetical order; "Premier Designers" at the top of the left-hand navigation, followed by "Lifestyle," and then "All Women's Apparel."

RECIPE A (DEFAULT)

Figure 1 The default version of the Women's Apparel page.

- **Recipe B.** "All Women's Apparel" categories in alphabetical order; "Premier Designers" incorporated into the "Lifestyle" links as the top category, and "Lifestyle" placed above "All Women's Apparel."

- **Recipe C.** "All Women's Apparel" categories in alphabetical order; "Premier Designers" incorporated into the "Lifestyle" links as the top category, and "Lifestyle" placed below "All Women's Apparel."

- **Recipe D.** "All Women's Apparel" categories ordered by traffic volume; "Premier Designers" incorporated into the "Lifestyle" links as the top category, and "Lifestyle" placed above "All Women's Apparel."

- **Recipe E.** "All Women's Apparel" categories ordered by traffic volume; "Premier Designers" incorporated into the "Lifestyle" links as the top category, and "Lifestyle" placed below "All Women's Apparel."

RECIPE A (DEFAULT)	RECIPE B: +2% conversion rate	RECIPE C: -14% conversion rate	RECIPE D: FLAT	RECIPE E: +13% conversion rate

Figure 2 Wireframes for the default and tested versions of the left-hand navigation on the Women's Apparel page.

This test was run for several weeks, with Recipe E being the clear winner, with a 13 percent lift in the order conversion rate. Recipe C led to a 14 percent decrease in the conversion rate, whereas Recipes B and D led to little or no lift. Although it's difficult to say exactly why Recipe E won, the new design was soon made visible to all visitors to the page.

Global Free Shipping A/B Test: Free Shipping Thresholds

This was one of a series of tests run to determine the impact of offering free shipping, at different thresholds, on customer behavior. This test was run during a promotional period that offered free shipping on orders of $150 or more. The default and alternate versions of the experience appear in **Figure 3**:

- ▶ **Default.** Free shipping on orders of $150 or more.
- ▶ **Recipe B.** Free shipping on orders of $200 or more.
- ▶ **Recipe C.** Free shipping on orders of $400 or more.
- ▶ **Recipe D.** Free shipping on all orders.

Both Recipes B and C raised the AOV, by 8 percent and 6 percent, respectfully. This is likely because customers purchased more in order to get free shipping. Recipe D lowered the AOV by 8 percent, meaning offering free shipping on all orders did not encourage enough purchasers to spend more. Tests like this one help us to make more balanced and informed business decisions, including those related to competitive dynamics around when and for how long to offer specific types of promotions.

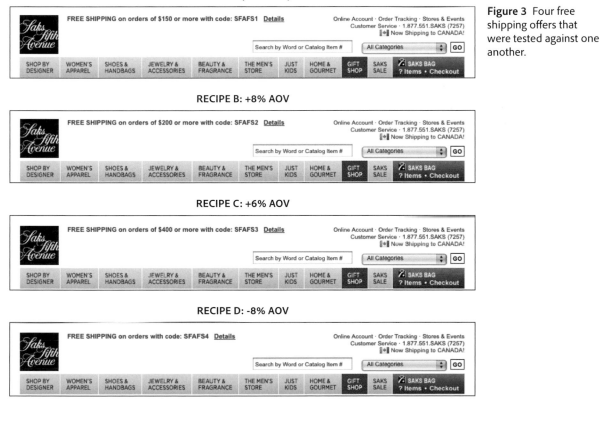

Figure 3 Four free shipping offers that were tested against one another.

Ryan Pizzuto, Web Test & Optimization Strategy Manager | Onsite Search Product Manager

T-Mobile's core optimization team is an army of one: Ryan Pizzuto. Ryan's mission is to help T-Mobile's internal business owners get the most out of their product, email, or webpage. He does this by helping them to gain a better understanding of their customers, educating them about T-Mobile's internal analytics and testing tools, and helping them run tests.

T-Mobile

T-Mobile serves approximately 43 million wireless subscribers and provides products and services through 70,000 points of distribution.

What are your business's goals?

We have business goals for E-Service and E-Commerce. E-Service is about helping the customer conduct self-service online because calling us costs us a lot of money. E-Commerce is about getting the sale through a purchase conversion, and new customer acquisition is the priority. This metric is hard to measure because the final transaction happens offline. Customers can purchase on our site, but when they get the unit, they have to activate it, and something might go wrong in between the two; for example, they might cancel the subscription. After new customer acquisition, adding a line of service or upgrading a plan are our next most important sales goals. There are also accessory sales, but those are not a priority.

What are your customers' goals?

Customers want to get what they need out of cell phone service at the lowest cost possible. We want to make sure people can easily understand the plans

and that they're on the right one. If applicable, we also want to make sure people can get their families on the same plan. It's a complicated industry, and we need to help customers easily understand the services we're selling. For example, customers might get less from another provider and pay more for it.

T-Mobile started a huge shift in March 2013 when we announced we're the "Un-carrier," which means customers don't have to get locked into rate plans. We used to have 17 or 18 different plan choices. We now say there's only one plan, but there are actually three subplans within the one. We're trying to make it simple for customers to understand the choice between T-Mobile and the other carriers.

Can you tell us a bit about T-Mobile's optimization program?

When I started, testing was a closed-off program for a specific group, and they didn't share their results. I called it the "Secret Society of Testing." Over the years, I've expanded the program while engraining testing more in our culture. I still see resistance to testing when people are afraid their idea may fail. I try to explain that there are no failures; we're always learning. If we didn't test, we could be failing; now we can ask why a recipe didn't work and iterate.

Good testing is about having the courage to step out of the organization's comfort zone. Rather than make a "perfect experience" that's "on brand" and "on everything," people should present crazy ideas. Some of our best performing recipes were ones that were thrown in as "that weird recipe C." Either they perform really well, or they totally tank.

I feel lucky that I was able to take on the optimization program, and I like it so much. With other jobs, I haven't found that to be the case, but with this job it really clicked.

Is your optimization program ROI positive?

We are amazingly ROI positive. To date, for the first four months of 2013, the annual projection is $4.6 million in incremental revenue. In 2012 it was $16 million, and in 2011 it was $15 million. Of course, a test may not perform the same way for an entire year, but these calculations show the value that a winning campaign could bring. However, we're not great at capitalizing on the successes of our tests because it's up to each business owner to decide whether to make the changes. Unfortunately, we don't implement all of the winners.

What is your opinion of more standard, full-site redesigns conducted outside of controlled experiments?

Needing to do a full-site redesign is a testament to the fact that a business hasn't been doing a good enough job optimizing. Over time, businesses that don't optimize create disjointed experiences. Each business owner controls their area, and when the different experiences try to come together as one site, it doesn't work. When a business gets to this point, I call it a "Frankensite," because pieces of the site get added on and stitched together over time. The experience can get so bad that they end up having to start over through a full redesign.

Visual Examples

Prepaid Activation Multivariate Test: Input Fields

This design change was incredibly simple, but the impact was very large. We considered it a throwaway test and only ran it because it was easy to set up while we were working on larger tests.

The default prepaid activation process is pictured in **Figure 1**. This experience is for customers who have purchased a prepaid phone, which means they have already paid for the phone but they haven't yet paid for the service. In order to start using the phone they need to activate it, and then fund their account. Although we make money from the phone sale, we really want them to fund the phone. After a customer has gone through this process once, they won't have to again. They can save their credit card and automatically refill their phone in the future. A phone can be activated in several ways, including online and by calling T-Mobile. We prefer people to activate their phones online because it costs us much less money.

The business owner came to me and said that 60 percent of the customers were dropping out of the process between step 1 and step 2. Of the customers who got to step 2, 95 percent completed the process by making it through steps 3, 4, and 5, which meant they funded their accounts. Based on that data, getting more customers to step 2 would be a huge victory.

We weren't sure why customers weren't completing step 1. Perhaps they weren't sure what to do. Each step has instructions, and a more detailed explanation would appear by clicking the tooltips to the right of each entry field. Our objective was to identify a layout that would drive a higher conversion rate to step 2 in the prepaid activation path. Our hypothesis was that adjusting the size or orientation of the input fields on the first step of the activation process would increase conversions to step 2.

RECIPE A (DEFAULT)

RECIPE B: -1.83% funded accounts

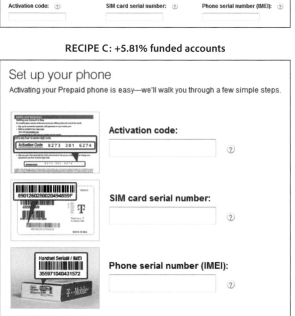

RECIPE C: +5.81% funded accounts

Figure 1 The default and alternate tested versions of the phone activation page.

RECIPE D: -1.91% funded accounts

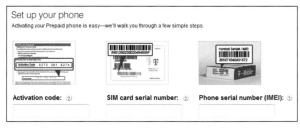

We ran a full-factorial multivariate test with two elements and two variations:

▸ **Orientation.** Vertical or horizontal

▸ **Text field and text within field.** Small or large

Recipe B (Figure 1) changed the orientation of the fields from vertical to horizontal. The next two recipes were just like Recipes A and B but with larger text fields. In addition to the size of the fields, when you typed in the text fields, the text would also be larger. Recipe C (Figure 1) used the vertical layout with the larger fields, and Recipe D (Figure 1) used the horizontal layout with the larger fields.

What we found out was pretty awesome. Just having those large fields increased customers converting from step 1 through step 5, which included funding an account, by 5.81 percent. Annually, that could mean 25,770 additional funded accounts and $2.2 million in incremental revenue. Our conclusion from this test was that customers might have had trouble seeing what they were typing, because the fields, and the fonts within the fields, were too small. We were also able to determine that the orientation of the text fields mattered, because the vertical alignment won. I really like this test because it was simple and had an unexpected result. Thankfully, after the test, we were able to implement the winning recipe.

Phone Details Page A/B Test: Payment Options

In late March, T-Mobile changed business models so that unlike other carriers, we were no longer perpetually charging customers for phones and no longer requiring that they sign two-year commitments. This is one of many tests we conducted around how to communicate this new business model.

People generally think that phones are free or that really great phones cost only $100 or $200. In reality, when phone companies give away phones for free, or for very low prices, the customer ends up paying

a lot more in the long term. The reason is that the carrier subsidizes the phone by increasing the cost of the customer's monthly rate plan, and they don't start charging the customer less once the cost of the phone has been recovered.

T-Mobile is trying to change that model by being more transparent with our customers. Rather than giving the customer a "free" phone, the customer can pay for the phone upfront or pay for it over time. If the customer chooses to pay for the phone over time, those payments stop once the phone has been paid off. Also, whether the customer chooses to pay upfront or over time, they benefit from a low monthly plan that doesn't include a subsidy for the cost of the phone.

We need to educate our customers, which takes a lot of work, because we're changing the way the telecommunications industry is running. In order to do so, we're relying on good design that is clean and simple.

The default experience is pictured in **Figure 2**. As you can see, if a customer chooses to pay over time, we don't charge them interest. In this example, it's either $99.99 upfront, plus $20 per month over 24 months, or $579.99 upfront. Both payment options come out to be the same price over time.

There are pros and cons for T-Mobile in both methods. The pro of a customer paying over time is that they're far more likely to stay with T-Mobile, and continue their service, during the 24 months that they're paying off the phone. The con of this method is that if people stop paying their bills, which is common, then T-Mobile is stuck with bad debt, which hurts us.

The pro of a customer paying all upfront is that we get $579.99 right away, so we don't risk accruing bad debt, but the customer can then take their phone and go to another carrier after a month. Before this model, when a customer wanted to leave it would be like a messy divorce. We don't want to force customers to stay with us; we want them to have a choice.

RECIPE A (DEFAULT)

RECIPE A (DEFAULT)

RECIPE B: +16.71% checkout conversions, +56.54% AOV

RECIPE C: +11.12% checkout conversions, +10.29% AOV

Figure 2 The default and alternate designs for how to display T-Mobile's new plan offering across all phone details pages.

In March, we rolled out this model and we started losing conversions at a pretty alarming rate. Customers would get down to almost the final step before they complete a purchase, and then they would bail. The objective of this test was to increase conversions, and our hypothesis was that better educating customers higher in the funnel would increase their likelihood to convert. Perhaps customers were looking at the default in Figure 2 and thinking, "Hey, this phone is $99," and not noticing the $20 per month or the $579.99 option. Once they got further down the funnel they were surprised by the final price because we had confused them. We think they didn't realize they had two options until the very end of the process.

We tested two different treatments of the payment options element across all phone details pages. In Recipe B (Figure 2), we tried to make it clear that there are two different options. We still emphasized the $99.99 over the $579.99, but we made the $579.99 larger than it was in Recipe A and drew attention to it by separating it with whitespace. We also inserted the word "OR" as a horizontal divider. In Recipe C (Figure 2), we tried to separate the two different options vertically and give both prices equal prominence.

The results were extremely surprising. Recipes B and C had higher conversion rates and higher average order values. Recipe B won, providing a 16.71 percent lift in conversions and a 56.54 percent lift in AOV. These results indicate that by better explaining the new model, customers were more likely to make a purchase, and they were also more likely to choose to pay for the phone upfront.

Conventional wisdom is that people are going to be scared by the large prices, and that turned out not to be the case. By better explaining the two options, customers were able to make the choice that was best for them, and several chose to pay upfront. We were able to accomplish this through a simple layout change. The design was critical, and the test has more than already paid for itself.

This test shows the importance of thinking through the full customer journey. If we had just focused on the one point where customers were dropping off—the next-to-last conversion step—we wouldn't have ever run this test. So, if a page has a high bounce rate, the cause may not be the page customers are bouncing from but a page that set their expectations beforehand.

It can be very difficult to substantially increase final conversions and AOV by just changing an element earlier in the funnel, but that's what happened here. We did this by setting the right expectation with customers ahead of time, so by the time they got to the final conversion step, they knew there were two payment options. In Recipes B and C, fewer customers entered the funnel, but more customers made it all the way through the funnel. This means we were sending more qualified traffic down the funnel. This also shows the importance of collecting multiple success metrics. If we had just looked at the metric of click-through rate into the funnel, we would have thought Recipe A was the winning design, even though it was losing us a lot of money.

Eileen Krill, Research Manager

For the last nine years, Eileen has overseen customer research for The Washington Post's media businesses, initially for the digital side of the business, and in more recent years for all print and digital products.

The Washington Post

The Washington Post is a global media company specializing in newspaper print and online publishing. The print newspaper was founded in 1877 and is the most widely circulated newspaper published in Washington, D.C. (source: Alliance for Audited Media).

Would you please tell us a bit about your role?

As part of the research and analytics team, I manage the primary research that we do in support of our print, digital, and mobile businesses. We track usage, satisfaction, opinions, and feedback across all of our current products, as well as new products and features that are always in development. My team oversees all the surveys and in-person qualitative research, and we partner with another internal team who conducts all the A/B testing.

My team also supports our sales department by pulling from syndicated data sources to profile our audience versus the competition. We also run custom research projects on behalf of some of our larger advertisers to provide them with additional value. These may include copy testing or ad effectiveness surveys; brand awareness studies to understand what kinds of advertising resonate with different audiences; or national polls on a topic of interest.

It's important to us that research and analytics is not part of any other department. We are not part of marketing, the Newsroom, or IT. We are

independent, and we roll up right to the president. We have no incentive for the data to turn out a certain way. We are truly an unbiased group conducting research for the benefit of our customers and the company overall.

What are your primary products?

The Washington Post print newspaper is our flagship product. Our digital products include the washingtonpost.com website and several different iOS and Android apps for phones and tablets. We also support *Express*, which is a free print newspaper that's given out at metro stations, and the *Capital Business*, which is focused on local business. Currently, we support *Slate* and its properties, which include *The Root*, although we'll soon no longer be part of the same company as part of the sale to Jeff Bezos.

For each of these businesses, we talk with existing customers and test out new products and features, although *The Washington Post* newspaper and website are our primary focus areas.

Who are your customers?

The Post serves two very different audiences. We have an audience based locally in Washington, D.C., which is very valuable to us because of their high level of engagement with our products, and because of the high concentration of opinion leaders and policy makers in the area. This local audience uses our products not only for political news and opinions, and all the things we're famous for, but also to help go about living their lives in the D.C. area—for example, planning entertainment, like looking up restaurants, movies, and events; finding a job; and all sorts of things like that.

Our other very important groups of customers are our national and international readers. They are obviously much larger and currently have near-infinite potential for growth. They typically come to us for very specific items and are less engaged across the breadth of our products than our local audience.

What types of research do you conduct?

My team runs online surveys, as well as live user testing, like one-on-one interviews, on-site observational user research, and remote qualitative user research with people on their computers at their homes. We also still occasionally conduct telephone and mail surveys.

The online surveys are mostly run with our user panel, which is composed of about 7,000 customers. It includes both print and digital customers; local and nonlocal customers; mobile, desktop, and tablet customers; and so on. We collect a wide range of information about our users when they first join the panel, including demographic and employment information, their Post consumption, and what devices they use so that we can better target surveys. It's a voluntary panel so the data isn't necessarily a statistically representative sample of our entire possible audience, but it gives us a good picture of what our most engaged users think, because those are the ones who tend to join the panel. For other surveys we'll mail to subscriber lists, or sometimes we'll buy email lists. For example, if we're looking for job seekers in the D.C. market who aren't necessarily our customers already, we'll have to buy access to those prospects.

We run surveys with our user panel across a variety of topics to get feedback on a feature, to get a reaction to design comps, or to even generate open-ended ideas for new products. We may ask questions like, "What would make you more likely to continue subscribing to the Sunday paper?" "How are you currently using the website?" "Which features do you find the most valuable?" "What's missing?" "What competitors are you using?" and, "What do they do better than us?" Those are just a few examples. We launched and continue to manage the panel ourselves, including programming and distributing the surveys and crunching all the data.

Live interviews and testing with our users is also very important. About a year ago we built our own research lab in our building, so we're able to do quite a lot of qualitative research in a much more cost-effective manner, because we no longer have to pay for renting out a facility. We have our own focus group room and a second room for one-on-one interviews and user testing. There's also an observation room, which seats between 12 and 15 people. Two members of my team have gone through training to moderate and conduct qualitative user testing, so we no longer have to outsource moderators for most of our projects. All we need to pay for is respondent recruitment and incentives. As a result, we're now able to do a whole lot more of this kind of research.

Having the lab in the office also makes it much easier for people around the company to come watch the live sessions. In the middle of a busy day, a stakeholder can travel down one floor in the elevator and catch a session or two. Before, people might have missed out on the sessions entirely because they didn't have time to travel somewhere outside of the office. Even though we provide a report of the results and tape all the sessions so people can watch later, there's nothing quite as useful as sitting and watching real customers.

For qualitative research, we always start the sessions in an open-ended way. We have the customer play around with the product unprompted for a few minutes. That helps us understand what their more natural reaction might be in the real world. We also ask them to talk about what they're thinking the whole time.

Not every task we're looking to understand comes up naturally, so afterwards we talk with them and probe into certain areas of their experience. We may ask specific questions like, "Did you notice this setting?" or "Can you find this feature?" We only ask them to do things that are relevant to them. For example, if we know through the recruitment process that they never go to the movies, we're not going to then say, "Can you find movie times in the app?" Throughout the process we listen to what they say and watch how they interact with the product very carefully.

After conducting any form of research, we'll analyze the results, put together a presentation, and then usually sit down with our internal client to talk them through our recommendations. It's then up to them to decide how to act. Sometimes people follow our recommendations, and sometimes they don't. Our internal clients have to incorporate business considerations along with our advice when deciding what actions to take.

It's wonderful that you have your own user testing lab. How were you able to help make that happen?

Forces aligned for that to happen. My former boss and I used to always say, "Wouldn't it be nice if we had our own lab?" A few years ago we had extra money in our budget, and my manager was able to sell the idea based on cost savings. I then spoke with the research facilities and moderators I had worked with in the past to ask for any advice they had on building a lab. People were able to put me in touch with two guys who had built the focus group rooms for the two or three big facilities here in D.C. I worked with them to design the space, buy the furniture, and purchase and install all the equipment. We were able to recoup our costs within a few months.

What is the range of products you research in your lab?

We encourage people in the company to have us conduct live user sessions for all new products and features whether in print, digital, or mobile. For example, we recently tested a new print paper for people looking for apartments to rent. The plan was to make it a free paper distributed each Saturday. We created several different prototypes of the paper, and we had people come in and use them in the lab. We looked to understand their initial overall reactions, whether they would read through certain pages and features, and whether they found the product to be clear and useful.

We also research our mobile apps. Ideally, we want to make the app experience so totally intuitive that people can figure it out themselves. But that's sometimes not so easy on smaller screens. Something we've learned in the labs is that people totally miss features the first or second time they're going through an app. Customers may not understand whether to swipe from right to left or from top to bottom, or what's behind each of the icons. We can ask those questions on a survey, and people might say, "Yeah, I get it." But watching them interact with it is more revealing because you can observe all their actual behaviors, which has been very helpful in increasing engagement within our apps.

As another example, we recently conducted user sessions to test our online subscription sign-up process. In 2013, we started to require a paid online subscription for readers who read over 20 articles per month online. Prior to launching the new system we had frequent Post website visitors in our lab walking through the process of signing up on desktop computers and mobile devices. We wanted to make sure they understood the pricing options and could easily complete the sign-up process, and to observe whether they noticed features like the reminder letting them know how many free articles they had left that month. We also tested several different versions of the messaging explaining to customers that we would soon be charging for continued access. Several of these messages were then tested on the live website through A/B testing.

What's the volume of customer research that you conduct?

We run research during the entire product life cycle, both pre- and post-launch. We're always collecting feedback, looking to understand satisfaction as well as areas of confusion with our existing products:

▶ **Surveys.** We run about 40–60 surveys each year. We almost always have a survey out there, and sometimes we're running up to five at once.

▶ **User labs.** We run an average of two projects per month. Each project includes eight to ten sessions per day; each session lasts 45 minutes. You can pretty much see patterns start to emerge after three to four users, but we typically conduct eight to ten sessions just to be sure. We may then add on an extra day to focus on a specific device, like mobile.

▶ **A/B testing.** We're also always running iterative A/B tests to optimize the products across all the main site areas. A/B testing is more easily scalable.

How do you evangelize internally about all the great research you're doing?

The Washington Post has great capabilities across research, analytics, and optimization, but not everyone around the company is aware of them. There's no official requirement that products be tested. I take every opportunity I can to tell people about our services and to share results. Whether I'm presenting at a senior staff meeting or working with people on a smaller project, I'm always reminding people of the various services we offer.

The fact that I have to evangelize these services sometimes amazes me. It seems like common sense that we should be talking to our customers about everything that we're doing. The Washington Post is all about providing products and services for our readers. We wouldn't have a business without them!

I couldn't agree more. What do you think about the recently announced acquisition of The Washington Post by Jeff Bezos?

In light of Jeff Bezos's comments about how we need to be completely "reader focused," I think it's very exciting to see what the future will bring, particularly for our team.

Visual Examples

Sign-in and Registration A/B Test: Page Redesign

These case studies are from when we started our testing program back in 2009. At the time the registration and sign-in process was our top priority. Analytics showed that, on average, registered visitors view more stories and return more often to the site. When visitors register, they have the chance to subscribe to breaking news alerts and topical newsletters. News alerts and newsletters give our readers information they're looking for, provide us with an opportunity to learn a bit more about our readers' preferences for stories, and also lead to increasing page views and advertising revenue on the site.

In 2009, registration provided unlimited access to the online paper for free; it's only now, in 2013 that we've moved to a subscription model where customers pay to read more than 20 free articles each month.

In the default version of the page, the CTA to register was the "Click here" link on the right side, and we hypothesized that it might be hard to find (**Figure 1**). Sign-in also took up most of the real estate on the

RECIPE A (DEFAULT)

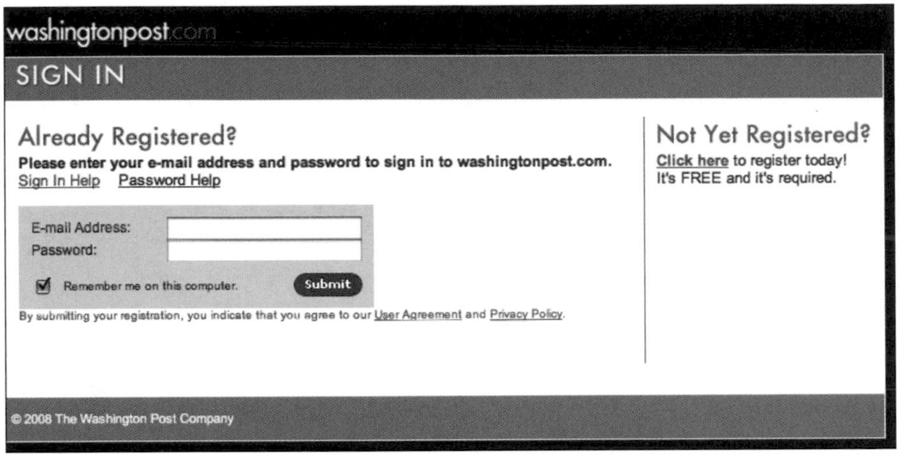

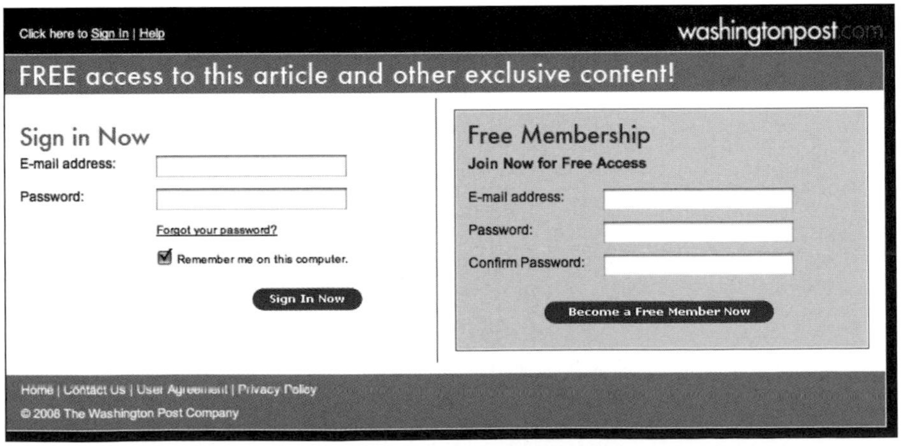

Figure 1 Recipes A, B, and C for the sign-in and registration test.

RECIPE B: -8% completed registrations

RECIPE C: +21% completed registrations

page, and we hypothesized that making registration more prominent might increase the likelihood that readers would register. The alternate designs included:

▶ **Recipe B** gave equal prominence to the sign-in and registration actions by splitting the page in half. The registration CTA changed from being a subtle "Click here" link within a sentence to being a large prominent button that read, "Become a Free Member." The benefits of registering were also added to the page.

▶ **Recipe C** substituted the value proposition bullets introduced in Recipe B with three form fields allowing the user to start the registration process right on that page. After this page, there were several more steps in the registration process.

The hypothesis of this recipe was that allowing users to start registering would be more compelling than any value proposition bullets. Value proposition bullets don't give an indication of the next step, whereas the form fields let the user know exactly what's expected of them. There have also been some studies showing that users' eyes are attracted to blank form fields, so we thought they might find this recipe enticing. There was a risk that visitors would get confused by the two sets of form fields, to sign in or register, or they would get frustrated once they realized the registration process was more than three steps.

We measured many metrics, but the primary conversion metric was final completed registrations. Recipe B dropped the registration completion rate, but Recipe C increased completed registrations by 21 percent! Both recipes led to a slight drop in the sign-in rate, but recipe C had the smallest drop. Recipe C also provided a substantial lift in page views. Our recommendation was to push Recipe C live to all visitors and to immediately run a series of follow-up tests starting with finding a way to raise the sign-in rate to reach the default levels, and then to redesign subsequent steps in the registration process to make them easier to accomplish.

Classified Jobs Listings A/B Test: Page Redesign

As everyone likely knows, over the last several years the newspaper business has seen a decline in the number of classified job listings purchased. This was one of several tests we ran to try to lessen the drop in classified sales and was run on the page an advertiser would visit to post a job listing (**Figure 2**).

There were several packages for posting job listings. They could be posted both online and in the print newspaper, only online, or only in the print newspaper. There was also a package offering online-only listings in bulk for a discount. In this A/B test we wanted to try to communicate the key value propositions of posting a job listing with The Washington Post, including our circulation size, and the ability to purchase discounts in bulk:

▶ **Recipe B** modified the layout of the page, grouping the different packages into tiles (**Figure 3**). The three ways to purchase a single job listing were placed in the same row and sorted by price from left to right. The first two tiles also featured images of the products in which the jobs would be posted: an image of the print newspaper on the left and an image of the online site in the middle. The second row allowed for purchasing online listings in bulk and used large fonts in an attempt to communicate the value. Rather than listing out several prices like the default, Recipe B aimed to simplify the messaging by making the calculator feature the most prominent element of the tile.

▶ **Recipe C** modified the page even further (**Figure 4**). Although it contains the same bulk-listing tile as Recipe B at the bottom of the page, the majority of the page has been redesigned to be a comparison grid. The goal of this page was to make it easy for customers to compare products while also emphasizing the combined print and online product as having the best value. Just like Recipe B, this layout builds in price from left to right.

RECIPE A (DEFAULT)

Figure 2 The default jobs listings page.

RECIPE B: +25% RPV

Figure 3 Recipe B.

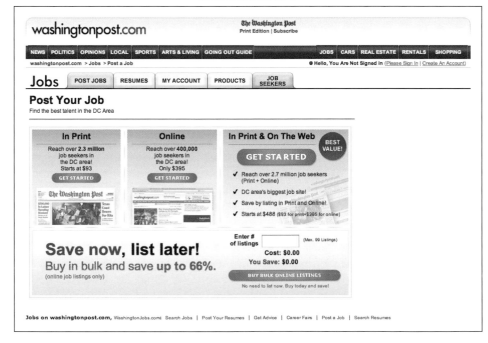

RECIPE C: +1% RPV

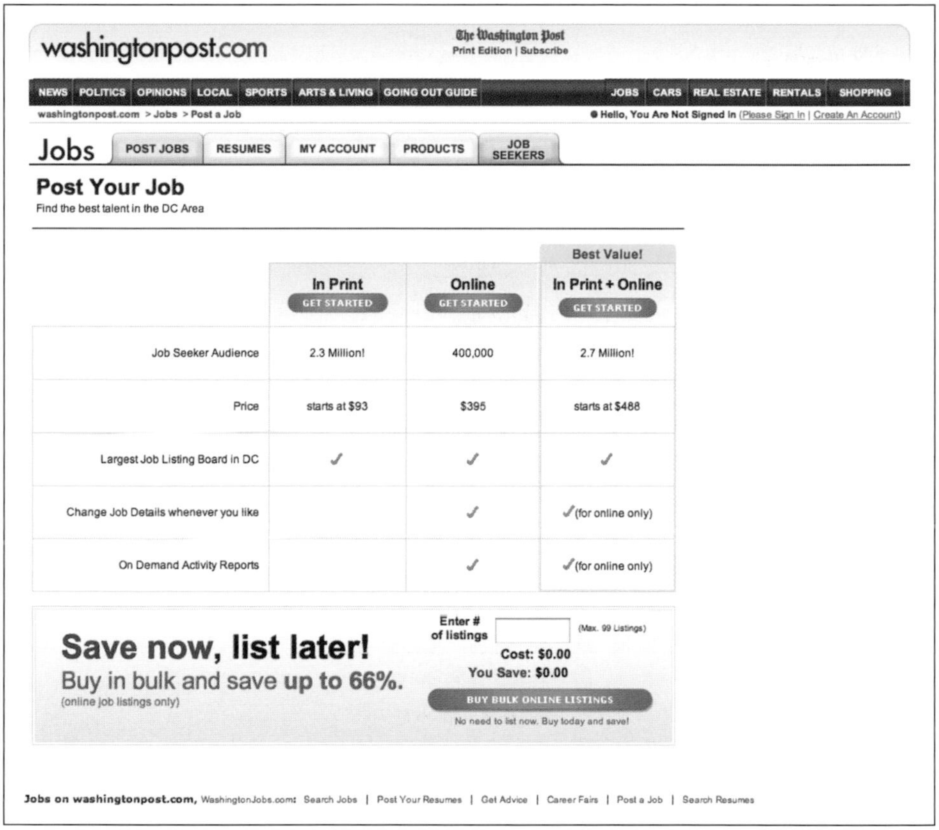

Figure 4 Recipe C.

The primary success metric was revenue per visitor (RPV), which was based on visitors completing a job listing purchase several steps down the funnel. Recipe B was by far the winner, providing a 25 percent lift in RPV. Recipe C provided only a 1 percent lift, which was surprising, because grid layouts like this one were very common on the web in 2009, and they still are today, in 2013. At the end of the day, the 25 percent RPV lift from Recipe B was a huge win. Our recommendation was to push it live to all visitors and to run a series of follow-up tests to simplify the entire funnel.

Going out Guide Homepage A/B Test: Calendar Redesign

The Going out Guide is a popular section of the site for finding information about local D.C. restaurants, entertainment, and events. Analytics showed that the section front to the Going out Guide had an extremely high bounce rate, but that once visitors clicked through, they generated multiple page views.

The default version of the Going out Guide homepage included search functionality, prominent left-hand navigation, and an events calendar (**Figure 5**). This was the first of a series of tests on the Going out Guide section and focused on the calendar feature. In any of the designs, visitors could switch back and forth between the weekly or monthly views.

The default version of the calendar showed the current week, with a detailed listing of the events happening each day. Recipe B selected the monthly rather than weekly calendar view (**Figure 6**). The hypothesis behind this design was that it might entice clicks from visitors who weren't interested in events happening during the current week, but who were interested in events happening within the next month. Recipe C was exactly the same as recipe B, except instead of highlighting the current day on the calendar, all future dates were highlighted (**Figure 7**).

RECIPE A (DEFAULT)

Figure 5 The default Going out Guide homepage.

Both recipes increased the primary success metric of overall page views within the Going out Guide section. Recipe B provided a 9 percent lift in page views while recipe C provided a whopping 15 percent lift in page views. We thought this was a nice achievement from such a simple test, and our recommendation was to push Recipe C live, and then to run follow-up tests throughout the Going out Guide.

RECIPE B: +9% Going out Guide pageviews

Figure 6 Recipe B defaulted to the monthly rather than daily calendar.

RECIPE C: +15% Going out Guide pageviews

Figure 7 Recipe C defaulted to the monthly calendar and highlighted future dates.

INDEX

A

A/B testing. *See also* testing
  Adobe's use of, 143–145
  Ally Bank's use of, 147–149
  best practices for, 114
  Caesars' booking module, 154–156
  Comcast's, 160–161, 162
  defined, 29
  Dell's use of, 168–169, 170–171
  email design for Dollar Thrifty, 173–176
  Foursquare's, 191, 193, 194–195
  Hightail's homepage test using, 211
  LinkedIn's, 223–225
  Marriott International, 227–230
  multivariable tests in, 81
  Obama for America, 231, 232, 233–234, 236–248, 249–250
  PetCareRx messaging and banner, 252–257
  product storage limits, 211–212
  redesigned customer loyalty pages, 157
  segmentation and, 235
  specifying in methodology, 109
  T-Mobile phone payment options, 265–267
  Washington Post's, 271–277
address fields, 216
Adobe, 143–145
  business and customers' goals for, 143
  use of A/B testing, 143–145
advertising banners, 69
Ahmed, Zimran, 177–184
algorithm for News Feed displays, 187–188
Ally Bank, 146–149
  balancing creativity with research, 146
  business and customers' goals for, 146
  homepage testing by, 147–148
  promoting social links at log-off portal, 148–149
American Express, 150–152
  business and customers' goals for, 150
  designing multiple product displays, 151–152
  offering customer incentives, 151
  optimization program for, 150
  testing impact on business strategies, 150–151
analysis paralysis, 88
AOV (average order value), 92, 166, 267
assembling wireframes, 119–120
auto-focusing feature, 246
auto-optimizing tests, 109, 116–117
autocomplete feature, 194–195, 209
average order value (AOV), 92, 166, 267
Axelrod, David, 234

B

banners
  A/B testing of size, messaging, and images for, 253–255
  ignored by customers, 69
best practices
  customer service, 121–122
  Foursquare's, 193
  Hightail's, 211, 212
  Saks Fifth Avenue's, 258
Bezos, Jeff, 11, 268, 271
Blakeley, Rob, 66, 86
blue-sky approach, 120
Bolt, Nate, 34, 35, 78, 185–190
borders of wireframes, 119
bounce rate, 92

D